KEY CONCEPT

Palgrave Key Concepts

Palgrave Key Concepts provide an accessible and comprehensive range of subject glossaries at undergraduate level. They are the ideal companion to a standard textbook, making them invaluable reading for students throughout their course of study and especially useful as a revision aid.

The key concepts are arranged alphabetically so you can quickly find terms or entries of immediate interest. All major theories, concepts, terms and theorists are incorporated and cross-referenced. Additional reading or website research opportunities are included. With hundreds of key terms defined, **Palgrave Key Concepts** represent a comprehensive must-have reference for undergraduates.

Published

Key Concepts in Accounting and Finance
Key Concepts in Business Practice
Key Concepts in Human Resource Management
Key Concepts in International Business
Key Concepts in Management
Key Concepts in Marketing
Key Concepts in Operations Management
Key Concepts in Politics
Key Concepts in Strategic Management
Linguistic Terms and Concepts
Literary Terms and Criticism (*third edition*)

Further titles are in preparation

www.palgravekeyconcepts.com

Palgrave Key Concepts
Series Standing Order ISBN 1–4039–3210–7
(*outside North America only*)

You can receive future titles in this series as they are published by placing a standing order. Please contact your bookseller or, in case of difficulty, write to us at the address below with your name and address, the title of the series, and the ISBN quoted above.

Customer Services Department, Macmillan Distribution Ltd,
Houndmills, Basingstoke, Hampshire RG21 6XS, England

Key Concepts in Strategic Management

Jonathan Sutherland and Diane Canwell

palgrave
macmillan

First published 2004 by
PALGRAVE MACMILLAN
Houndmills, Basingstoke, Hampshire RG21 6XS and
175 Fifth Avenue, New York, N.Y. 10010
Companies and representatives throughout the world

PALGRAVE MACMILLAN is the global academic imprint of the Palgrave Macmillan division of St. Martin's Press, LLC and of Palgrave Macmillan Ltd. Macmillan® is a registered trademark in the United States, United Kingdom and other countries. Palgrave is a registered trademark in the European Union and other countries.

ISBN 1–4039–2135–0

This book is printed on paper suitable for recycling and made from fully managed and sustained forest sources.

A catalogue record for this book is available from the British Library.

Library of Congress Cataloging-in-Publication Data
Sutherland, Jonathan.
    Key concepts in strategic management / Jonathan Sutherland and Diane Canwell.
        p. cm. – (Palgrave key concepts)
    Includes bibliographical references and index.
    ISBN 1–4039–2135–0 (pbk.)
    1. Strategic planning—Dictionaries. I. Canwell, Diane. II. Title.
III. Series.
    \00712251\5 ⟨
    HD30.28.S913 2004
    658.4'012'03–dc22   2003070657

10   9   8   7   6   5   4   3   2   1
13 12 11 10 09 08 07 06 05 04

Printed and bound in Great Britain by
Creative Print & Design (Wales), Ebbw Vale

Contents

Introduction

The vast majority of textbooks written on strategic management focus on the ways in which senior management run their organizations. They focus heavily on techniques and procedures particularly related to long-term planning, and focus on the importance of mission statements or vision statements. Strategic management, however, is a much broader discipline and requires the creation of shared cultures, consistency, uniformity and order. Strategic management should, theoretically at least, reduce the amount and the extent of unpleasant surprises for an organization. Strategic management, therefore, suggests the creation of a level of predictability in the future, thereby improving the organization's ability to control its own destiny.

Strategic management is a vibrant and controversial area of management which is not simply restricted to the actions of senior managers at board level. Strategic management requires intuition and judgement to work alongside structure, rules and procedures. Strategic management is about dealing with ambiguities, uncertainties and those ever-present surprises. Strategic management is about perfecting techniques to deal with inconsistency, culture clashes and conflict. It is also concerned with dealing with irregularities, differences, disorder and instability.

Inevitably, strategic management, its objectives and applications are contradictory and many approaches could not be considered in any way to be conventional. Strategic management is at the hub of organizational dynamics and provides a means by which the managers of an organization can understand the nature of its business, the behaviour of its systems and the importance of its internal and external environment. It is also concerned with cause and effect, and the identification of patterns which can affect the organization in its attempts to assemble policies, implement those policies, evaluate and amend, and seek to fulfil its objectives and obligations successfully.

The structure of the glossary

Every attempt has been made to include all of the key concepts in this discipline, taking into account currently used terminology and jargon common throughout strategic management in organizations around the world. There are notable differences in legislation and procedure when we compare different forms of business organization. Some definitions of strategic management terminology and developments have more, or less, application and relevance to the United Kingdom, Europe, the United States and Japan. Increasingly in Europe, for example, there is a harmonization process in train which is gradually seeking to standardize regulations and procedures, yet the strategic management process is, essentially, an individual affair, organization-by-organization.

The key concepts have been arranged alphabetically in order to ensure that the reader can quickly find the term or entry of immediate interest. It is normally the case that a brief description of the term is presented, followed by a more expansive explanation.

The majority of the key concepts have the following in common:

- They may have a reference within the text to another key concept identified by a word or phrase that is in **bold type** – this should enable readers to investigate a directly implicated key concept should they require clarification of the definition at that point.
- They may have a series of related key concepts which are featured at the end of the definition – this may allow readers to continue their research and investigate subsidiary or allied key concepts.
- They may feature book or journal references – a vital feature for the reader to undertake follow-up research for more expansive explanations, often written by the originator or by a leading writer in that particular field of study.
- They may include website references – it is notoriously difficult to ensure that websites are still running at the time of going to print, let alone several months beyond that time, but in the majority of cases long-established websites have been selected, or governmental websites that are unlikely to be closed or have a major address change.

Glossary terms – a guide

Whilst the majority of the key concepts have an international flavour, readers are cautioned to access the legislation, in particular, which refers to their native country or to the country in which they are working. It is also often the case that there are terms which have no currency in a particular country as they may be allied to specific legislation of another country. Readers should check whether the description includes a specific reference to such law, and should not assume that every key concept is a generic one that can be applied universally to strategic management.

In all cases, references to other books, journals and websites are based on the latest available information. It was not always possible to ensure that the key text or printed reference is in print, but most well-stocked college or university libraries should have access to the original materials. In the majority of cases, when generic business books have been referenced, these are, in the view of the writers, the best and most available additional reading texts.

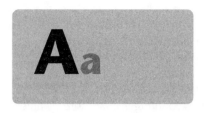

Absolute cost advantage

The term 'absolute cost advantage' is largely associated with one of the many **barriers to entry** which prevent businesses from entering new markets. Absolute cost advantages are the benefits which a larger, more established business can achieve through **economies of scale** or as a result of an innovation which has allowed them to reduce costs. Typically, a new competitor entering the market may face a price war, which often causes new entrants to fail, whilst the incumbent, having the absolute cost advantage, manages to survive.

The incumbent, having taken account of relevant opportunity costs, will expend resources and secure a **first-mover advantage** in a new market or with a new innovation, and thus will be able to enjoy, relatively speaking, monopoly profits. Any potential entrant into the market must devise a profitable entry plan. The scale of these costs is often referred to as a measure of the height of an entry barrier.

Absorptive capacity

The absorptive capacity of a business represents its abilities to identify, and to value, assimilate and then utilize, any new knowledge. In other words, it is the ability of the business to recognize the value of new, often external, information, then assimilate it and use it to its own commercial advantage. Businesses have increasingly realized that outside sources of knowledge are important, if not crucial, in continuing to innovate.

It is believed that there is a negative relationship between a business's absorptive capacity and the practice of **outsourcing**. Businesses which carry out their own research and development are more likely to achieve absorptive capacity as a by-product of this activity.

Cohen, W. M. and Levinthal, D. A., 'Absorptive Capacity: a New Perspective on Learning and Innovation', *Administrative and Science Quarterly*, 35(1) (1990).

Accounting

Accounting, in its more general sense, involves the communication of a business's financial position to its providers of capital and, for tax purposes, to governments. It is also used to evaluate performance, control expenditure and make forecasts and plans.

In international business, however, accounting is a far more complex discipline as businesses will need to adapt their accounting procedures to fall in line with the local demands in each environment in which they operate. There are a number of national differences in both accounting and auditing standards. As markets have become increasingly globalized over the past few decades, there has been a distinct lack of comparability between the accounting demands in each area in which a business operates. It is therefore difficult for a business to show why financial information appears to be different, depending on the accounting practices of each country in which it has an interest.

There have been attempts to institute a form of accounting standard harmonization, notably from the International Accounting Standards Committee (IASC). To date, their attempts have been rather limited. A multinational business, with subsidiaries in foreign countries, would be required to keep their accounting records and prepare financial statements in the currency of the country in which it is located. It is only when compiling consolidated accounts of the multinational that the subsidiaries' financial statements have to be translated into the home country's currency. This, in itself, is a difficult task as exchange rates fluctuate and assets which are valued in a foreign currency also have to be translated into the home currency, but usually at the exchange rate that was current when the assets were purchased. This leads to difficulties in making a multinational's balance sheet balance.

Inevitably there are distortions in both budgets and performance data when the results are translated into another currency. Increasingly, multinational businesses are seeking ways whereby they can streamline this process, and make the assumptions required more transparent.

Madura, Jeff, *International Financial Management*. Mason, OH: South Western College Publishing, 2002.

Acquisition and restructuring strategy

The term 'acquisition and restructuring', in formulating a business strategy, makes the presumption that a business which has a superior internal governance system can create value simply by acquiring less efficient, or poorly managed, businesses and improving their efficiency.

An acquisition can be differentiated from either a merger or a take-over in as much as it is a transaction where one business buys another with the primary purpose of using that business's **core competence** by making it a subsidiary.

There are a number of reasons why businesses choose to acquire other businesses. These include:

- Increased speed to market – which is an expression closely related to **barriers to entry** as it allows market entry more easily.
- Diversification – which allows the business to move quickly towards gaining experience and depth, although this does depend on the organization's position.
- Reshaping competitive scope – which relates to acquisitions being a primary means by which a business can restrict its dependence on only a few products or markets.

Effective acquisitions can be achieved by addressing the following issues:

- Complementary assets and resources – in buying businesses with assets that meet current needs and help build competitiveness.
- A well-considered selection process – which incorporates an evaluation as to the ease of integration and whether **synergies** will be built.
- Maintaining a financial reserve – so as not to forgo any other profitable projects which may appear, through having spent all the reserves and available cash on the acquisition.

Normally there are three different forms of restructuring, which can be best summarized as in Table 1.

Table 1   Different types of restructuring

Restructuring alternative	Short term	Long term
Downsizing	Reduced labour costs	Loss of human capital
Down-scoping	Reduced debt costs	Potentially lower or higher performance
Leveraged buy-out	High debt costs	Higher performance but higher risk

Acquisitions

The most common use of the term 'acquisition' is in describing the process of one business purchasing another business, or indeed individuals purchasing an existing business.

'Acquisition' can also refer to the process of obtaining a loan or another form of finance.

'Acquisition' can equally be applied to the purchase of a property by a business.

In international business, all acquisitions are subject to local and national laws and regulations in respect of how businesses are acquired or shares are purchased. In many cases businesses which are acquired by another company continue to operate as independent organizations, maintaining their original name, personnel and **organizational structure.**

Weston, J. Fred and Weaver, Samuel C., *Mergers and Acquisitions.* New York: McGraw-Hill, 2001.

Action planning

Action planning is an integral part of both goal-setting and problem solving, yet in many business contexts it is a neglected area. Action planning can assist a business in planning for the future, ensuring that as future situations change they can be controlled. At its most basic, action planning is the conversion of goals or objectives into a series of steps, in order to ascertain what has to be done, by whom and by when. This is variously known as either an action planning process or an event track. The process of formulating the event track follows a set series of procedures:

1 Decide a goal or objective.
2 Identify sequence of actions required to achieve this.
3 Refine the initial plan by identifying where it may go wrong.
4 Having identified what may go wrong, formulate plans or actions to deal with these problems.

A

The action plan should describe how the business is to get from where it is now to where it wishes to be, describing in detail how it proposes to do this. There needs to be a secondary process running alongside the action plan, which checks to see whether the plan is working.

Effective action planning requires the participation of all relevant **stakeholders**, who need to be aware of their role in the process. A full action plan event track is likely to incorporate the following aspects:

1 Development of a rough action plan, which combines individual

work from the participants, listing the activities they propose in order to reach the goal. Once this has been completed, all of the activities are discussed, and, perhaps using a voting technique, the most appropriate ones are chosen. These then need to be arranged in the correct sequence.

2 The action plan now needs to be refined. Above all, the action plan needs to be robust; each event needs to be detailed in terms of what, when and who.

3 Checks need to be carried out regarding any assumptions made in the creation of the action plan. This may include skills, time, finance and materials. There may also be assumptions regarding coordination. Above all, the participants need to consider how unexpected problems may be dealt with if they arise.

4 Contingency plan – no matter how complex the creation of the action plan may have been, it is imperative that a contingency plan is created, which may need to be instituted in the event of the action planning going off track. This means that a monitoring process needs to be put in place, together with a clear idea of how to solve potential problems as they arise, in order to ensure that the goal is finally reached.

Kaplan, Robert S. and Norton, David P., *The Balanced Scorecard: Translating Strategy into Action*. Boston, MA: Harvard Business School Press, 1996.

Activity ratios

Activity ratios are a means by which an assessment can be made as to how well a business is managing its assets. Typically, the activity ratios would include the following:

- **Inventory turnover** – which shows whether a business is holding excessive stocks of inventory.
- Fixed assets turnover – which shows whether the assets are being used at close to near capacity.
- Total assets turnover – which indicates whether a sufficient volume of business is being generated for the size of the asset investment.
- Working capital turnover – which indicates whether funds are being used efficiently.

The activity ratios combine information which can be found on a business's balance sheets or income statements, and are considered to be very useful analytical tools in understanding the financial position. Effectively, the ratios revolve around turnover, or may perhaps include calculations regarding issues such as the average collection period.

Temple, Peter, *Magic Numbers: The 33 Key Ratios that Every Investor Should Know.* New York: John Wiley, 2001.

Adaptive culture

Edgar Schein originally proposed the notion that **organizational culture** is framed by what a business assumes to be true about itself and the environment in which it operates. He also suggested that culture is unconscious, but can be learned and reinforced when problems are repeatedly solved using the same approach.

An adaptive culture is that of an organization which recognizes that it is not the strength of its culture which matters but its adaptability. An adaptable culture is one which allows the adoption of strategies or practices which are able to respond to changing markets and new competitive situations. Such businesses are forward-looking and tend to be guided by positive change. Research has shown that organizations which do not have adaptive cultures can be short-term successes, but as markets change, they cannot change quickly enough to adapt to new business conditions. The main differences between organizations with

Table 2 The value of adaptive cultures

Organizations with high-performance adaptive cultures	Organizations without high-performance adaptive cultures
Ability to maintain a fit between the culture and the business context.	Short-termism.
Active support within the organization to identify problems.	Emphasis on structure and systems.
Active support within the organization to identify problems and find workable solutions.	Inability to focus on multiple stakeholders.
Feeling of confidence amongst employees.	Biased perception of the competition.
Trust.	Inability to deal with negative suggestions or observations.
Risk taking.	Feeling of invulnerability.
Proactivity.	Alternative strategies ignored.

A

high-performance adaptive cultures and those without high-performance adaptive cultures are outlined in Table 2.

Kotter, John and Heskett, J. L., *Corporate Culture and Performance*. New York: Free Press. 1992.

Advanced factors of production

Advanced factors of production tend to be created rather than inherited. They include factors which have been created through sustained and sophisticated investment such as:

- managerial sophistication and expertise;
- high-quality human capital assets (skilled labour);
- physical infrastructure (including roads, railways and ports);
- technological knowledge;
- sophisticated capital equipment.

Over time, countries that have inherited basic factors of production move to a situation where their competitiveness is based on advanced factors of production. These may also include:

- research and development;
- innovation;
- education;
- technical infrastructure.

Porter, Michael E., *The Competitive Advantage of Nations*. Basingstoke: Palgrave Macmillan, 1998.

Agency, markets and hierarchies

Examining agency, markets and hierarchies is an alternative way of looking at the coordination of economic activity. It is most closely associated with a strand of economics known as either information economics or organizational/neo-institutional economics.

It is generally agreed that perfect markets exist when:

- the businesses involved make decisions based on local information;
- they can also formulate production and consumption plans;
- the prices of products and services include all the information required to make decisions.

This approach, however, recognizes that market failure can occur when:

- factors arise from production costs;

A

- factors arise from transaction costs;
- information is too complex and not understood;
- there are insufficient businesses in the market.

The theory suggests that two different forms of market may evolve: namely, an oligopoly or an assisted market. There are three different associated hierarchies:

- Team-based – where the businesses have a common interest.
- Supervisory – where the businesses' interests conflict and one of the groups exercises control over the other businesses.
- Agency-based – where one of the businesses delegates a form of discretionary power to an agent.

Ansoff, Igor

The Ansoff matrix (see Figure 1) is one of a number of classic marketing concepts. It encapsulates the future vision of a business.

Igor Ansoff has made major contributions to the concepts surrounding corporate strategy ('A Practical System of Objectives' in *Corporate Strategy*). However, it is for the growth vector matrix that he is best known. The matrix examines the potential strategies available to a business in four areas, cross-referenced as new or existing markets and new or existing products. The matrix suggests the marketing strategies available to the business in each of these areas:

- *Market Penetration – Existing products into existing markets.*
  Management seeks to increase its market share with the current product range. This is considered to be the least risky strategy of all the available options. Existing customers are encouraged to buy

Figure 1 The Ansoff matrix

more products and services; those at present buying a competing brand are persuaded to switch; and non-buyers are convinced to begin to make purchases. Any readily recognizable weaknesses in the portfolio of the business need to be addressed and strengthened.

● *Market Development – Existing products into new markets.*
Systematic market research should reveal new potential markets for the existing products. Clearly defined segments are then targeted individually, either using existing marketing and distribution channels or, by setting up new ones to service the new segments. As the business is moving into new markets, it needs to be aware of potential differences in reactions, expectations and other factors.

● *Product Development – New products into existing markets.*
Assuming the business has sufficient resources, either new products or developments in the existing products can be brought onto the market. Provided the business has closely matched the new products with the requirements of the existing markets, risks are minimized. The major concern is 'time to market', which means the time it will take to develop the new products, and whether it will be possible to defray the development costs quickly.

● *Diversification – New products into new markets.*
This is considered to carry the highest risk of all of the strategies. Essentially, there are two options available to the business: the first is synergistic diversification, which relies on the business being able to harness its existing product and market knowledge (production processes, channels of distribution, etc.). The other option is known as 'conglomerate diversification', which means that the business departs from its existing product and market knowledge. This form of diversification is often achieved by merging with, or taking over, a business operating in another unrelated area (which in fact converts conglomerate diversification into synergistic diversification).

Ansoff, H. Igor, *Corporate Strategy* (The Library of Management Classics). London: Sidgwick & Jackson, 1986.

A

Asset reduction strategy

An asset reduction strategy, also known as a harvest strategy, is a means by which an organization seeks to limit or decrease its investment in its business by extracting as much cash from the operation as it can. Typically, an asset reduction strategy would be employed in a declining market or industry, allowing the business to optimize its **cash flow** levels.

Aston Group

The Aston Group was set up in Birmingham, England, in the 1960s. It is concerned with the study of organizational behaviour. Its work is exemplified by the following:

- Attempts to identify all of the variables used for describing organizations and their environment.
- Painstaking measurement (including reliable data and multiple scales).
- The breadth of investigation (which includes most of the different sectors of the economy).
- The levels of analysis (including groups and roles).

The Aston Group collected their data from informants and from already published data. They managed to create a number of concepts, notably problem-solving models, team working and early versions of **quality circles**.

Pugh, Derek S. and Hickson, David J., *Writers on Organizations*. London: Penguin Books, 1997.

Average collection period

The 'average collection period' is also known as the 'collection ratio'. It is the average time during which receivables are outstanding. It is calculated by taking the figure for accounts receivable, divided by the average daily sales.

A

Balanced scorecard

Robert Kaplan and David Norton developed the balanced scorecard system in the 1990s. The balanced scorecard seeks to assist businesses in clarifying their visions and strategies and provide them with a means by which they can be translated into action.

The balanced scorecard consists of four separate perspectives which aim to allow the business to develop measurement systems, data collection mechanisms and means by which information can be analysed. The four perspectives (see Figure 2) are:

- *Financial* – which includes metrics such as **cost–benefit analysis** and financial **risk assessment**.
- *Internal business processes* – which aim to identify how well the business is performing and whether the products and services offered meet customer expectations.
- *Learning and growth* – which seek to identify where employee training budgets can be best deployed with the objective of ensuring continued individual and corporate improvement.
- *Customers* – which focuses on the analysis of different types of customers, their degrees of satisfaction and the mechanisms or processes which are used by the business to deliver products and services to customers.

Kaplan, Robert S., Lowes, Arthur and Norton, David P., *Balanced Scorecard: Translating Strategy into Action*. Watertown, MA: Harvard Business School Press, 1996.

Barriers to entry

'Barriers to entry' is a term used to describe the way in which a business, or group of businesses, seeks to keep competition out of markets in which it is currently operating. There are four main ways in which this is achieved:

- A business may have control over a specific resource, such as oil, or may have an exclusive licence to operate, such as a broadcast agreement.

Figure 2 A balanced scorecard

- A large business which has significant **economies of scale** will have a **competitive advantage** because it can produce products and services at lower costs than those of its rivals.
- A business may protect its market by investing considerable sums in advertising and marketing, making it very difficult for competitors to make any impression in the marketplace.
- Large and powerful businesses can render a competitor's venture into their market far more risky by raising the exit costs. In this respect, they may have established specific ways of hiring employees, perhaps on long-term contracts, which have become the industry norm. It is therefore expensive for a newcomer to the market to try, and then fail, as dispensing with staff would become prohibitively expensive.

B

Barriers to imitation

It would be reasonable to assume that where technological innovations and new ideas can be brought onto the market much more swiftly than was hitherto thought imaginable, there would be little opportunity for competitors to copy. None the less, businesses are increasingly aware that competitors are not only able to imitate their products, but can also take significant advantage of the ways in which successful businesses operate.

Creating barriers to imitation involves attempts to sustain a **competitive advantage**. This can be done in a number of different ways, including:

- Legal restrictions, including patents, copyrights and trademarks.
- Superior access to inputs or to customers, either by having cost or quality advantages in inputs that are difficult for competitors to imitate, or in the case of customers, by having access to the best distribution channels or the most productive retail locations

Base/baseline

'Base' or 'baselines' can refer to either metrics or indices. Typically, a baseline is established reflecting the measure at the start of a particular period, or on the adoption of a new process. The baseline then operates as the comparator for future measurement. These measurements are expressed as changes from the baseline, to show improvements (or otherwise) in the results from that baseline figure and time.

The baselines can also be used as historical figures with which all future metrics and measurements can be compared.

Behavioural theory

The concept of behavioural theory is derived from the field of psychology and is often referred to as 'behaviourism'. In essence there are two forms of behaviourism, the first of which is known as classical conditioning; this suggests that individuals behave on the basis of reflex learning. They are conditioned by repetition to continue to behave in a particular way in similar circumstances. A slightly more sophisticated version is known as operant conditioning, which states that when individuals exhibit a particular behaviour and understand the consequences of what they have done, this is reinforced, making it more likely that they will do it again.

For the purpose of management, particular behaviours can indeed be reinforced in order to ensure that the correct response in certain circumstances is largely guaranteed. Equally, if individuals are not given encouragement and praise for particular behaviour, then it is likely that this form of behaviour will cease. Managers using this form of psychology theory are concerned with behaviour modification, using praise and discipline, and perhaps rewards, in order to reinforce desired behaviour. It is suggested that praise is a far more potent form of reinforcement than criticism or punishment and that feedback is of prime importance in order to ensure behaviour modification.

B

Benchmarking

A benchmark is a predetermined set of standards against which future performance or activities are measured. Usually, benchmarking involves the discovery of the best practice, either within or outside the business, in an effort to identify the ideal processes and prosecution of an activity.

The purpose of benchmarking is to ensure that future performance and activities conform with the benchmarked ideal in order to improve overall performance. Increased efficiency is key to the benchmarking process as, in human resource management, improved efficiency, reliability of data, and the effectiveness of activities will lead to a more competitive edge and ultimately greater profitability.

Damelio, Robert, *The Basics of Benchmarking*. Portland, OR: Productivity Press, 1995.

Bonus plan reward system

There is a wide variety of bonus schemes in operation in various businesses. Bonuses usually consist of additional payments made on a monthly or an annual basis, as a reward for good work, as compensation for dangerous work or as a share of the profits.

Other businesses will offer bonuses in relation to referrals. This is an integral part of human resource departments' methods of finding new employees for hard-to-fill jobs, particularly those with special skill requirements. Many businesses will offer a referral bonus payment to existing employees for recommending qualified candidates who are subsequently employed by the business. Clearly, there are strict regulations in respect of the suitability of the candidate and the length of service that the referred candidate actually completes (usually part of the payment is held back until the referred candidate has been working for the business for six months).

There are difficulties in using this system – especially, as there may be conflicts of interest. Some human resource departments come under intense pressure from existing employees to shortlist candidates that they have referred. In many cases there is also a system set up to ensure that improper promises or assurances of employment to prospective candidates are not made by existing employees.

Keenan, William, *Commissions, Bonuses and Beyond: The Sales and Marketing Management Guide to Sales Compensation Planning*. New York: McGraw-Hill Education, 1994.

B

Boston growth matrix

The Boston Consulting Group (BCG) was founded in 1963 by Bruce D. Henderson as the Management and Consulting Division of the Boston Safe Deposit and Trust Company (the Boston Company).

The theory underlying the Boston matrix is the product life cycle concept, which states that business opportunities move through life-cycle phases of introduction, growth, maturity and decline. The Boston classification, or BCG matrix, is a classification developed by the Boston Consulting Group to analyse products and businesses by market share and market growth (see Figure 3). In this, **cash cow** refers to a product or business with a high market share and low market growth, **dog** refers to one with a low market share and low growth, **problem child** (or 'question mark' or 'wild cat') has a low market share and high growth, and a **star** has high growth and a high market share.

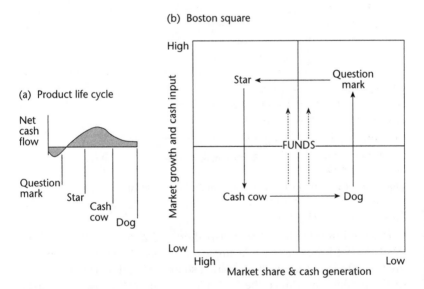

Figure 3 Linkage between the product life cycle and the Boston matrix

These phases are typically represented by an anti-clockwise movement around the Boston matrix quadrants (see Figure 4) in the following order:

● From a market entry position as a 'question mark' product.

Products are usually launched into high-growth markets, but suffer from a low market share.

- To a 'star' position, as sales and market share are increased. If the investment necessary to build sales and market share is successfully made, then the product's position will move towards the 'star' position of high growth/high market share.
- To a 'cash cow' position as the market growth rate slows and market leadership is achieved. As the impact of the product life cycle takes effect and the market growth rate slows, the product will move from the 'star' position of high growth to the 'cash cow' position of low growth/high share.
- Finally to a 'dog' position as investment is minimized as the product ages and loses market share.

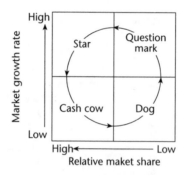

Figure 4 The anti-clockwise movement around the Boston matrix

At each position within the matrix there are a number of opportunities open to the business. For example, at the cash cow stage the options are either to invest to maintain market share, or to minimize investment in the product, maximize the cash returns, and grow towards market dominance with other products.

www.bcg.com

Bottom–up planning

Bottom–up planning is a form of consultative management style. The planning system encourages employee participation in both problem solving and decision making. In effect it is a form of **empowerment**, which aims to encourage flexibility and creativity across the organization. Bottom–up planning is also closely associated with organizations which have a **flat structure**. In other words, the hierarchy of the organization has few tiers of management, allowing employees far greater access on a day-to-day basis with key decision-makers within the organization. Bottom–up planning is the opposite of what is known as a **top-down planning** approach.

Brand loyalty

Brand loyalty is a consumer's preference to buy a particular brand in a product category; it is also the ultimate goal a business sets for a branded product.

Customers tend to become brand loyal when they perceive that the brand offers them the right mix of product features and images. Of equal importance is an appropriate level of quality at the right price. Having established this link, the customers are then more likely to use this as the foundation of their buying habits.

Typically, a customer would make a trial purchase of the brand, and if fully satisfied, would continue to buy the brand in the knowledge that this is a safe and reliable purchase. Loyal brand purchasers will be prepared to pay higher prices and they will actively recommend the brand to other purchasers.

Brand loyalty is an important concept, and reality, for businesses for the following reasons:

- It has been estimated that in the US, for example, an average business loses 50% of its customers every five years (around 13% annually). In any attempt to make a modest increase in growth of 1% or 2%, the business has to add the annual loss to the equation. Reducing these customer losses can dramatically affect business growth, and brand loyalty is seen as a major tool in achieving this goal.
- As brand loyalty grows, customers become less sensitive to price increases, making it possible for the business to charge premium prices for its products and services. Brand loyalists recognize that the brand offers them some unique values that they could not enjoy from a competing brand. Brand loyalist may be encouraged to buy more by the introduction of promotions, but money-off deals only tend to subsidize purchases that were already being planned by the loyal customers.
- Brand loyalists are willing to search for their favourite brand and are less sensitive to promotions offered by competitors. The busi-

B

ness offering the products or services which enjoy brand loyalty also reap the benefits of lower costs in advertising, marketing and distribution.

Given that it has been estimated that it costs some six times as much to attract a new customer as to retain an existing one, businesses constantly seek means by which to foster brand loyalty. The following approaches are typical:

- Consumers must like the product in order to develop loyalty to it, therefore positive brand attitudes are important.
- To convert occasional purchasers into brand loyalists, habits must be reinforced.
- Consumers must be reminded of the value of their purchase and encouraged to continue purchasing the product in the future.
- To encourage repeat purchases, advertisements before and after the sale are critical.
- The business needs to become a customer-service champion.
- Advertising shapes and reinforces consumer attitudes; these attitudes mature into beliefs, which need to be reinforced until they develop into loyalty.
- The business needs to make sure that customers get what they want from the product.
- To give customers an incentive to repeat-purchase, offer them the chance to win a prize, a gift (with proofs of purchase) or in-pack discounts.
- Tie up the distribution so that it is easier for the customers to buy the brand than competing brands.

Freeland, John G. (ed.), *The Ultimate CRM Handbook: Strategies and Concepts for Building Enduring Customer Loyalty and Profitability*. Maidenhead: McGraw-Hill, 2002.

B Broad differentiator

The term 'broad differentiator' refers to businesses which have developed ranges of products or services specifically targeted at particular market segments or niches.

According to P. Ward, D. Bickford and G. Leong (1996), a business can attempt to adopt any of three different configurations, namely:

- cost leader/differentiator;
- broad differentiator;
- niche differentiator.

The relationships between the three different approaches can be seen in Figure 5.

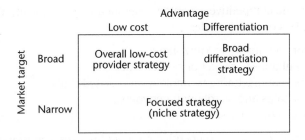

Figure 5 Approaches to differentiation

Ward, P., Bickford, D. and Leong, G., 'Configurations of Manufacturing Strategy, Business Strategy, Environment and Structure', *Journal of Management*, 22(4) (1996), pp. 597–626.

Bureaucratic costs

Bureaucratic costs arise in an organization as a result of problems related to coordination and motivation. Typically, bureaucratic costs arise from:

- supervisory monitoring;
- motivational problems;
- coordination activities;
- opportunism and information distortions.

There are also bureaucratic costs associated with the internalizing of activities: ultimately businesses may face the point where the costs of continuing to undertake all bureaucratic activities (both those required and those which have grown out of control) outweigh the transaction cost savings that would be afforded to them by **outsourcing** certain functions.

B

Business level (competitive) strategy

Clearly, businesses are concerned with the ways they can compete on every level of their activities. The primary goal is to establish a **competitive advantage** over their rivals and to be able to protect that advantage as best they can. Businesses not only aim to identify and gain this competitive advantage, but also seek an advantage which can be sustained.

Most businesses will focus upon their distinctive **core competences**, considering that these are vital to their success and will enable them to gain a sustained competitive advantage over their rivals. Typically, these core competences may include:

- superior technology or know-how;
- better/enhanced product or service features;
- superior manufacturing technology and related skills;
- superior sales and distribution networks;
- enhanced customer service provision.

Above all, business level competitive strategy involves conveying the notion that in some way the business is different, better in some respects. In other words, the business offers a unique mix of values – both perceived values and actual added value.

Business level strategy

Business level strategy is based on three key considerations:

- customer needs (what is being satisfied);
- customer groups (who is being satisfied);
- distinctive competitiveness (how customer needs are to be satisfied).

Customer needs can be satisfied through the characteristics of a business's products or services. Product differentiation can be seen as the process of creating a **competitive advantage** in designing product characteristics to satisfy those customer needs.

Defining customer groups, in essence **market segmentation**, involves grouping customers according to important differences in customer needs or preferences, to gain a competitive advantage. There are three approaches:

- Concentrate on the average customer, without segmenting at all.
- Develop products or services specifically for each identified group.
- Only serve selected segments.

Further, a business may decide to develop various versions of a given product or service in order to attract customers from different groups, and then focus on the most profitable groups.

The third issue regarding business strategy is to decide what type of distinctive competence to pursue in order to satisfy customer needs. Some businesses may focus on their production technology (developing distinctive manufacturing competences), others may focus on technological competence or sales and marketing competence. In all cases, the

B

business needs to combine and organize its resources to pursue this competence in order to gain and retain a competitive advantage.

Finlay, Paul, *Strategic Management: An Introduction to Business and Corporate Level Strategy*. London: Financial Times, Prentice-Hall, 2000.

Business principles

In effect, business principles are not unlike a **mission statement**, but perhaps they are more adequately described. The vast majority of statements of business principles tend to include some five related business principles, placing the more encompassing (and at times rather vague) mission statement at the top (see Figure 6).

MISSION STATEMENT

CORPORATE VALUES
(Policies and goals to be shared)

CORPORATE VISION
(Policies and goals to be shared)

CORPORATE CHANGE PROGRAMMES
(Programmes instituted to achieve goals)

CORPORATE ETHICS AND CODES OF PRACTICE
(Action guidelines to achieve goals)

Figure 6   The typical structure of a statement of business principles

See also **mission statement.**

B

Business process

Business processes are the activities undertaken by a business which allow it to function. The business processes within an organization carry its operations forward in a smooth and, hopefully, a profitable manner. Frequently, business processes are grouped by department or division, such as:

- Procurement – obtaining resources.
- Product development – planning, designing and refining products and services.
- Production – the manufacturing or providing of products and services.
- Delivery – receiving, fulfilling and tracking shipments.
- Accounting – the trailing of transactions and investments.
- Human resources – the hiring and firing of employees and the management of payroll and benefits.
- Marketing – the promotion of products or services.
- Customer service – the solving of customer problems.

Managers contribute to the business process by identifying and eliminating potential inefficiencies and bottlenecks in the business. They are actively involved in:

- elimination of flaws in the systems;
- the reduction of time spent on particular tasks;
- cost reduction;
- reduction in the use of resources;
- improvements in efficiency;
- improvements in quality;
- increasing customer satisfaction;
- increasing employee satisfaction.

Smith, Howard and Fingar, Peter, *Business Process Management: The Third Wave*. Tampa, FL: Meghan-Kiffer Press, 2003.

Business system

The term 'business system' is used to describe the way in which economic activities are organized and developed. Typically, a dominant institution or business system would develop in market economies. Business systems tend to have three key functions:

- governing the nature of the market relations between businesses;
- maintaining the coordination between businesses;
- overseeing the control systems within the businesses.

The business system both develops and governs the economic activities within the market, and established conventions are created, which tend to relate to the following:

- notions of trust between the exchange partners;
- whether there are dominant forms of identity and loyalty;
- norms which regulate relations.

State structures and policies can also have an impact upon the business itself, as can the way in which the financial system is organized in relation to the business system. Other considerations include the availability and development of labour skills. There is a strong interdependence between changes in the businesses that are involved in a market and this will affect the way competition is undertaken in these markets.

Buyer–supplier relationships

Given the fact that the average business spends more on supplied resources than on the resources it employs within the organization, the relationship between suppliers and the business is a vital concern.

The buyer–supplier relationship has a distinct strategic importance and, increasingly, studies have sought to understand the relationship. The creation of partnerships or relationships tends to revolve around the following aspects:

- trust;
- the length of relationship;
- the number of suppliers involved;
- the types of assets acquired from suppliers.

The two key considerations in regard to these relationships are:

- Supplier coordination – gaining an understanding and a **synergy** between the buyer and the supplier in order to anticipate and satisfy each other's needs.
- Supplier development – bringing the supplier into the decision making at the earliest stage to ensure the quantity and conformity of supplied items.

The overall relationship can be typified as in Figure 7.

Nellore, Rajesh, *Managing Buyer–Supplier Relations: The Winning Edge Through Specification Management: Tools and Techniques for Corporate Management.* London: Routledge, 2001.

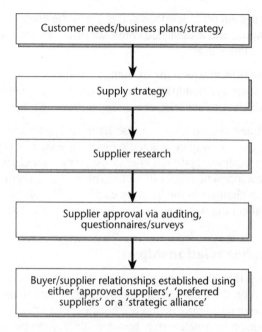

Figure 7 The development of relationships between buyer and supplier

B

Capabilities

'Capabilities' refers to the key skills which allow organizations to utilize and coordinate their resources. The capabilities allow businesses to use these resources at an optimum level in order to maximize their productivity and profitability.

See also **core competences.**

Capable competitors

'Capable competitors' is a term describing other businesses that can supply products or services which directly compete with a business on quality, delivery and service (and many other aspects).

The existence or non-existence of capable competitors often determines the business strategy of an organization, such as in the following examples.

- An absence of capable competitors, making imitation difficult, enables a business to be an aggressive sole provider of a product or service, if the business possesses the required skills and resources, and if there are suppliers of complementary products.
- Passive multiple licensing is possible when there are capable competitors, when the **barriers to imitation** are low, but where the other businesses lack the skills and resources required.
- Aggressive multiple licensing (combining licensing with aggressive positioning) can take place when businesses have the required skills and resources, the barriers to imitation are low and there are several capable competitors.
- Selective partnering occurs when the barriers to imitation are high, other businesses lack the required skills and resources, but there are potentially several different capable competitors.

Capacity control strategies

Simply, capacity is the maximum rate of output for a given process. It is usually measured in output per unit of time. Businesses will tend to use different units of time in order to calculate their capacity, such as per minute, per hour, per day or per shift. In truth, the maximum capacity is much better described as being the demonstrated capacity, as this is the true level of capacity which has been achieved. Some organizations and analysts will attempt to calculate a theoretical capacity, which is largely based on the capacity of the machines involved and rarely takes into account any variables which may affect the capacity. Businesses will attempt to operate at their optimum capacity. This means that they will attempt to reduce the costs or loss of capacity associated with waiting time.

Capacity management is best described as achieving the maximum output, content or performance of a given system or component. Capacity management is often applied to the area of information technology, describing or defining in both business and technical terms the requirements of a business's information technology. An efficient information technology infrastructure must be able to deliver, at the optimum cost, the ability to deal with specified levels of capacity. Capacity, in its simplest form, represents the probable volume of activities which the information technology infrastructure is able to cope with given normal circumstances. Clearly, capacity management needs to ensure that there is sufficient capacity, plus additional reserve capacity.

Capacity requirements planning (CRP) is the process of determining the short-term output demanded of an organization or one of its production processes. CRP is a computerized system that projects the load from a material requirements plan (MRP) onto the capacity of the system and then identifies under-loads and over loads. CRP is used by an organization to assess whether it can start new projects in the future, or whether it can produce an immediate order for a customer. Normally CRP will require information about when orders are required, details of equipment and labour, as well as orders which are already in the pipeline. The CRP will then be able to provide the organization with a profile for each operation in the production system. It will make an assessment of the work that needs to be completed and the work already in progress, in relation to the system's capacity. CRP relies on accurate information, defining capacity through the use of the following formula:

Number of machines or employees × number of shifts × utilization of machines and workers × efficiency

CRP is therefore used to calculate the ability of the organization to meet its orders.

Capital structure

Capital structure is a means by which the balance between a business's debt and its equity can be expressed.

Cash cow

Cash cows are part of the **Boston growth matrix** and represent established products or services which are likely to be in the mature phase of their product life cycle. Cash cows are well entrenched, with sales that have grown to a stable level.

Cash cows are considered to be profitable products or services which are making positive contributions to the business's **cash flow**. Businesses that have the advantage of having a cash cow or a number of cash cows as part of their portfolio are often encouraged by the income to consider launching product variants on the theme of the cash cow. This often ends in failure as it only serves to fragment the market and undermine the general sales and profitability of the cash cow. Instead, many businesses use the cash generated by the cash cow to develop and launch new products and services. They will inevitably target growth markets, while continuing to support the cash cow and its hard-won market share.

Some businesses also attempt to strengthen the position of their cash cows but this is often a costly and unsuccessful strategy. This leads to businesses recognizing that they need to set an upper limit on the support, providing the product maintains its market position.

Cash cows are vulnerable to cheaper substitute products which offer better or equal benefits. Equally, cash cows, being older than more recent substitutes, may have less technically developed means of production. This can make the unit costs of the cash cow less attractive than those of a newcomer. If a new competing product is successful, the cash cow's product life cycle will be shortened, reducing its financial return.

C

Cash flow

'Cash flow' is a term used to describe the net funds which have flowed through an organization over a period of time. Traditionally, cash flow is usually defined as earnings. The identification of when those earnings were received and when payments had to be made defines the parameters of cash flow. Calculating the cash flow figure is often complicated by the actual value of the cash received in a given period. Cash flow does not take into account expenses which may have been incurred by the organization prior to the period the cash flow covers, yet during this period the organization is benefiting from those costs in the past. Equally, the reverse is true; payments may now be due on equipment or stock from which the organization has already profited, and that has been noted on a previous cash flow account.

Cash flow calculation also has a difficulty in dealing with outstanding debts and money owed by creditors. These do not appear on the cash flow as neither has been paid, yet they are important considerations, as they may have a negative or a positive effect on the available working capital of the organization. The available funds which are calculated and identified within the cash flow have enormous implications for the business, particularly as the available working capital determines the organization's ability to pay subsequent debts promptly and to make necessary investments.

Graham, Alistair, *Cash Flow Forecasting and Liquidity*. New York: Amacom, 2000.

Centrality

Centrality is usually taken to mean the importance of a particular part of a business, perhaps a department or division, in terms of its involvement in the activities of other parts of the organization.

Centrality, therefore, measures or identifies key functional or service areas of a business upon which the rest of the organization may rely. Typically, divisions or departments with a high level of centrality are at the heart of resource transfers in the business.

Centralization

Centralization is a measure of how concentrated the decision-making processes are within an organization. The greater the concentration, the more centralized the organization is considered to be.

Chaining strategy

The term 'chaining strategy' has different meanings in different contexts. One of the most basic definitions relates to a business establishing a number of linked outlets which are so interconnected and reliant upon one another that they are able to function cooperatively as a single business entity.

W. C. Jordan and C. S. Graves (1995) suggested a means of chaining strategy which would allow businesses (particularly in manufacturing) to create flexible configurations. These flexible configurations combine, or chain, the stages of production effectively, helping to eliminate inefficiencies. Their approach suggests chaining strategies are ideal in dealing with multi-stage supply chains through which raw materials, components and finished goods pass.

Jordan, W. C. and Graves, C. S., 'Principles on the Benefits of Manufacturing Process Flexibility', *Management Science*, 41(4), (1998), pp. 577–94.

Clarity of expectations

Sound planning not only ensures focus, but also ensures clarity of expectations. In this sense clarity of expectations is an integral part of the structuring of tasks and the setting of deadlines. 'Clarity of expectations' refers to managers being precise regarding their instructions and communications in respect of ensuring that subordinates comprehend what is expected of them and what the likely outcome of a task is expected to be from the point of view of the performance.

Clarity of expectations is an integral part of enhanced communications, information-sharing and delegation.

Close substitutes

Close substitutes tend to be products or services which have some or all of the following features:

- They provide similar, the same, or equivalent product performance characteristics.
- They have broadly equivalent characteristics in terms of the occasions for which they are used.
- They are available for, or are targeted at, the same broad geographical market.

Cognitive biases

Essentially, cognitive bias is the tendency for individuals, however intelligent or well informed, to do the wrong thing.

Because certain issues or occurrences come to the mind more easily than others, individuals tend to use these occurrences as benchmarks for decision making rather than a better and more efficient alternative.

The human brain, it is said, is built for interpersonal relationships rather than statistics. Because of cognitive bias, managers need discipline, tools and quantitative methods in order to make the correct decisions.

Kahneman, Daniel and Tversky, Amos, 'Subjective Probability: a Judgement of Representativeness', *Cognitive Psychology*, July 1972.

Commission system

A commission-based pay is an incentive-based pay structure, which is widely believed to produce better results from employees than a traditional pay structure. Typically, sales staff are placed on commission-based pay. Their income is directly related to their performance and in most cases there is no ceiling to the amount of money they can earn. Commission-based pay structures are seen as a viable means of identifying those who are under-performing and who may require either redeployment or training. One of the many associated problems, however, with commission-based pay structures is that employees tend to focus on the sale of items which provide them with the largest return in relation to their time. Commission-based salaries tend to work when the products or services sold by a business have few variations. This means that employees will focus on building relationships with customers in order to provide steady commission payments.

Torkelson, Gwen E., *Contribution-Based Pay: Tools to Identify, Measure and Reward Performance.* Lincoln, NB: iUniverse.com, 2001.

Company infrastructure

Typically, the company infrastructure, or organizational infrastructure, is taken to mean the sum total of the following aspects of a business:

- Its **organizational structure** (as detailed and defined in the organizational chart).
- Its control systems (management, accountability, policies, procedures, rules and regulations).
- Its **organizational culture** (how it perceives issues, handles them and seeks to instil these ideas in its management and employees).

In essence then, company infrastructure details the means by which the business carries out all of its operations and applications to create value.

Competitive advantage

The term 'competitive advantage' refers to a situation where a business has a commercial advantage over the competition by being able to offer consumers better value, quality or service. Normally, a competitive advantage would result in lower prices, but where more benefits and greater quality are offered, higher prices are possible as a result of the competitive advantage enjoyed.

Porter, Michael E., *Competitive Advantage: Creating and Sustaining Superior Performance.* London: Simon & Schuster, 1988.

Competitive bidding strategy

Competitive bidding strategy is concerned with the offering of short-term contracts to suppliers on the basis of their ability to honour particular contracts won via a bidding system. Usually, but not exclusively, the winning bidder is the supplier who offers to fulfil the contract at the lowest price. Competitive bidding is an integral part of any project's cycle. Following the initial decision to pursue a project – which is a decision made by senior management in conjunction with sales personnel – and once demand has been established, an assessment is made of the requirements for the project.

The initiating business specifies the precise nature of the requirements of the contract. It then either approaches possible suppliers, or offers the contract out to wider supplier groups, usually by advertising the fact that the contract is available. Suppliers expressing an interest in the contract become involved in the first instance by obtaining tender specifications. The bidding phase consists of setting up a proposal, after having received an invitation to bid. The negotiation phase starts with the opening of bids and finishes with the signing of the contract. There is then an implementation phase, during which the supplier and the buyer identify and solve problems which may possibly arise.

Cova, B., Ghuari, P. and Salle, R., *Project Marketing: Beyond Competitive Bidding*. New York: John Wiley, 2002.

Ioannou, Photios and Leu, Son-Sen, 'Average Bid Method: a Competitive Bidding Strategy', *Journal of Construction, Engineering and Management*, 119(1) (1993), pp. 131–47.

Tweedy, Neil, *Winning the Bid: A Manager's Guide to Competitive Bidding*. London: Financial Times, Prentice-Hall, 1995.

Competitive environment

The most important aspect of a business's external environmental factors is its industry or competitive environment. Clearly, each different industry has its own characteristics, but in more complex organizations which are involved in a number of different markets, or a number of different overseas environments, the complexity of dealing with the competitive environment becomes all the more crucial.

It is widely believed that in order to assess the industry or competitive environment, a business has to consider seven key issues:

- The nature of the industry's dominant features, particularly the economic features.
- The nature and strength of the competition.
- Change factors which are having an impact on the industry's competitive structure and general environment.

- An identification of the major competitors and their relative competitive strength.
- An anticipation of any strategic initiatives which competitors are likely to make.
- An identification of any key factors which could determine competitive success.
- The attractiveness of the industry in drawing in new competitors and the ability of the business to attain a reasonable (sustainable) level of profitability.

Whilst the most often used model for diagnosing either the industrial or the competitive environment is Porter's **Five Forces model**, it does require a degree of detailing, particularly in relation to any relative strengths of importance, or specific forces relevant to a particular industry. Typically, any form of competitive analysis will begin with an investigation of the rivalry amongst existing businesses. In this respect the rivalry concerns direct competition and perhaps this is the most important of all the five forces. Specifics regarding such rivalry include the following:

- The rate of market or industry growth – in fast-growing markets, businesses may not be overtly competitive, as there is sufficient demand for all. However, should a market be in decline, or be experiencing slow growth, then it is inevitable that the businesses in that market will seek to seize market share from their competitors.
- The existence of capacity surplus – in many cases, since businesses are forced to fund their fixed costs, or are reluctant to leave a market because of the high exit costs, they are in a position where they have excess capacity. This means that supply exceeds demand. In these cases the price expected for products and services is depressed and consequently a business's profits suffer.
- The size and number of competitors – when business competitors in a market are broadly equal in their capabilities and size, there is a tendency for competition to increase. Customers will also switch from one supplier to another when there are sufficient numbers of options available to them. In these cases rivalry is at a high level.
- New competitors – this aspect of the competitive environment concerns what may be known as either diverse or relatively new competitors. In effect, these new competitors challenge both one another and the existing businesses, as they may have different ideas regarding competition. Dangerously, there are unknown factors. New competitors come into the market without a precise knowledge of the competitive boundaries and may well adopt

strategies which were hitherto unknown in the industry. Whilst smaller new competitors can be easily dealt with, comparatively speaking, larger firms that have acquired a business which will compete more vigorously in the market are a much more dangerous proposition, as they have the funds and the resources to back their competitive bid.

- **Standardization** of products and services – it is clearly the case that as similar products and services appear, a greater definition needs to be made in order to retain customers. When products and services are, to all intents and purposes, interchangeable, businesses tend to be more competitive and will resort to drastic pricing or promotional strategies in order to gain a **competitive advantage**.
- High **exit barriers** – if it is particularly difficult for businesses to leave an industry or market because of the high costs involved, they are left with one simple option. This option is to compete, and perhaps, to compete on a more extreme basis than they have done before.

Another significant aspect of investigating the competitive environment is an analysis of any potential new entrants to the market or industry. Some industries are less susceptible to this form of additional competition, as customers may be reluctant to switch from one supplier to another, or there may be especially high **barriers to entry**. Typical barriers to entry include the following:

- The requirement to acquire specific or specialized resources, such as financial backing, technology, or **economies of scale**.
- Highly differentiated products or services, so that it may be difficult for potential new entrants to find a ready market, as customers are already using the most appropriate products or services offered by existing businesses.
- High capital requirements – significant investment in relation to possible returns can be a major dissuading factor for potential entrants.
- Limited access to distribution channels – when many of the distribution channels are already dominated by existing businesses and there are no viable alternatives to the traditional channels, it may deter new entrants as they will find no easy way of getting their products and services to the end-user.
- Regulatory restrictions – in certain cases public or private monopolies exist which effectively bar new entrants from specific markets. This has been particularly the case in many infrastructure-based industries, notably transport.

- Tariffs and trade restrictions – in certain cases, under the terms of the General Agreement on Tariffs and Trade (GATT), countries may erect tariffs, quotas, or other forms of trade restriction, to effectively protect their domestic markets from overseas competition. Whilst such protectionist policies are on the decline, they are still a considerable impediment to potential new entrants to a market if their products or services become too expensive as a result of tariffs, or if the volume of their exports is reduced because of quotas or other restrictive trade practices.

New entrants tend to be successful and represent a good competitive risk if they can create a **synergy** with their existing lines of business. Equally, they are a threatening prospect if they have access to considerable financial resources, alternative technology and government assistance, or if they can penetrate the distribution channels.

Competition in the form of substitute products or services is also a concern. These substitute products may either be new, or may already exist. In the case of an existing product being used as a substitute, this is brought about by that product or service being transferred into a new market with which, hitherto, it was not necessarily associated. Prime examples include email, which has become an effective substitute for postal services. New products or services are strictly those which did not exist before, and which represent a major improvement over the products and services that were originally available. Prime examples from the recent past include the virtual replacement of typewriters by computers or word processors, and electronic watches replacing traditional mechanical watches. In recent years, music and film, for example, have seen a number of major changes. Cassette tapes provided an alternative to the traditional vinyl record, and both have gradually been replaced by CDs, which in turn are in the process of being replaced by internet music files.

The other major consideration concerning the competitive environment is the strength of the suppliers to the businesses operating in a given market. Some suppliers are more powerful and can dictate the course, or fortunes, of the competition within the market, usually under the following circumstances:

- They are strong when there are few suppliers and demand for their products or services is high.
- They are also strong when they have a large number of customers and have options open to them as to who they sell to and at what price they sell their products.

- Strength can also be found in cases where suppliers produce unique products or services, which cannot be obtained elsewhere.
- Strength can be derived from circumstances where the suppliers have access to greater financial resources than the other businesses operating within the market.
- Another consideration regarding supplier strength is that these firms could decide to engage in forward integration

The final factor in assessing the competitive environment is the buyers themselves. Buyers can be other businesses or they can be consumers, and in cases where buyers have numerous available sources for the products they need, they have a relatively strong position. They are also significant where there are actually very few buyers and demand is considerably less than supply. In cases where buyers can easily substitute one product or service for another, they have relative strength, provided that the products and services are not in themselves sufficiently differentiated. Another major consideration regarding buyers is the fear that they may decide to engage in backward integration.

Thompson, Arthur A. and Strickland, A. J., *Strategic Management*. New York: McGraw-Hill Education, 2001.

Competitive intelligence

Competitive intelligence (CI) is increasingly seen as a distinct business management discipline, which provides an input into a whole range of decision-making processes.

There are four stages in monitoring competitors, known as the Four Cs:

1 Collecting the information.
2 Converting information into intelligence (CIA: Collate and catalogue it, Interpret it, and Analyse it).
3 Communicating the intelligence.
4 Countering any adverse competitor actions.

Competitive strategies, development of

This is a potentially complex area of study, but includes all of the activities of a business aimed at maintaining a competitive edge in the market. The overall competitive strategy options are summarized in Table 3.

Table 3 Competitive strategies

Characteristics	Introduction	Growth	Maturity	Decline
Sales	Low	Rapidly rising	Peak	Declining
Costs	High per customer	Average per customer	Low per customer	Low per customer
Profitability	Negative	Rising profits	High profits	Declining profits
Customers	Innovators	Early adopters	Middle majority	Laggards
Competitors	Few	Growing number	Stable, but beginning to decline	Declining numbers
Marketing objectives	Create product awareness and trials	Increase market share	Maximize profits and defend market share	Milk brands and reduce costs
Product	Basic product	Product extensions	Diversification	Eliminate weaker products
Price	Cost plus	Penetration	Competitive or matching the competition	Price reductions
Place	Selective	Intensive	More intensive	Eliminate unprofitable areas of the distribution
Advertising	Build product awareness among early adopters and dealers	Build product awareness and interest in the mass market	Focus on brand differences and benefits	Reduce to level needed to retain loyal customers
Sales promotion	Heavy use to encourage trials	Reduce as mass market begins to make purchases	Increase to encourage and discourage brand switching	Reduce to a minimum

Doyle, Peter, 'The Realities of the Product Life Cycle', *Quarterly Review of Marketing,* Summer 1976.

Wasson, Chester R., *Dynamic Competitive Strategy and Product Life Cycles*. Austin, TX: Austin Press, 1978.
Weber, John A., 'Planning Corporate Growth with Inverted Product Life Cycle', *Long Range Planning*, October 1976, pp. 12–29.

Competitiveness, determinants of

An analytical framework can be created which assumes that overall innovativeness and competitiveness are determined by industry-specific determinants:

- technology;
- the characteristics of the markets;
- corporate strategies;
- the organization of transactions.

The technological component refers to the tools available in producing the services and then transferring them to the end-user. Market-induced competitiveness refers to the economic performance which results from the structural characteristics of the market and the strategies of the businesses operating in it. The relationships can be seen in the diagram in Figure 8.

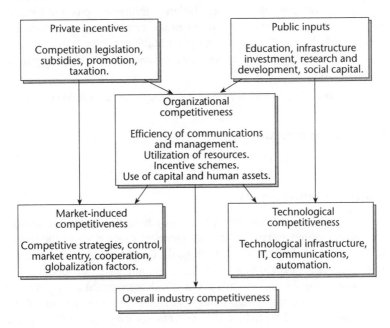

Figure 8 Business competitiveness

Competitiveness of related and supporting industries

The competitiveness of related and supporting industries is one of Michael Porter's key determinants of national competitiveness, along with factor and demand conditions, and business strategy, structure and rivalry. Increasingly, international suppliers and related industries have increased the level of competition in both upstream and downstream industries. Porter, amongst others, suggests that whilst these competing related and supporting industries offer both benefits and potential threats to a business, it is access to a domestic market which is of primary concern. Businesses that can obtain efficient, early and rapid (and in some cases preferential), access to cost-effective inputs, have a significant advantage.

Porter, Michael, *Competitive Advantage of Nations*. Basingstoke: Palgrave Macmillan, 1998.

Complementors

The power of complementors arises when the value of a business's products or services depends upon the availability of others. Toothpaste on its own, for example, would have no value without toothbrushes. Complementors directly influence the profitability of a given market. In the absence of the correct complementors, or if those complementors develop slowly or are of poor quality, profitability can be harmed.

The concept of complementors was probably first introduced by Andy Grove of Intel.

Grove, Andrew, *Only the Paranoid Survive*. New York: HarperCollins Business, 1998.

Conflict aftermath

See conflict management.

Conflict management

Conflict management involves situations where there may be opposition, incompatible behaviour and antagonistic interaction, or the blocking of individuals from reaching their goals. Conflict behaviour can range from questioning or doubting, to a desire to annihilate the opponent.

Typically, conflicts will arise out of disagreements, disputes or debates. Conflict is not always a negative aspect for a business and there is no specific need to reduce all conflicts, as they ebb and flow and become an inevitable part of organizational life. Indeed, many consider conflict to be essential for growth and survival. Therefore, conflict management includes both decreasing conflict and increasing it.

There are various forms of conflict but they can be broadly distinguished as being either functional or dysfunctional. Functional conflict, or constructive conflict, was first suggested in 1925 by Mary Parker Follett. It increases information and ideas, encourages innovative thinking, allows different points of view to be raised and reduces organizational stagnation.

Dysfunctional conflict, on the other hand, usually arises from tensions, anxieties and stresses. It reduces trust, and often poor decisions are made because of distorted or withheld information. Management tends to be obsessed with dysfunctional, high-conflict situations.

There is also a sub-division, which is dysfunctional low conflict, which again is negative in the sense that few new ideas are presented, and there is a lack of innovation and of sharing of information, all of which leads to stagnation.

Conflict management involves three levels of conflict: there could be conflict between organizations; there could be group conflict within the organization; and also conflict between individual members within the groups.

Generally it is considered that there are three kinds of conflict episodes. These are:

- Latent conflict – which is behaviour which starts a conflict episode.
- Manifest conflict – which is the observable conflict behaviour.
- Conflict aftermath – which is the end of a conflict episode; this can become the latent conflict for another episode in the future.

Clearly, it is conflict management, appearing between the manifest conflict and the conflict aftermath, which seeks to lower the level of the conflict itself. A more complete view of conflict episodes and the place of conflict management within this system can be seen in Figure 9.

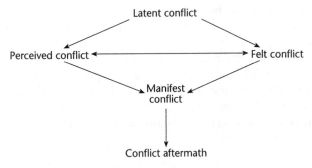

Figure 9 The place of conflict management

As can be seen in the diagram, perceived conflict occurs when individuals become aware that they are in conflict. Conflict can be perceived even when no latent conditions exist. A prime example is the misunderstanding of another person's position on an issue. Felt conflict is the emotional or personalizing part of the conflict and is exemplified by oral or physical hostility. These are the hardest episodes for managers to control.

The various episodes link the conflict aftermath to future latent conflict, and effective conflict management breaks this connection by discovering the latent conflicts and removing them. An ideal conflict management model, which would seek to maintain conflict at functional levels, would include the following:

- no complete elimination of conflict;
- an increase in dysfunctional low conflict;
- choosing a desired conflict level based on perceived conflict requirements;
- a tolerance to conflict.

Mayer, Bernard S., *The Dynamics of Conflict Resolution: A Practitioner's Guide*. New York: Jossey-Bass Wiley, 2000.

Congruence

See goal congruence.

Consolidated industry

Consolidation is a measure which is often applied to the study of particular industries. In the UK, for example, some 85 per cent of all retail sales are achieved by just 500 different businesses. It is therefore imperative for businesses in a competitive environment to understand the dynamics of the market. Highly consolidated industries are typified by a dominance of the market by a handful of businesses, relatively speaking, though these may appear to the consumer to be a broader range than they actually are. Consolidation has gradually been achieved in many areas of industry by large multinational businesses through mergers and acquisitions. In order to give the impression that there is still considerable choice and competition, these businesses have tended to retain old company names, and continued to trade under these names, despite the fact that they are enjoying all the **economies of scale** associated with a larger business enterprise.

Consumer-oriented business definition

Consumer or customer orientation is a marketing principle followed by businesses which view their entire operations in terms of the end-user. All product development, production, distribution and marketing are aimed at fulfilling consumer needs and wants. This marketing concept is diametrically opposed to a product or production orientation, which seeks to find markets, and persuade consumers to buy existing products and services that have not been initially designed to match their needs.

Continuum of business activities

The continuum of business activities addresses the important role of capital and labour in the production process. The continuum addresses the extent to which capital and labour influence the production process and the physical properties of the outputs. As can be seen in Figure 10, industries very reliant on labour are located in categories A and E. The other categories are, to a greater or lesser extent, capital-dominated manufacturing industries or capital-dominated services.

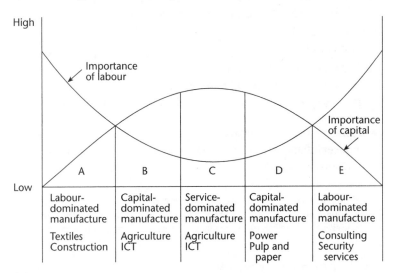

Figure 10 Continuum of capital and labour roles

Cooperative strategies

Cooperative strategies, as the term implies, involve competitive strategies based around mutual assistance between businesses. Effectively, any cooperative strategies could be deemed to be **strategic alliances**. These forms of strategy involve the following:

- An agreement or an alliance between two or more businesses.
- The desire to achieve specified objectives.
- The fact that the alliance is mutually beneficial.

There are a number of reasons why businesses may choose to become involved in a cooperative strategy; the following list addresses some, but by no means all, of the possible reasons:

- to obtain or share in technology;
- to share the benefits of particular manufacturing capabilities in a synergistic way;
- to share a degree of access to a particular market;
- to reduce risks (such as market risk, or political or financial risks);
- to achieve a form of competitive advantage which would be otherwise unobtainable if tackled alone.

The exact nature of the cooperative strategy will very much depend upon the objectives of the business, and perhaps, upon the nature of the markets and competition. Some of the possibilities for cooperative strategy include:

- Mutual service groups or consortia – which occur when businesses pool their resources to obtain high-value capital assets.
- Straightforward licensing agreements.
- **Joint ventures** – where a new business entity is brought into existence in order to achieve particular objectives.
- **Value chain** partnerships and agreements – such as **just-in-time** supplier relationships or the **outsourcing** of certain value chain functions.

Beamish, Paul W. and Killing, Peter (eds), *Cooperative Strategies: North American Perspectives*. New York: Jossey-Bass Wiley, 1997.
Boyce, Gordon H., *Co-operative Structures in Global Business: Communicating, Transferring Knowledge and Learning Across the Corporate Frontier*. London: Routledge, 2000.

Coordination and control

Although economists view coordination and control as being, effectively, either the **invisible hand** or conscious coordination by businesses (entrepreneurs or bureaucratic structures), there are other views on the subject. Notably, there are two other major attempts to explain the coordination and control of markets. These are:

- Cognition-based coordination and control – using the transfer of knowledge via standards or methods of working, where effects and professional skills are evaluated.
- Relation-based coordination and control – which is achieved by a business hierarchy, or a power or leadership structure. This brings about a gradual adjustment in the form of coordination and control.

In fact, of course, the coordination and control of any market or series of markets is a mixture of all of these drivers. Increasingly, however, coordination and control has to be dynamic and flexible enough to deal with a constantly changing environment, which displays differing levels of competitiveness at different times.

Core and complementary assets

Core and complementary assets are a key feature of ensuring that a business can build a strong strategy to manage its operations. The overall core and complementary asset structure in relation to the main elements of a business is best described as in Figure 11.

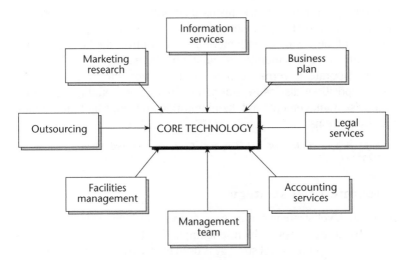

Figure 11   Core and complementary assets

Assuming the core technology is viable, the complementary assets need to be identified and provided. Often the business will consider making partnership decisions or acquisitions to secure essential assets.

Core competences

Core competences have two specific definitions. The first is the identification of the key skills, knowledge and experience required of an individual to carry out a specific job role.

The other definition refers to the ability of employees or managers to be adaptable in the sense that they could work in an alternative remote location, in particular abroad. In these cases core competences examine the adaptability and resourcefulness of the managers in operating in what may be an unknown overseas environment.

> Stone, Florence M. and Sachs, Randi T., *High-value Manager: Developing the Core Competences Your Organization Demands.* New York: Amacom, 1996.

Corporate governance

The three key aspects of corporate governance mechanisms are:

- ownership structure;
- monitoring and controlling mechanisms;
- management performance.

Corporate governance mechanisms deal with the ways in which the management structure, as determined by the ownership and overall structure of the business, both monitors and controls the business while at the same time it is monitored and controlled itself.

The corporate governance mechanisms cover: the board structure and composition; disclosure standards; financial accounting and standards; risk management; and the monitoring and control of information and transactions.

> Monks, Robert and Minow, Nell, *Corporate Governance.* Oxford: Blackwell Publishing, 2003.

Corporate level strategy

Corporate level strategy can be seen as the overarching strategy, put in place by a business, which encompasses the deployment of its resources. Corporate level strategy is used to move the business towards its goals in various areas of activity, including production, finance, research and development, personnel and marketing.

> Lynch, Richard, *Corporate Strategy.* London: Financial Times, Prentice-Hall, 2002.

Corporate planning, process of

At any level of management, a planning process must be undertaken in order to outline, monitor and implement, and then to continue to monitor and assess the outcomes of, any plan. In order to do this the senior management must first identify and agree performance levels, both operational and financial. Typically they will also identify when these particular performance levels should be reached. Clearly, at corporate level the planning process can be fairly complex; not only does it have to incorporate a series of both qualitative and quantitative objectives or measurements, but it also has to achieve the overall support of those within the organization. Whilst there is no definitive model of the corporate planning process, the conceptual model in Figure 12 indicates the overall series of steps which need to be undertaken in a specific order to achieve a viable corporate level plan.

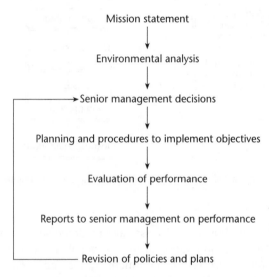

Figure 12   Conceptual model of the planning process

The business needs to formulate a plan which is in broad accord with the organization's posture and position, otherwise it will be impossible for the organization to have any hope of achieving the performance objectives. The planning process should also indicate the journey upon which the organization is about to embark, in order to achieve the objectives and to achieve its new position and posture in the future.

None of this planning can take place without due attention to the organization's external environment. The organization needs to analyse the environment and use this information as the basis for its forecasting.

It is only then that the business can begin to develop performance objectives and, above all, decide how these performance objectives will be achieved. In other words, the business must apply a series of rational criteria, linked to the current position and posture, in order to move forward. In many respects the model for any planning process is in essence a process which incorporates issue management, as can be seen in Figure 13.

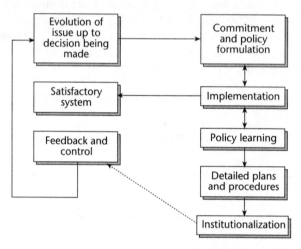

Figure 13   Conceptual planning model incorporating issue management

This model shows how the business can at first recognize that a decision needs to be made in relation to the overall plan. The issue cannot be advanced until there is a commitment by the organization and a policy formulated in order to deal with it. Only at this point can that element of the plan be implemented.

There are two factors which can now develop in relation to the issue. The policy implementation may be satisfactory, in which case regular feedback and control may reveal new issues for which commitment and policy formulation need to be developed. However, it is rare that the implementation policy is a smooth process and there may be a period, which can be called a policy learning phase, where the business and its employees and management gradually incorporate the new policy into their day-to-day thinking. At this stage the detail of the plan can come into operation, with detailed procedures regarding the new policy. Eventually the policy will become, in effect, institutionalized and an integral part of the overall business operations. Again, regular feedback and control systems will identify new issues, for which policy formulation and implementation will have to follow.

Johnson, Gerry and Scholes, Kevan, *Exploring Corporate Strategy: Text and Cases.* London: Financial Times, Prentice-Hall, 2001.

Corporate raiders

A corporate raider is an individual or a group of investors who make investments in a business purely on the basis that they will resell the business, either as a whole or in pieces.

Corporate raiders are, in effect, extractive investors. They spot inefficient businesses whose asset value is greater than their stock market valuation. They attempt a take-over of the business by quietly buying the shares at the prevailing (low) price.

The raider then tenders a bid to the board of directors of the target business to buy up the outstanding shares at a price higher than the market price, but lower than the 'break-up' value.

Usually, the raider will use borrowed capital to finance the deal. The target businesses have a high equity to debt ratio as a result of the purchase, so assets can be sold off. Capital can be raised by:

- the sale of profitable units;
- the drawing of cash reserves;
- relocation to cheaper premises (perhaps overseas);
- job cuts.

With the disposal of these assets, the business now reports a stronger profit and the business is resold at a higher market value than that for which it was originally purchased.

Corporate social responsibility

Corporate social responsibility reflects any sense of obligation that an organization may feel it is appropriate to include as an integral part of its strategic decision making. The options and application can best be summarized as in Table 4.

Corporate social responsibility is important in the following senses:

- It can avoid adverse publicity.
- It can avoid law suits or legislative procedures.
- It can resolve issues before they reach a critical stage.

Social issues clearly include a wide variety of environmental issues. Businesses seek to formulate policies to deal with them. These policies can come about either through the business's own actions or by government legislation. Typically, the following steps outlined in Table 5 would be taken by a business.

Table 4 Corporate social response

Factor	Corporate social responsibility	Corporate social responsiveness
Initiation	Business itself and managers	Stakeholders
Time frame	Long term	Medium term
Motivation	Trusteeships	Stakeholder power
Action	Philanthropic Paternalistic	Practical response to demands of stakeholders

Table 5 Possible policies relating to social issues

Steps	Detail
Identification of issues/trends/ public expectations	Scanning the environment for trends and issues; tracking these trends and issues as they develop; identification of those applicable to the business.
Evaluation of impacts and setting of priorities	Assessing impacts and the probability of occurrence; assessing organizational resources needed to respond; preparation of priorities for further analysis.
Conducting research and analysis	Categorization of issues; ensuring that priority issues have staff assigned to them; involvement of functional areas; development and analysis of position strategies.
Development of strategy	Analysis of position and strategy options; decision on strategic options available; integration with overall business strategy.
Implementation strategy	Dissemination of agreed policies and strategies; development of tactics which are consistent with overall strategies; development of alliances; establishment of internal and external communication flows.
Evaluation of strategy	Assessment of results; modification of implementation plans; undertaking of additional research (if necessary).

Harvard Business Review, *Harvard Business Review on Corporate Responsibility*. Boston, MA: Harvard Business School Press, 2003.

Corporate strategic change

Attempting to understand and manage change at a corporate level has become all the more important with the advent of global markets. Originally, scientific management approaches were used to track strategic change in organizational development and the management of human resources. The most important approach today uses a more strategic focus, namely:

- There is an assumption that in all markets there are clear competitors vying for control.
- Managers, at their core, are rational decision-makers.
- Organizations are passive in themselves, but subject to planning changes by senior management.

Unfortunately there is no universally approved means of looking at corporate strategic change – change itself can be either radical or incremental. There are, however, some common strategic change drivers, as can be seen in Figure 14.

	New	**Change**
Future	Market development Product development New technologies	Strategic development of HR Organizational change Process development
	Customers/Products	**People processes**
Present	Orders Service Account management Market requirements	Manufacturing Reporting (financial operations) Audits HRM
	External	Internal

Figure 14 Strategic drivers of change

A basic model for corporate level strategic change could be exemplified as in Figure 15.

Thompson, John, *Strategic Management: Awareness and Change*. London: Thomson Learning, 2001.

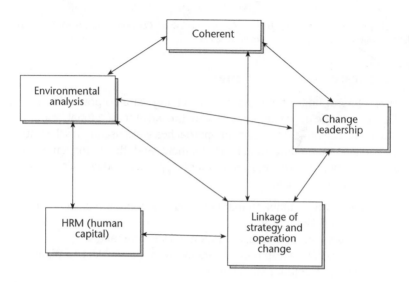

Figure 15   Basic model of strategic change

Cost-leadership strategy

Cost-leadership strategy, although it is more often thought of as a generic marketing strategy, has considerable implications for human resource management and strategic management. Cost-leadership strategy aims to provide the business with a competitive advantage by lowering the costs of its operations. This inevitably means that since the drive is towards increased profitability via a reduction in costs, which could also lead to a reduction in prices, there will be pressure on employees in many different areas of their work. Clearly a policy can be adopted which seeks to reduce the overall demands on the business in terms of pay, either by a reduction in the workforce, or by requiring each individual to show a higher degree of productivity and contribution towards profit. Another inevitable implication is the use of outsourced labour in order to provide products and services at a lower cost than could be achieved by employing a workforce directly. Businesses will seek to find means by which the human resource department can identify cost savings, either by reducing staff numbers, by job enlargement or by multiskilling.

Pohlmann, Randolph, Gardiner, Gareth S. and Heffes, Ellen M., *Value Driven Management: How to Create and Maximize Value Over Time for Organizational Success.* New York: Amacom, 2000.

Crisis management

For most organizations, crisis management is an unavoidable situation where the business's survival or well-being is threatened by an unexpected problem. Most organizations will have established a series of contingency plans in order to ensure that specific steps have been outlined to deal with similar, predicted situations. In most cases the business will appoint an individual, probably from the board or senior management, to deal with the situation. This individual will be given the full support of the board and may be granted considerable authority to deal with the crisis. Swift decision making is essential in crisis management as immediate remedies are required in order to ensure the business's continued survival.

Fink, Steven, *Crisis Management: Planning for the Inevitable*. Parkland, FL: Universal Publishers, 2000.

Critical business issues

Critical business issues are part of organizational **process mapping**. They represent the differences between the current position of an organization and its desired future position. There is a strong linkage with **critical business needs** (specifically **critical success factors** and **core competences**). Critical business issues are used to define potential deficiencies in the organization at the process level.

See also **process mapping**.

Critical business needs

The critical business needs are identified within a strategic planning process. They consist of the **critical success factors** and the **core competences** and, above all, what the business needs to do in order to support them within the context of the business process.

Critical success factors

A business may identify critical success factors (CSFs) as a means by which to determine its own strategic objectives. Each of the major objectives has associated CSFs, which in theory should be achieved *en route* to the principal objective or objectives. In other words, these CSF criteria are major milestones along a continuing process towards the objectives as identified by the business.

Sashkin, Marshall and Sashkin, Molly G., *Leadership that Matters: The Critical Factors for Making a Difference in People's Lives and Organizations' Success*. San Francisco, CA: Berrett-Koehler, 2003.

Cross-cultural communication

Cross-cultural communication has become an increasingly important concern for businesses engaged in international trade. The desire is to pay regard to the customs and business etiquette of other countries in which a business may trade. Increasingly, multinational businesses are trying to understand cultural differences and how these affect the way in which business is practised. Cross-cultural communication requires sensitivity to the customs and culture of other nations, without which potentially important business opportunities would be lost.

Although English has become the dominant business language in the world, the speaking of foreign languages would not only be beneficial, but may often be expected in other cultures in order to cement positive business relationships.

Current ratio

The current ratio is used as an indicator of whether a business has the ability to meet its short-term debts. Typically, it is calculated by dividing the current assets by the current liabilities.

The current assets include all cash, or assets which can be easily converted into cash (stock, debtors etc.). By dividing the current assets by the current liabilities, a business will be able to assess the coverage it has with which to meet its obligations. For example, a business may have current assets valued at $950,000 and current liabilities of $450,000. In this case the current ratio can be calculated as:

$$\frac{950,000}{450,000} = 2.11$$

This figure can be expressed as 2.11:1. The ratio shows that the business has $2.11 of current assets for every $1.00 of current liabilities. If the industry standard current ratio was 2:2, then this business would be considered to have a satisfactory current ratio.

Fridson, Martin and Alvarez, Fernando, *Financial Statement Analysis: A Practitioner's Guide*. New York: John Wiley, 2002.
Temple, Peter, *Magic Numbers: The 33 Key Ratios that Every Investor Should Know*. New York: John Wiley, 2001.

Customer defection rate

According to the American Management Association, the majority of profits of a business come from its loyal customers and, typically, loyal customers account for 65% of an organization's revenue. It further suggests that a 5% cut in the customer defection rate could lead to a profit increase of between 25% and 85%. In other words, by reducing the number of customers lost to competitors, a business could double its growth in a year.

Given that it costs five times as much to obtain new customers as it does to retain a current customer, businesses are increasingly concerned with customer retention figures. Having said this, the vast majority of businesses do not know their own customer defection rate.

Typically, businesses will wait to improve their services until it looks as if customers are going to defect to another business; usually by this time it is too late – the decision has already been made. To combat this, database marketing seeks to identify average customer behaviours and, in effect, set up a trip-wire event to warn the business that a customer is considering defecting to a competitor.

Customer delight

In essence, 'customer delight' is a measure of how much a product or service exceeds the expectations of customers. Normally, customer delight will be measured in terms of quality and service. It is a prime measure of customer satisfaction.

Typically, customer delight is achieved by:

- being cost effective;
- being better than the competition;
- responding faster to customers.

The attainment of customer delight therefore involves the following areas of the business:

- partnerships with distributors/suppliers;
- the management (as defined as a commitment to customer delight);
- the commitment of employees;
- responses to customer feedback;
- quality monitoring and management.

Keiningham, Timothy L. and Vavra, Terry G., *The Customer Delight Principle: Exceeding Customers' Expectations for Bottom-line Success.* New York: Contemporary Books, 2001.

C

Customer response time

Customer response time is a measure of a business's ability to provide products or services to its customers. Customer response time is also known as 'waiting time in line' (WTIL). Waiting time in line describes the usually non-productive time during which customers have to wait before being served or having their orders processed. There are essentially three costs that must be balanced in a waiting line system: the cost of service and the cost of waiting, as well as the cost of a scheduling system. Theoretically, a scheduling system is a management strategy designed to avoid waiting lines.

In cases where the cost of service and the cost of waiting are known and measurable, the organization can attempt to determine the optimal, or close to optimal, waiting system configuration and rate of service. However, the cost of service has a positive relationship with the rate of service; conversely, the cost of waiting has a negative relationship with the rate of service. In other words, the faster the service rate, the higher the cost of service, and the faster the service rate, the lower the cost of waiting. The opposite applies with a slower service rate meaning a lower cost of service but a higher cost of waiting.

Dshalalow, Jewgeni H. (ed.), *Advances in Queuing: Models, Methods and Problems.* London: CRC Press, 1995.

Chen, H. and Yao, D. D., *Fundamentals of Queuing Networks: Performance, Asymptotics, and Optimization* (Applications of Mathematics). New York: Springer-Verlag, 2001.

Customer responsiveness

Customer responsiveness is a measure of a business's ability not just to identify, but also to satisfy, the needs or requirements of its customers. Various reports suggest that up to 40% of businesses fail to respond to even simple customer requests. In a survey carried out by RDMP (a UK-based marketing company website) in 2003, 250 of the top 500 FTSE businesses, including those in finance, insurance, communications, utilities and manufacturing, who had collectively spent £16.5bn a year on advertising, failed in basic consumer responsiveness measures. Some 92% failed to re-contact a customer who had made an initial enquiry, and only 24% of enquiries were replied to within 24 hours. In spite of the rise and importance of websites, some 66% of these businesses failed to respond to consumers who had requested information or asked questions via their websites.

www.computerweekly.com/article122826.htm

www.rdmp.co.uk

Customer satisfaction

Customer satisfaction is a means by which businesses can assess how their actions measure up to the expectations of their customers. Measuring customer satisfaction requires a continued survey of how customers perceive the business and the level of service, including response times, value, and other aspects of their dealings with the business.

Customization

Customization is a trend that has been slowly developing over recent years. It aims to create bespoke products and services which closely match the exact needs and wants of the customers.

Traditionally, customization and low costs were mutually exclusive; the period of mass production meant that unit costs could be driven down at the expense of providing specifically for customer needs. Uniformity was the key word. A premium price was charged by specialists or small suppliers for supplying bespoke products and services.

Interactive technologies, such as the internet, now allow customers to purchase products and services to their own specifications, by automated systems. This means that customers can be encouraged to specify their exact requirements, for which an additional, but not crippling, extra charge is levied. This allows marketing activities to revolve around this aspect of the offering, focusing on the personalized nature of the product or service. The process has also become known as 'mass customization' as, in point of fact, the specifications are often prescriptive and the variations from the norm not as wide as one might expect.

Kelly, Sean, *Data Warehousing: The Route to Mass Customization*. Chichester: John Wiley, 1996.

C

Day's sales outstanding

The day's sales outstanding (DSO) is calculated by dividing the total amount owed to a business, by the sales achieved per day. Businesses simply calculate the daily sales by dividing their annual sales (on credit) by 365.

If a business has a yearly turnover of $1,000,000 then the daily sales figure is $2,739.7. If the business is currently owed some $10,000 then the calculation is:

$$\frac{10,000}{2,739.7} = 3.65$$

Should the business improve this DSO then it simply multiplies the amount still owed by the percentage improvement in the collections. It would then subtract the resulting figure from the amount still owed, before repeating the DSO calculation.

In the US, for example, DSO is calculated per quarter in which case the formula is: the accounts receivable, divided by the sales, and then divided by 91.

Debt to assets ratio

The debt to total assets ratio seeks to measure the extent to which lenders and creditors are contributing to the financing (of the assets) of a business. The debt to total assets ratio is:

$$Debt\ to\ total\ assets = \frac{Total\ debt\ (long/short\ term)}{Total\ assets\ (fixed\ and\ current)} \times 100$$

A business may have a total debt of some $2,100,000 and fixed and current assets currently valued at $5,700,000. Its ratio looks like this:

$$\frac{2,100,000}{5,700,000} \times 100 = 36.84\%$$

This particular ratio reveals that lenders and creditors are contributing nearly 37% of the total funds which the business has used to finance the purchase of its assets.

Fridson, Martin and Alvarez, Fernando, *Financial Statement Analysis: A Practitioner's Guide.* New York: John Wiley, 2002.

Temple, Peter, *Magic Numbers: The 33 Key Ratios that Every Investor Should Know.* New York: John Wiley, 2001.

Debt to equity ratio

The debt to equity ratio is primarily concerned with the relative contribution of debts and equities (for ordinary shareholders) in financing the operations of a business. The ratio is:

$$Debt\ to\ equity\ ratio = \frac{Total\ debt\ (long\text{-}term\ and\ short\text{-}term\ liabilities)}{Total\ equity\ (ordinary\ share\ capital\ plus\ reserves)}$$

If a business had a total debt of some $2,100,000 and a total equity of $3,600,000 then the ratio would be:

$$Debt\ to\ equity\ ratio = \frac{2,100,000}{3,600,000} = 0.58$$

This means that for every $1 contributed by equity shareholders, the lenders and creditors have contributed $0.58. The higher the ratio, the less protected the lenders.

Fridson, Martin and Alvarez, Fernando, *Financial Statement Analysis: A Practitioner's Guide.* New York: John Wiley, 2002.

Temple, Peter, *Magic Numbers: The 33 Key Ratios that Every Investor Should Know.* New York: John Wiley, 2001.

Decentralization

Decentralization involves a gradual dispersal of decision-making control across an organization. Integral to the dispersal of decision making is the movement of power and authority from the higher levels of management, or a single headquarters unit, to various divisions, branches, departments or subsidiaries of the organization. At its very core, decentralization implies **delegation**, by transferring the responsibility and power from senior management to individuals at lower levels. The purpose of decentralization is to encourage flexibility and, above all, assist faster decision making, which, in turn, means faster response times.

Decentralization is also strongly associated with the concept of **empowerment**, affording to frontline staff the power, authority and

D

responsibility to make immediate decisions without reference to senior management.

Decision Making Units (DMUs)

A decision making unit is a group of people, usually taken to mean a business or perhaps a department, who make collective decisions with regard to purchasing. A DMU can, of course, be a household although the term is usually more closely associated with business-to-business marketing and sales.

Stereotypically, a DMU would have individuals who fulfil the following roles: a specifier, an influencer, an authorizer, a gatekeeper, a purchaser and a user.

Decision support systems are usually a computerized series of flexible menus which include models and decision aids that can be used in conjunction with current and relevant data. These support systems are designed to assist managerial decision making at all levels of an organization.

Decision tree

Decision trees are tools which assist managers in deciding between several different courses of action. These graphical representations make possible the investigation of outcomes which would be associated with the different options. Decision trees can therefore be used to form a balanced picture.

In order to create a decision tree, a small box is drawn at the left-hand side of a page. Lines are then extended to the right, which relate to each possible solution or option. The name or description of the solution is written along the line. If the result of taking a decision is unclear, a circle is drawn at the end of the line. Alternatively, if the initial option leads to the need for another decision to be made, another square is drawn and the procedure is repeated. Squares on a decision tree represent decisions and circles represent uncertain outcomes.

It is now possible to note on each of the lines what the relevant option means. All of the possible options can then be compared. Normally a business or a manager would assign a cash value or a score to each possible outcome. At each of the points represented by a circle, an estimate of the probable outcome needs to be calculated. These can be either fractions, which add up to 1, or percentages.

Once the value of each outcome has been calculated, the actual values of all of the decisions or options can be calculated in monetary terms. An example of a decision tree is shown in Figure 16.

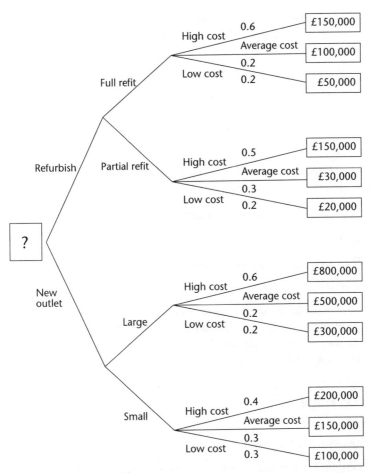

Figure 16 Decision tree for the question: 'Should we open a new outlet in London or refurbish our existing one?'

D

The calculations therefore are:

Full refit   0.6 × £150,000 = £90,000
          0.2 × £100,000 = £20,000
          0.2 × £50,000 = £10,000
                        ─────────
                         £120,000

Partial refit 0.5 × £50,000 = £25,000
          0.3 × £30,000 = £9,000
          0.2 × £20,000 = £4,000
                        ─────────
                          £38,000

Large new outlet 0.6 × £800,000 = £480,000
0.2 × £500,000 = £100,000
0.2 × £300,000 = £60,000
£640,000

Small new outlet 0.4 × £200,000 = £80,000
0.3 × £150,000 = £45,000
0.3 × £100,000 = £30,000
£155,000

Using the following maximum cost figures as examples, it is now possible to calculate the cost savings of each option:

Full refit   £150,000 – £120,000 = £30,000

Partial refit   £50,000 – £38,000 = £12,000

Large new outlet £800,000 – £640,000 = £160,000

Small new outlet £200,000 – £155,000 = £45,000

Clearly, the new large outlet offers the greatest cost savings, but the full investment is four times higher than any of the other alternatives. The business may ultimately decide that the investment costs are actually more significant than the apparent cost savings.

Decline stage

This is the final stage of the standard product life cycle. As sales decline, the business has several options:

- Maintain the product, possibly by adding new features and finding new uses.
- Try to reduce costs and continue to offer it, possibly to a loyal segment.
- Discontinue the product, selling off any remaining stock (if it is a product) or selling it to another business that is willing to continue the product.

An alternative to accepting the inevitable end of a product's life cycle is to consider re-launching the product, perhaps with a new image or identity. However, many businesses will consider terminating the product entirely, or perhaps take the option of dumping the product (often continuing the production) in another country.

D

Deconstruction analysis and management

Originally, deconstruction analysis and management was used as a form of literary criticism. It is now used to provide new interpretations of cause and effect. Deconstruction analysis is often used to investigate the hidden meanings of management messages, revealing the true purpose and nature of the statements beneath the rhetoric.

Delegation

Delegation is not only an issue for management; it is of considerable importance to human resources, as it involves the active use of the skills and experience of employees in subordinate positions. Delegation usually begins with the identification of an individual suitable to perform a particular task. This person needs to be prepared, and above all given the authority, to carry out the job properly. Delegation does mean that the manager needs to support and monitor progress and, once the task is completed, to acknowledge that the job has been completed success-fully. Delegation is a means by which pressured key members of staff can reduce their workload in the certain knowledge that vital tasks will still be performed. It is not always possible to delegate all tasks to other individuals, but delegation can mean greater efficiency, increased **motivation**, skill development, and a more equitable distribution of work throughout a team.

Smart, J. K., *Real Delegation: How to Get People To Do Things for You and Do them Well.* New York: Prentice-Hall, 2002.

Developmental change

Developmental change is considered to be the lowest in the hierarchy of forms of organizational change, as it effectively limits changes to improvements. In 1972 Larry Greiner suggested that organizations go through five stages of growth (see Figure 17) and that they need appropriate strategies and structures to cope.

The stages of the growth of organizations and the various crises and solutions are:

1 *Growth through creativity* – ideas and creativity are the driving force and therefore a simple entrepreneurial structure is all that is required. The organization reaches a stage where it cannot cope and a revolutionary crisis of leadership leads to a need for direction.

2 *Growth through direction* – the new systems and procedures provide direction through a functional structure. The procedures eventually

D

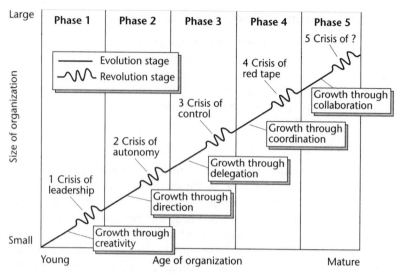

Figure 17 The five stages of growth possible

encourage smoother creativity; this leads to a crisis of autonomy as the systems cannot cope with individuality.

3 *Growth through delegation* – a new, decentralized decision-making system allows more autonomy. Employees can use their initiative to make and take decisions quickly. The organization has adopted a form of 'holding company' structure, but if the decision-makers in the units begin to move in their own direction there will be fragmentation, leading to a crisis of control. The decision-makers can be brought back into line through a process of re-centralization, but this simply takes the organization back to the problems which led to autonomy being granted in the first place. The answer is to proceed to phase 4.

4 *Growth through coordination and monitoring* – controlled centrally through a divisional structure, this allows the decision-makers to operate freely but within the overall control of the organization. Coordination needs to be at arms' length, otherwise a crisis of red tape can occur.

5 *Growth through collaboration* – a matrix structure develops to facilitate the use of small teams to accomplish tasks. However, new crises may occur.

Greiner, Larry E., 'Evolution and Revolution as Organizations Grow', *Harvard Business Review*, July–August 1972.

Devil's advocacy

Devil's advocacy is a method used to improve decision making. Normally the organization would generate a plan to tackle a particular situation. This would then be discussed, and any possible problems arising out of the plan would be addressed. Devil's advocacy takes the view that a critical analysis of the plan should be written while the plan is being formulated. This provides the organization with a ready set of criticisms and factors to take into consideration while contemplating the plan itself.

Dialectic enquiry

In situations where there are irreconcilable analyses of situations, a formal structure known as dialectic enquiry can be employed. Aided by facilitators, a group can identify the assumptions behind their options and then all of the participants attempt to arrive at a negotiated settlement or conclusion. In effect, this is a compromise, preferably a synergistic synthesis of opinion which integrates all the differing viewpoints.

Attempts to reconcile the opinions will fail if the manager intentionally, or unintentionally, encourages the holding of diametrically opposed views, with no compromise.

Mitroff, I. I., Emshoff, J. R. and Kilmann, R. H., 'Assumptional Analysis: A Methodology for Strategic Problem Solving', *Management Science*, 25 (1979), pp. 583–593.

Diamond

See **Porter's four generic competitive strategies.**

Differentiation strategy

The purpose of differentiation strategy is to achieve a **competitive advantage** by creating a product or service that is, essentially, perceived to be unique in some way. By achieving differentiation, a business is able to charge a premium for its products and services.

In seeking to produce differentiated products or services, businesses tend to aim for a high level of differentiation and produce a wide range of these goods. Differentiation can also be achieved with innovation, technological competence, superior after-sales service, wide distribution, and other key customer-service functions.

Differentiation has the following advantages:

- Potential entrants to the market must develop unique products to compete.

D

- Differentiated businesses have a high level of **brand loyalty**.
- The threat of competitors is only based on their ability to produce truly substitute products and services.

The following disadvantages relate to differentiation:

- The business must maintain the perception of uniqueness in the eyes of the customer.
- The business must continue to innovate, or will be caught up by the competitors.
- Uniqueness can be eliminated as a factor by a change in customer tastes and demands.
- The business needs to be aware of new marketing opportunities at all times, to exploit its uniqueness.

Aaker, David A., *Brand Portfolio Strategy: Creating Relevance, Differentiation, Energy, Leverage and Clarity.* New York: Simon & Schuster, 2004.

Diseconomies of scale

Diseconomies of scale are said to be the point at which a manufacturing process simply becomes too large, and the normal rules of **economies of scale** cease to apply. In certain cases, as capacity continues to increase, a manufacturing organization may encounter the problem of average unit costs increasing, rather than falling. There are usually three reasons for this:

- The different stages within the manufacturing process may have already reached their optimum capacity and be unable to produce any more, thus causing difficulties for other areas which are capable of a higher rate of production. This means that various parts of the production process are literally starved of parts and components by these bottlenecks.
- As the organization grows, there are difficulties related to the coordination of activities. To support the production process there is an attendant increase in administration and a proliferation of bureaucratic procedures which may inhibit the production process itself, while adding indirect costs to each unit of production.
- Provided that the capacity levels of the organization could, up to a point, be supplied by other organizations within a viable geographical area, as production increases the manufacturing organization may need to cast its net wider in order to secure a sufficient supply. Compromises may also be needed as to the lead times, quality and delivery costs of these additional supplies. All of these issues

will add cost overall, which in turn are applied to each unit of production.

Diseconomies of scale, therefore, occur as a mixture of internal and external diseconomies.

Distinctive competence

The term 'distinctive competence' usually describes any specific specialism or advantage a manufacturing organization may possess. It is these distinct competences or abilities which mark the organization as having a competitive edge in a specific aspect of its operations.

Diversification

Diversification involves the movement of a business into a wider field of activity, with the primary objective of spreading risks and reducing its dependence on a single market or product range. Diversification can be achieved in a number of ways, including purchasing other businesses already servicing targeted markets.

Businesses which are involved in diminishing markets, such as tobacco, or seasonal markets, such as ice creams, are keen to move into new markets in order to ensure their continued growth. Strategic decisions are made to diversify either through purchase or through development of new areas within the business itself.

The key advantages include the improvement of the long-term survival prospects of the business, a movement away from a saturated marketplace in order to ensure sustained growth, and the provision of new opportunities for the business's existing skills and resources.

There are also clear disadvantages attached to diversification, which could include the business's failure to understand its new customers and market or the nature of the new competition. Diversification may also bring about **diseconomies of scale**, through being involved in too many different areas to enjoy true efficiency in any one aspect of the operations. A business may also find diversification weakens its core business, as it may be required to divert resources away from traditional areas in order to support the new business activities.

D

Divestiture

'Divestiture', in strategic management terms, refers to the process by which a business decides to exit from a particular industry or market. By its very nature divestiture implies that the organization sells its entire sub-division, or subsidiary, which had hitherto been involved in that industry or marketplace.

Divestment strategy

Theoretically, at least, an organization's divestment strategy involves the selling off of a business's assets, perhaps in the form of a subsidiary or an entire **division** of the organization, prior to there being a steep decline in the industry or market in which it was involved. Organizations will continually monitor the progress of what they perceive to be declining industries. By selecting the correct time to carry out the **divestiture**, the business will hope to maximize its income from the sale, or at least cover its net investment. It is necessary for the organization to time this procedure correctly as by the time the industry has gone into steep decline, the value of the assets may be significantly reduced and the residual income derived from the sale may be negligible.

Since the early 1980s divestment has become an integral part of corporate refocusing and, therefore, it has taken place on a voluntary basis. The exact timing and extent of divestment is usually chosen for one of two reasons:

- The business possesses an optimal level of **diversification**.
- A number of multinational businesses in particular have already exceeded this optimum level and correspondingly reduced the spread of their activities by divestment

Howell, Sidney, Stark, Andrew, Newton, David, Paxson, Dean, Cavus, Mustafa and Pereira, Jose, *Real Options: Evaluating Corporate Investment Opportunities in a Dynamic World*. London: Financial Times, Prentice-Hall, 2001.

Dividend yield

The dividend yield is, in effect, the annual dividend per share, but expressed as a percentage of the current market price of that share. Since share prices fluctuate in the marketplace, a share which increases in value will see a proportionate fall in yield. Dividend yields are an important consideration for those who seek an income from their shares. The normal formula used is:

$$\frac{Dividend\ per\ share}{Market\ share\ price} \times 100 = Dividend\ yield$$

Suppose that a share which has an average value of £20 over a given trading period pays out a dividend of £1. Using the formula, the dividend yield is 5%. However, if the share falls to £10, yet still pays out $1 in dividends, the dividend yield has in fact increased to 10%. Conversely, if the share increases in value to £40, yet still pays out £1 in dividends, the dividend yield has fallen to 2.5%. It is normally the case that more established companies offer higher yields, whilst younger companies that are still growing offer lower dividends. It is also the case that many smaller, growing businesses are unable to pay any dividends to their investors.

Spare, Anthony and Ciotti, Paul, *Relative Dividend Yield: Common Stock Investing for Income and Appreciation*. New York: John Wiley, 1999.

Division

A division is, essentially, a business unit of an organization which tends to operate in a distinct business area. Organizations create divisions in order to:

- ensure that they serve different market segments;
- provide different products or services to those markets;
- create geographical divisions to focus on specific markets;
- ensure that they utilize different production processes.

Whilst the divisions' responsibility and function may overlap, they are designed to be semi-autonomous, integrated mechanisms, with their own management structure.

However, as the number of these business units increases, the **span of control** of the chief executive at corporation level becomes too unwieldy. As a result, divisions may themselves be grouped with their own hierarchies. This, however, causes new centres of power and simply increases problems with coordination. Typically, there is also growing tension between individuals at corporate level and those who control the divisions.

Many businesses have shifted from replicating functional specialisms in each of the divisions, to a more centralized series of corporate services. Typically, finance and accounts, personnel, marketing, purchasing, and research and development would all be centralized, leaving the divisions to deal with operational issues. This means that the autonomy of each of the business units is limited and the number of management layers within the organization as a whole is restricted.

D

Dog

'Dogs' are one of the four parts of the **Boston growth matrix**. Products in segments in which the business is not one of the leaders, and in which the market is not growing, are classified as dog products. These products are likely to be in the mature phase of their product life cycle. Their markets exhibit slow, static or even negative growth. There will be little new business to compete for and any strategic moves to increase market share are likely to provoke a vigorous competitive reaction.

Dogs may be linked to low profits, and the prognosis for investment is generally low. Unless some new competitive advantage can be introduced it is likely that these products or businesses will not be able to compete and will not attract the resources necessary to improve their position within the market. If future market demand is considered likely to last for some years, then the commercial risk of building market share may be worthwhile. Generally, however, alternative more attractive investments could probably be found elsewhere. Therefore dogs should remain within the portfolio only so long as they contribute something to the business. Dog products should:

- provide a positive cashflow;
- contribute to overhead expenses;
- fulfil a strategic need.

If (as is often the case with dog products) the opportunity is moribund, decisive action should be taken, such as:

- diverting attention and resources to other segments that will provide a better return;
- focusing attention and resources on other segments which can be ring-fenced;
- maximizing **cash flow** from the product by reducing to a minimum all production and marketing costs;
- disposing of the product, or selling the rights to the product or the business.
- dropping the product from the portfolio.

Double loop learning

Double loop learning, which was proposed by Chris Argyris, relates to learning to change underlying values and assumptions. He believed that in solving complex and ill-structured problems, individuals can change the way in which they solve problems. In effect, double loop theory is based on the ability to learn while doing. While concentrating on the specific tasks in hand, or carrying out the role of leader, the manager is actually learning about the skills involved in leadership and management. Thus double loop learning means that a secondary learning process is being undertaken while the duties of a manager are being

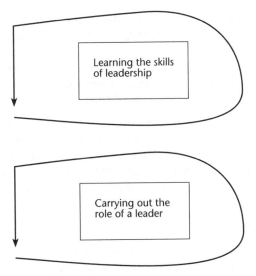

Figure 18 Double loop learning

carried out. Effective problem solving is learned, provided the manager is involved in situations where it is possible to examine and experiment with different ways of solving problems.

A simplistic managerial double loop learning experience is shown in Figure 18.

Argyris, Chris, *Increasing Leadership Effectiveness*. New York: John Wiley & Sons, 1976.

Argyris, Chris and Schon, D., *Theory in Practice: Increasing Professional Effectiveness*. San Francisco, CA: Jossey-Bass Wiley, 1992.

Downsizing

The term 'downsizing' refers to an organization's need to streamline its activities, perhaps involving the closure of certain operations, along with the associated loss of employees engaged in those areas. Vital in the concept of downsizing is the quality, as opposed to the quantity, of employees.

The downsizing process needs planning by the human resources management as the implications are that some employees will be offered voluntary redundancy. Often, those who opt to take this method of dismissal will be those who are valued by the organization because they have the qualifications, skills and expertise that make them potentially more attractive to competing organizations. While planning the downsizing process the human resources management would have to consider:

- the legal implications with regard to redundancy;
- the implications to the organization of losing key members of staff to competitors;
- how they will communicate their intention to downsize;
- what alternatives are available to them apart from redundancy, e.g. retraining or the redeployment of employees

Fear of downsizing can be stressful for employees, and the human resources department needs to ensure that it is communicating with them through appropriate and effective channels. Certainly consultation with trade union or employee representatives is essential, as is the provision of an employee assistance programme (EAP).

Dumbsizing

Dumbsizing is the attempt by organizations to streamline or engage in a de-layering process which strips out levels of management. Dumbsizing, whilst attempting to cut the fat from an organization, which would benefit the business in terms of cost saving, actually only succeeds in cutting out some of the organization's muscle in respect of critical functions and responsibilities that are no longer being covered.

Dumbsizing is also known as **flattening** and can have a serious and negative impact on the business's ability to operate. It is also typified by a gradual, but severe, reduction in the overall workforce of an organization, to such an extent that the business becomes not only inefficient but also unprofitable. It is a radical restructuring process which breaks many of the rules of considered and logical restructuring exercises.

D

Economies of scale

Strictly speaking, economies of scale is an economics-related issue. However, it has considerable implications for **operations management** and production. The basic concept revolves around the fact that a business needs to build up a critical mass. In other words, it must be large enough to be able to enjoy the benefits associated with larger-scale production or distribution. As the size and scope of the business increases, the generally held view is that the unit costs are driven down. The corollary is that having achieved economies of scale, the business has more funds available to further improve its market position and efficiency.

Jackson, Dudley, *Profitability, Mechanization and Economies of Scale.* Aldershot: Ashgate Publishing, 1998.

Economy of scope

'Economy of scope' is an economics term which puts forward the proposition that a business will enjoy a lower unit cost as it increases the variety of products it offers. Rather than receiving the benefits associated with **economies of scale**, the business derives advantages from the **synergies** (similarities) in the production of similar products. The unit costs are driven down by the fact that several products share the same resources, and a number of the same components may be used to produce a variety of products which have common features.

Ashton, John Kevin, *Cost Efficiency, Economies of Scale and Economies of Scope in the Retail Banking Sector.* Bournemouth: Bournemouth University School of Finance and Law, 1998.

Effectiveness

'Effectiveness' in both management and strategic management refers to programmes, projects or tasks with already established performance criteria attached to them. Effectiveness is measured by the ability to determine not only the result, both quantitatively and qualitatively, but also what the result actually suggests. At its simplest, effectiveness can also mean correctly following specific steps or completing particular tasks. Above all, any of these accomplishments needs to be consistent with the organization's **mission statement**, its **vision statement**, its **values** and its goals and **objectives**.

Normally, effectiveness relates to the outcome of an event, rather than any **efficiency** measures which contributed to the outcome.

See also **outcome measure**.

Efficiency

Efficiency is a means by which an organization can compare the average time taken to carry out a particular process on a production line against a standard processing time. In other words, if a particular process normally has a standard time of 30 minutes per production unit and the current production time is 25 minutes, then the efficiency of that part of the process is 30 ÷ 25 = 1.2; this is normally expressed as a percentage, in which case this would be 120%.

Wheelwright, Steven C. and Clark, Kim B., *Revolutionizing Product Development: Quantum Leaps in Speed, Efficiency and Quality*. New York: Free Press, 1992.
Coelli, Tim, Prasada Rao, D. S. and Battese, George E., *An Introduction to Efficiency and Productivity Analysis*. Dordrecht: Kluwer Academic, 1997.

Embryonic industry

An embryonic industry is typified as an industry in its first stages of development. In the past, tourism, information technology, recycling, forestry management and a host of other industrial and service areas were described as 'embryonic'. An embryonic industry can be a difficult area for a new business to break into. Often there are few rules, the expectations of customers are unclear, and the extent of the competition is unknown.

Businesses that are part of an embryonic industry, therefore, have no distinct benchmarks upon which to base their structure or their business operations. Inevitably, businesses tend to adopt approaches learned from industries that are broadly similar in some respect to their own business. Equally, existing or emerging embryonic industries tend to cluster around a specific area in a given country in order to enjoy **synergies** and to engage in **strategic alliances** where appropriate.

Emergent strategy

Emergent strategies are unplanned strategies. They are unplanned in the sense that they are a response to unforeseen circumstances.

E

However, the majority of possible sets of circumstances which would need an emergent strategy to be framed might have been considered in advance, under some form of contingency plan.

Emergent strategies tend to take one of two forms:

- A form of incremental strategic change occurs when intended strategies are implemented and managers adapt from experience.
- Adaptive strategies can be put in place when managers respond to either opportunities or threats as they present themselves, in the external environment (or in some cases, in the internal environment).

As with any form of decision making, there are two elements: individuals and information. These are inextricably linked, as no matter how much information is available, it is managers or employees who must interpret that information and act upon it. Therefore emergent strategies mean that managers and employees must learn and change in what can be called a dynamic environment. In other words, emergent strategy is about innovation on the part of managers, who have accepted a form of delegated responsibility, who might otherwise be known as **intrepreneurs**.

In order for managers to become intrepreneurs and engage in the formulation of emergent strategies, a degree of freedom needs to be afforded to them in order that they can gather information, analyse it and then act upon it.

See also **Fiedler contingency model.**

Emotional intelligence

According to Daniel Goalman, emotional intelligence is a collection of psychological attributes which enable individuals to excel. Typically, they include the following:

- self-awareness;
- impulse control;
- persistence;
- **empathy**;
- self-regulation;
- **motivation**.

Goalman suggests that many of the best leaders exhibit these characteristics. He claims that some 90 per cent of all outstanding leaders could attribute their success to emotional intelligence, which he believes is twice as important as intellectual intelligence (IQ).

E

In the UK, the Centre for Applied Emotional Intelligence can be found at www.emotionalintelligence.co.uk

Goleman, Daniel, *Emotional Intelligence: Why It Can Matter More than IQ*. London: Bloomsbury, 1996.

Goleman, Daniel, *The New Leaders: Emotional Intelligence at Work*. New York: Little Brown, 2002.

Empathy

An empathetic manager attempts to listen to and respect a subordinate's feelings and values. This requires managers to be flexible, experimental and creative in the way in which they deal with subordinates. Empathy also implies: a suggestion of equality (in as much as the subordinate does not feel inferior); spontaneity, in communication; a problem orientation, which allows managers to deal with problems as they arise. It is also descriptive, in the sense that empathetic managers are clear about their perceptions and describe situations in a fair manner.

Empowerment

The term 'empowerment' refers to individual employees being allowed to control their contribution within an organization. This means that they are given the authority and responsibility to complete tasks and attain targets without the direct intervention of management. The benefits of empowerment to the organization are that it reduces the importance of repetitive administration and the number of managers required at the various levels of the structure. Streamlining management levels often increases the effectiveness of communication. From the employees' point of view, empowerment increases their creativity and initiative, as well as their commitment to the organization, by allowing them to work with autonomy.

Engagement

The term 'engagement' can refer to both employees and customers. Engaged employees are encouraged to use their natural talents in order to assist the business in having a competitive edge. It is believed that, collectively, efforts involving employee engagement can actually assist in the engagement of customers. Employee engagement requires understanding of the business and also of the management, and of what they both hope to achieve. Managers within organizations must assist employees in realizing their expectations, which have been learned by the subordinates as being the primary motivators of the business itself.

Employee engagement, therefore, involves mobilizing the talent, energy and resources of employees. If done effectively, employee engagement delivers the following:

- It contributes to the development of a healthy and sustainable business
- It assists the business in identifying the needs of customers, and their solutions.
- It creates opportunities for dialogue with the business's stakeholders.
- It provides leverage for the business in the sense that it strengthens relations with stakeholders and leads to partnerships.
- It uses resources efficiently.
- It allows for the development of personal skills.
- It is an asset for leadership and team development.
- It assists in bringing any form of corporate culture into sharp focus, building morale, loyalty and pride in the workforce.
- It assists in the establishment and maintenance of the business's reputation.

Axelrod, Richard H., *Terms of Engagement: Changing the Way We Change Our Organizations*. San Francisco, CA: Berrett-Koehler Publishers, 2003.

Buckingham, Marcus and Coffman, Curt, *First, Break All the Rules*. New York: Simon & Schuster, 2001.

Entrepreneur

The term 'entrepreneur' suggests an individual who is prepared for a degree of risk taking and has a flair for identifying potential business opportunities. Entrepreneurs exist in almost every area of business and seek to identify gaps in the present market provision which can be filled with new products or services, often delivered in a radically different way from that in which the market already operates. Entrepreneurs place a great emphasis on **innovation** and will seek to design an entirely new business model, rather than relying on tried and tested business practices.

Entrepreneurial strategy is seen to be related to leaders who have the imaginative power to take decisions in conditions of uncertainty and ambiguity.

Dollinger, Marc J., *Entrepreneurship Strategies and Resources*. New York: Prentice-Hall, 2002.

Kao, J., *Entrepreneurship, Creativity and Organization*. New York: Prentice-Hall, 1989.

Escalating commitment

The term 'escalating commitment' refers to resources having to be poured into a specific project. Escalating commitment tends to occur when there has been a decision-making error at a strategic level. In this situation, businesses are faced with a stark choice: either they can escalate their commitment to the project, committing ever-more resources, on the basis that the project is failing or may fail, or they can seek to cut their losses and back out of the project. This latter choice represents a failure, and a loss of investment for the business, and in many cases decisions at corporate level would tend to favour continued and escalating commitment, rather than writing the project off. In effect, the escalating commitment is a reflection of the organization's inability to accept failure and loss of face.

Ethical decision making

Ethics and social responsibility related to business have become increasingly important and much-debated issues in recent years. Essentially, there are inherent conflicts between the desires of business, industry, society in general, and the consumer. All may have mutually exclusive goals and objectives. Ethical issues arise when one group's values conflict with those of another. In many cases there are multiple levels of conflict arising out of different sets of values.

The marketing industry has sought to pre-empt governmental intervention by establishing professional associations and accrediting bodies who are concerned with self-regulation. An example of these is the American Marketing Association (AMA), which suggests that marketing behaviour should follow the rules listed in Table 6.

There is considerable conflict between the main purposes of marketing, the ethical criteria as stated by organizations such as the AMA, and the goal of making a profit. Given the fact that the major promotional objectives include accentuating the value of the product, providing information, stabilizing sales, stimulating demand, and the differentiation of the product, it is clear from these inherent marketing responsibilities that it is difficult to retain an ethical balance.

Making ethical decisions is a complex procedure because there are often a number of considerations, including:

- a variety of alternatives;
- consequences that may have knock-on effects;
- uncertain circumstances;
- outcomes that can have economic, legal and social benefits;
- outcomes that can have economic, legal and social costs;
- personal implications for the managers and employees of the business, as well as implications for the business itself.

Table 6   Recommended marketing behaviour (AMA)

Guidelines	Description
Responsibility	The AMA urges those involved in marketing to accept responsibility for the consequences of their actions and activities. They are asked to consider their decisions, recommendations and subsequent actions in the light of satisfying and serving all stakeholders.
Honesty and fairness	The AMA urges marketers to show integrity, honour and dignity as professionals.
Rights and duties	The AMA suggests that there should be an inherent relationship between businesses and their customers, firmly based on the notion of trust. Products and services should be safe and fit for the uses for which they were intended. The AMA also stresses that marketing communications should be truthful and that products and services should be sold in good faith. In the case of disputes, a grievance procedure should be established.
Organizational relationships	The AMA also suggests that those involved in marketing should be clearly aware that their actions are intended to influence the behaviour of others. In this respect, given their persuasive role, they should not encourage unethical behaviour or apply undue pressure to those they target.

Ethical decisions can also often involve the business's **stakeholders**, who can have goals that are opposed to or conflict with the interests of the business.

Businesses often have innumerable complexities to unravel in order to ensure that they are not behaving in an unethical manner, including:

- ensuring that their goals are compatible with ethical considerations;
- ensuring that their route to meeting these goals is ethically acceptable;
- considering whether or not their motives for meeting their goals are selfish and non-ethical;
- considering the consequences of their activities for others, including the stakeholders.

E

Table 7 Terms associated with ethical standards

Ethical system	Problem
Eternal law	These are moral standards for which there are innumerable interpretations.
Ethical egoism	This could be interpreted as a contradiction in terms, as it revolves around cooperation and productivity and it is difficult to determine whether one business's (or an individual's) interests are more, or less, important than those of others.
Utilitarianism	These ethical standards relate to the outcome of a decision or an action and the effect on others. Again this can be difficult to determine, particularly if the business's actions have a positive impact on a number of other businesses or groups, or individuals, but a negative one on a few.
Universalism	This applies to the intention behind an action or a decision by a business or an individual, as opposed to the outcome of that action or decision.
Enlightened self-interest	Similar in many ways to utilitarianism, enlightened self-interest requires the business, or the individual, to ensure that their long-term interests conform to those of society at large.
Interdependence	This ethical system or belief applies to the ability to compromise in order to provide a dependent business or individual with what they need to achieve their goals.

As can be seen in Table 7, there are various terms associated with ethical standards.

Robin, D. P. and Reidenbach, R. E., 'Social Responsibility, Ethics and Marketing: Closing the Gap between Concept and Application', *Journal of Marketing*, 51 (January 1987), pp. 44–58.

Evolutionary theory

Evolutionary theory, when applied to organizations, proposes that organizations develop and behave very much in the same way as evolutionary models proposed in relation to the natural sciences. There are three key areas with regard to the biological analogies of evolutionary theory, most prominently suggested by Nelson and Winter. These are:

- selection – which has an impact upon the business's internal routines;
- mutation – which encompasses any changes in those routines;
- struggle for existence – which reflects the fact that businesses operate in a competitive environment.

Whilst Nelson and Winter do not necessarily suggest that there are absolute parallels between biological and organizational evolution, the fundamental theory is useful in suggesting how an organization does develop over a period of time.

Nelson, Richard R. and Winter, Sidney G., *An Evolutionary Theory of Economic Change.* Boston, MA: Harvard University Press, 1990.

Exit barriers

Exit barriers are factors which make it difficult for a business to contemplate leaving a particular industry or market. Exit barriers would typically include high capital investment, long-term contracts, government regulations or specialized assets. Many organizations have a distinct aversion to closing down businesses which have hitherto been successful, and in which they have invested much time and effort, not to mention capital. It is usually the case that one of the following holds true:

- If the **barriers to entry** are high, then exit barriers can be low because if industry profits are high, these high profits mean that businesses can afford to protect their positions.
- If entry barriers are high and exit barriers are also high: this is largely as a result of the potential for high profits, but there are usually higher risks, notably higher investment costs.
- If entry barriers are low and exit barriers are also low: this suggests that businesses enter or leave a market solely according to the availability of profit. Typically, profits would remain fairly low and businesses will move in and out of the market at will.

The relationship between entry barriers and exit barriers is best summarized as in Figure 19.

In February 2000 the multinational giant Unilever instituted its 'Path to Growth' five-year strategic plan, and estimated that the restructuring costs would run to some 5 billion Euros. In essence, the strategic plan was an exit strategy which would concentrate Unilever's resources behind 400 leading brands and 250 other brands – this was a significant reduction from the 1600 brands it had been offering up unitil 2000.

www.Unilever.com

E

Entry barriers

	High	Low
High	High profits	Worst-case scenario
Low	Best-case scenario	Low, but stable returns

Exit barriers

Figure 19 Entry and exit barriers

Experience curve

The term 'experience curve' has had a direct application for many businesses over a number of years, in as much as it describes the improved performance of both the organization and individuals within it, over a period of time, as they repeat and become competent at tasks. Experience curve analysis is the study of this phenomenon, and indeed it has an additional dimension in dealing with international trade, with the experience curve being steeper in the sense that there is more to learn and understand, and then practically demonstrate, when businesses deal with overseas markets.

It has been proved that there is a direct and consistent relationship between the growth in product volume and the reduction in unit cost. Each time production doubles, costs decline by between 20% and 30%. The experience curve itself relates the cost per unit output to the cumulative volume of output since a production process was first begun. Costs per unit of production decline as the cumulative volume of output increases. The production process, repeated time after time, allows the business and employees to learn from experience and adjust their activities in accordance with their acquired knowledge, thus reducing costs. Numerous studies suggest that these costs tend to decline by a relatively stable percentage each time the cumulative volume produced is doubled.

Clearly, the experience curve, or learning curve, of the organization and its employees has different dimensions, particularly in the case of setting up production facilities abroad. None the less, the fundamental phenomenon of the experience curve and its cost-saving implications are still ultimately enjoyed.

E

Explanation

'Explanation' is a term most closely associated with strategic decision making. 'Explanation' refers to the fact that any managers or employees, not to mention **stakeholders**, who may be affected or involved as a result of a strategic decision being made, should be informed of the rationale behind the decision. In other words, explanations should be given as to why specific ideas or inputs have been addressed, and others have been ignored.

External environment

Manufacturing organizations do not, of course, operate in a vacuum; there are issues which have a direct impact upon the capacity and the output of their manufacturing processes. External factors are usually taken to be events or issues which arise outside the industrial sector itself, and therefore do not normally include the availability of supplies, labour or demand. External factors tend to revolve around government legislation, such as health and safety issues, which may require the organization to amend or rethink the way in which it processes products. Equally, external factors can include union action, or agreements with unions as to how their members will be deployed and the conditions under which they work within the facility.

See also **Five Forces model**.

External stakeholders

External stakeholders are individuals who can either affect or be affected by the organization. There are clear indications that provided the organization acts in concert with, and pays attention to, the stakeholders, considerable **synergy** can be achieved.

Theoretically, at least, the relationship between the organization and its stakeholders should be mutually beneficial. Stakeholders exercise a series of controls or influences on the organization, in return for which the organization should engage with the stakeholders. The primary relationships are explained in Table 8.

E

Table 8 Relationships between business and stakeholder

External stakeholder	Influence on the business	Business response
Government	Regulatory compliance	Compliance
Investors	Capital providers	Risk reduction
Consumers	Demand for products or services	Quality products or services
Industry	Standards of practice	Fair dealing
International bodies	Best practices	Fair dealing
Local communities	Operating licences	Community relations programmes
Business partners	Transparency	Fair dealing

E

Factor conditions

Factor conditions are a measure of the costs and/or quality of the **factors of production**.

Factor endowments

'Factor endowments' refers to the primary factors of production of a given country. In essence this means the different ratios of capital to labour and the fact that goods differ in their input requirements, notably in ratios between rents and wages and the fact that some goods require more capital per man hour than others. Primarily the endowment factors include labour, capital, land, and in some cases, natural resources. The concept of factor endowments is very much based on the Heckscher–Ohlin model. A similar model, known as the Stolper–Samuelson Theorem states that as the price of goods goes up, the return on the factors used intensively in their production goes up by a larger percentage, while the return on other factors of production falls.

Lal, Deepak, *Unintended Consequences: The Impact of Factor Endowments, Culture and Politics on Long-Run Economic Performance*. Cambridge, MA: MIT Press, 1998.

Factors of production

In international trade, factors of production are significant as they represent the inherent nature of the economic activity of a given country. Typically, factors of production include the available assets in terms of land, labour, capital and enterprise. Each country has its own distinct blend of factors of production, often described as **factor endowments**.

Fayol, Henri

In 1916 Henri Fayol, a French industrialist, wrote of his views and theories about the problems commonly encountered by organizations. His

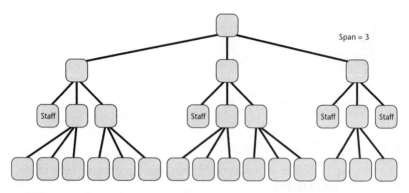

Figure 20 Structure of a top–down organization

view was that many of the root causes of industrial failure were down to management and personnel. Fayol was a 'top–down' theorist who believed that change must begin with the board of directors or the managing director (see Figure 20).

Fayol began by identifying the three main aspects of management, which are:

- the activities of the organization;
- the elements of management;
- the principles of management.

Fayol identified the six main categories of activities of an organization as being:

- Technical activities – which include production, manufacture and adaptation.
- Commercial activities – which include buying, selling and exchanging.
- Financial activities – which include the seeking of finance and deciding the best use of that finance.
- Security services – which include the protection of the organization, its employees and its property.
- Accounting services – which include the production of balance sheets, costings, statistical data and stock inventories.
- Managerial activities – which include forecasting and planning, organization, giving instructions, coordinating and controlling employees activity.

Fayol then identified 14 elements and principles of management which were key qualities and functions:

- Division of work – ensuring that all employees know what their duties are.
- Authority – the ability to give clear, complete and unambiguous instructions.
- Discipline – to be rigid and firm when appropriate but always to ensure understanding.
- Unity of command – to ensure that all aspects of management within the organization are uniform.
- Unity of direction – to ensure that the business has a clear corporate strategy.
- Subordination – the ability to put the organization first, and personal needs and commitments second.
- Remuneration – the need for a fair wage for a fair day's work.
- Centralization – to ensure that tasks are concentrated and not duplicated, in order to maintain cost effectiveness.
- Clear scalar chain – to ensure that all individuals within the organization know their position. Fayol suggested that this could be achieved through the production of an organization chart.
- Internal order – to strive to avoid internal conflict.
- Equality – to ensure equal opportunity within the organization and avoid discrimination by age, sex, sexual orientation, disability or religion.
- Stability of tenure – to ensure that employees feel their job is secure, so that they are not concerned about their own security.
- Initiative – to encourage idea creation and the acceptance of ideas from employees without, necessarily, enforcing senior management input.
- Esprit de corps – to encourage a company spirit where individuals are proud to support the objectives of the business.

Fayol also identified some rules which he considered management should follow. He wrote that an individual who specialized would become more skilled, efficient and effective, but he also considered that the manager should have the ultimate accountability for employees.

Boje, David and Dennehy, Robert, *Managing in the Postmodern World* (3rd edition, September 2000) at http://cbae.nmsu.edu/~dboje/mpw.html

A summary of Fayol's work can be found at www.comp.glam.ac.uk/teaching/ismanagement/manstyles1f.htm

F

Felt conflict

See **conflict management**.

Fiedler contingency model

Fiedler wrote on styles of leadership and the relationship between the leadership style and particular situations. His model depends upon the leadership style being described in terms of task or relationship motivation. The form of leadership depends upon three factors:

- the relationship between leader and members, which is concerned with how the leader is accepted and supported by the members of the group;
- the structure of the tasks and whether they are defined, with clear goals and procedures;
- position power, which details the leader's ability to control subordinates through punishment and reward.

Fiedler suggested that high levels of these three factors give the most favourable situation and low levels the least favourable. Leaders who are relationship-motivated are most effective in moderately favourable situations whilst task-motivated leaders are most effective at either end of the scale. Fiedler recognized that while it is difficult for leaders to change their style, what they must attempt to do is to change their situation in order to achieve effectiveness.

Fill in the blanks

The term 'fill in the blanks' is usually used to describe an opportunity which a business may encounter in relation to an improvement in its competitive position. Filling in the blanks usually relates to existing markets, where a business will leverage its **core competences** in order to improve its overall competitive position. As the term implies, 'fill in the blanks' means that the organization will have the answers to particular issues and be ready to deploy them.

F

First-mover advantage

The term 'first-mover advantage' is most closely associated with the competitive edge gained by a business which is first, or early, into a new market. Whilst businesses moving into a new market face the risk of failure (since they and no other businesses have experience of that market or those modes of operation), if successful they have a substantial competitive edge over those who may wish to emulate them.

In internet business terms, not only were both eBay and Amazon keen to establish clear distribution, promotion and fulfilment, but they were also concerned with measures to successfully combat competitors who might seek to enter or emulate their own market. In both cases these businesses have successfully used their first-mover advantage, being first into the market, and remaining the most dominant businesses.

First-mover disadvantage

Given the fact that it is often as important to know when to make a strategic move as it is to know what strategic move to make, **first-mover advantage** revolves around attempts by a business to make an early commitment, thus gaining the loyalty of first-time buyers – in effect, launching a pre-emptive strike against a particular market or industry. Whilst first-mover advantages are clear, there are also a number of disadvantages. The following are examples:

- A business makes a high financial commitment to pioneer a new market, but it transpires that the loyalty of first-time buyers is weak.
- Since technological change is hardly ever dormant, there is a distinct possibility that businesses which follow the first movers into the market can actually leapfrog them in terms of technological development.
- The skills and know-how which have been expensively acquired or learned by the first mover can be relatively easy to imitate.
- Latecomers to the market may find it considerably easier to find a place now that the market has been developed, as well as identified, by the first mover.

Five Forces model

Michael Porter developed a five-forces model for industrial analysis. He maintained that industries are influenced by five forces and that the model enables businesses to understand the industry context in which they operate. Porter's five forces consist of:

- The barriers to entry – including cost advantages, access to raw materials and components, **economies of scale**, switching costs and access to distribution channels.
- Buyer power – price sensitivity, brand identification, buyer concentration and volume.
- Degree of rivalry – concentration of industry, exit barriers, product differences, diversity of rivals and industry growth.
- Supplier power – concentration of suppliers, switching costs, possibility of forward integration, importance of buyer to supplier.

F

- Threat of substitutes – inclination of buyer to purchase substitutes, price to performance compared with substitutes, switching costs.

Porter went on to suggest that generic strategies could be followed in order to counter the impact of the five forces. He suggested that strategy could be formulated at three different levels:

- corporate level;
- business unit level;
- functional or departmental level.

His three generic strategies were:

- **Cost leadership strategy** – which was applicable in an industry-wide context.
- **Differentiation strategy** – which again was applicable industry-wide and rested on the uniqueness of the product
- **Focus strategy** – which was largely applicable in market segments, based on the offering of low costs and product differentiation.

Porter, Michael, *Competitive Advantage*. New York: Free Press. 1985.

Flat structure

A 'flat' organizational structure is a hierarchical structure in the sense that it is in the shape of a pyramid, but it has fewer layers. Often a hierarchical structure can be de-layered in order to create a flat structure. This de-layering process often allows decisions to be made more quickly and efficiently because the layers are able to communicate more easily with one another. This enables the organization to become less bureaucratic. It is a simple structure often used by organizations operating from a single site. The directors and other major decision-makers are more easily available for consultation with employees, who often find that they feel more a part of the process. This encourages **motivation**, particularly amongst junior managers, who are more likely to be given responsibility through delegation from the senior management level of the structure.

F

Flattening

Flattening or de-layering is a concept primarily related to the 1990s which saw businesses move to 'flatten' their organizational structure. This is achieved by effectively stripping out a number of layers of management in the organization. It became synonymous with a reduction in bureaucracy, faster decision making, shorter communication channels, and fostering high-involvement management.

The majority of organizations considered that in de-layering they would cut their overheads and for many this was the principal motivation. For others, the flatter organization represented team working and high-involvement working practices.

Flatter organizations are achieved by:

- eliminating or automating management activities (which could lead to these posts becoming redundant);
- reducing and reallocating unnecessary and costly overlaps of accountability.

There is no ideal way of undertaking the process, but the key influencing factors are:

- the pace of the de-layering;
- the extent of the imposition of the de-layering;
- the degree of employee involvement in the process;
- the degree of organizational re-design and analysis required.

The major aspects of attaining the benefits of de-layering are:

- Form should follow function.
- Provided de-layering eliminates situations where management does not add value, the process is credible.
- Loss of hierarchies could mean that new hierarchies must take their place.
- New accountabilities must be clarified.
- The commitment of employees must be won.
- Performance indicators must be in place and pilot de-layering is desirable.
- Managers deliver the de-layering but are also the targets of it, and they will require additional support.

Keuning, Doede and Opheij, Wilfred, *Delayering Organisations: How to Beat Bureaucracy and Create a Flexible and Responsive Organisation.* Harlow: Pitman, 1994.

F

Flexible machine cells

Flexible machine cells are usually designed to provide a business with the ability to produce low-volume special parts in small lot sizes. Flexible machine cells are usually controlled via a computer-integrated manufacturing system. They group various types of machinery together with a common materials handler.

Flexible manufacturing technology

Theoretically, a flexible manufacturing system is an integrated group of machines which have the capacity for automated handling between them. In other words, they share an integrated information system which automatically passes part-finished products between the machines for the next stage of the process to be carried out.

See also **lean production.**

Gunasekaran, A., *Agile Manufacturing: The 21st-Century Competitive Strategy.* Amsterdam: Elsevier, 2001.

Kidd, P. T. and Karwowski, W. (eds), *Advances in Agile Manufacturing: Integrating Technology, Organization and People.* Amsterdam: IOS Press, 1994.

Focus strategy

Focus strategies are also known as **niche strategies.** They aim to provide a targeted market, with a much better range of products, services and support functions than those offered by their competitors. Typically a business will choose a market niche for its focus strategy in which the buyers have the following characteristics:

- specific or distinctive preferences;
- special requirements;
- unique requirements or needs.

'Low-cost focus strategies' aim to provide products and services at a lower cost than their competitors. Alternatively, a focus strategy may choose to offer a differentiated product or service, in which case it is known as a **differentiation strategy.**

In order for a segment to be appropriate for a focus strategy, it needs to have the following characteristics:

- It must have the potentiality to be large enough to provide the business with a reasonable profit.
- The segment must appear to offer growth potential.
- It must not be of critical importance to major competitors.
- The business itself must have sufficient resources to service the segment.
- The business must be able to defend itself on the grounds of goodwill or a superior ability to serve the buyers in that segment.

Focus strategy tends to work best when it is more difficult for multi-segment competitors to operate in that segment to provide for the specialized needs of the target group. Ideally, there should be no other

F

competitors concentrating on that segment at the same time as the business using the focus strategy. The potential risks are that:

- Larger competitors may be attracted as a result of the business using the focus strategy appearing to show signs of success.
- The targets of the focus strategy may well develop a desire to change their preferences to a product or service which is more generic in nature.

Follett, Mary Parker

In her 1995 book, Pauline Graham describes Mary Parker Follett as being the prophet of management. Follett was born in the mid-nineteenth century and died in the 1930s. During the 1920s, her most productive period, she wrote extensively on leadership, power, conflict, behaviour, empowerment, teams, networking, relationships, authority and control. Her ideas were considerably ahead of her time and she has, quite rightly, been identified as one of the most influential management writers or creators of theory models.

See also **conflict management**.

Graham, Pauline, *Mary Parker Follett: Prophet of Management: A Celebration of Writings from the 1920s*. Watertown, MA: Harvard Business School Press. 1995.

Foreign market entry strategies

The decision whether to enter an overseas market is usually taken at strategic level. It represents a considerable challenge, not only in identifying potential overseas markets, but also in deciding how to supply the market with the relevant products or services. Clearly one of the first choices is whether to concentrate any provision within the overseas market itself, or whether to produce the products or services at the organization's existing manufacturing plants and then transport them to the new market. In essence this means that a strategic decision needs to be made regarding the benefits of exporting or of engaging in local production.

Clearly there are economic and strategic implications for both of these choices. On the one hand, exporting means involvement in customs procedures and possible duties and taxation, additional insurance, costs of freight and special packing. It is not always the case that setting up production in the overseas market means that production costs will be low enough to compensate for the additional costs that would have been incurred had the products been exported. This means that it is not

F

a foregone conclusion that higher production costs in an overseas market are necessarily disadvantageous when compared with the export option.

There are also considerable risks with regard to any form of foreign investment. These could include:

- political instability;
- currency fluctuations;
- management and employee training;
- hierarchical control;
- ordering.

A further alternative is to consider licensing the business's expertise, brands or patents in the overseas market, and entering into an alliance with another business to produce and distribute the products and services within that market.

Each of the options with regard to foreign market entry strategy has to be weighed up in relation to the various costs and benefits which may or may not be incurred. Equally, the business needs to consider the risks, comparatively speaking, in adopting each of the options. There is never an optimum choice, and the decision may be based upon how risk averse the business has been in the past.

Initially at least, the majority of businesses will choose exporting, perhaps licensing, and as a third alternative, foreign direct investment. Given the fact that, through globalization, the business no longer has to consider an overseas market as a completely separate operation, many businesses have begun to integrate their overseas activities with the rest of their core operations.

Foreign operations department

A foreign operations department is often created by larger multinational organizations that are predominantly, as far as core operations are concerned, centrally located in a home territory. The department is designed to oversee international sales and the fulfilment of orders for products or services which have been made in the domestic market.

Fragmented industry

A fragmented industry is an industry or market which is not dominated by any large businesses. The market is typified by a large number of small to medium-sized businesses. None of these businesses is in a position to dominate the market in any way.

Franchising

A franchise is a form of business in which a franchisor enters into a business relationship with a franchisee. The franchisor grants the franchisee a licence to use their common trade name, or trademark, in return for a fee, and during the association the franchisor will render assistance to the franchisee. It is essentially a licensing system which affords the franchisor the opportunity to expand, with the capital required to enable that expansion being provided by external sources.

In the US alone franchising generates some $800 billion per year and employs around 9 million people. Franchisees enjoy considerable benefits, which include:

- the ability to open a franchise business which is already a proven success;
- the right to receive full training and continued support from the franchisor;
- the ability to enjoy the benefits of national advertising;
- a guarantee that the franchisor will not sell a similar business to a competitor in the immediate area.

Free cash flow

Free **cash flow** is another means by which the general health of a business can be assessed, as it is concerned with the amount of cash which a business has to hand after it has dealt with its expenses and made any necessary investments. In many respects free cash flow reveals the actual working capital of a business. Free cash flow is used as a financial measurement tool, particularly in the US, where it has an associated ratio:

$$\begin{pmatrix} Operating \\ cash\ flow \\ (net\ income \\ +\ depreciation \\ +\ amortization) \end{pmatrix} - \begin{matrix} capital \\ expenditure \end{matrix} + dividends = free\ cash\ flow$$

Many financial analysts consider free cash flow to be a prime indicator of the way in which a business is being run and its overall financial condition. Free cash flow, however, can be misleading in some respects since many growing businesses plough the majority of their earnings back directly into new investments. This would obviously reduce their amount of free cash flow. Therefore a negative free cash flow may not be an indication that the business is in trouble, but it may reveal that the business is not earning a sufficiently high rate of return on the investments it has made. This may indicate that the business is simply spending too much.

Full integration

Full integration may be the ultimate desire of a truly multinational or multi-domestic business. In order to become fully integrated, a business needs to control all of its own inputs into its core business operations. In other words, this requires the business to acquire those suppliers of raw materials and components that were previously independent suppliers to the business. In addition, the business is also concerned with the acquisition of distributors and ultimately retailers, who will be able to sell its products and services straight onto the market, without involving any other external operation or business. In essence then, full integration involves both forward and backward integration, where a business controls all of its inputs and the disposal of all of its outputs through its own operations.

Functional level strategy

Functional level strategy aims to improve the operations of a business in respect of key function areas, such as:

- marketing;
- manufacturing;
- customer service;
- research and development.

See also **hierarchies of strategy.**

Functional orientation

'Functional orientation', at its simplest, refers to the preoccupation of management with regard to operational issues, rather than any of the other activities or requirements of the organization.

Functional operations can also involve an organization in:

- allowing the development of functional hierarchies;
- allowing these functional hierarchies to grow apart from one another;
- allowing them to then adopt radically different attitudes to strategic issues, which may also affect the organization as a whole.

The term is sometimes referred to as 'narrow functional operations', which alludes to the fact that the organization and management may be perceived as being somewhat blinkered in their views. Business processes such as **total quality management (TQM)** can be considered to have a cross-functional orientation.

Functional structure

A functionally based organizational structure is designed around specific sections of the organization, usually those that produce, market and sell the organization's product or service. Functional structures can be a sub-structure of either hierarchical or **flat structures** and similarly will be controlled by a managing director, supported by relevant senior function or departmental managers. The creation of positions and departments around a specialized function is an integral part of the functional structure. There will be common themes, in terms of function or process, within each department, enabling the management to concentrate on specific issues within their own technical area of expertise. This form of organizational structure has a number of advantages and disadvantages over other types of structure, as shown in Table 9.

Sutherland, Jon and Canwell, Diane, *Organisation Structures and Processes*. Harlow: Financial Times, Prentice-Hall, 1997.

Table 9   Advantages and disadvantages of a fundamental structure

Advantages	Possible disadvantages
Promotes skills specialization and reduces duplication of resources.	These organizational structures tend to limit the organization to a relatively short-term horizon.
There is a clearer career progression route.	Managers of each department could become parochial, thus limiting career advancement.
There are clearer lines of communication, which could lead to higher productivity and performance within the department.	There is a chance of restricted communication between departments.
	If one department does not reach expectations, this has a knock-on effect on other departments.

F

Funnel of development

The term 'funnel of development' suggests that a broad spectrum of ideas (both good, bad and indifferent) are offered to the business via various means. The organization needs a means by which these ideas can be filtered or reduced in number in order to ensure that only the most viable and practical ideas reach project development. The process takes the form of a narrowing funnel, as can be seen in Figure 21.

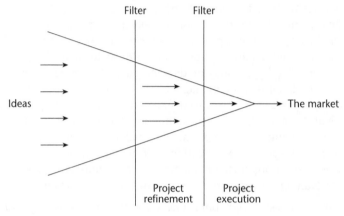

Figure 21   The funnel of development

F

Gg

General Electric screen matrix (the General Electric (GE) business screen)

The GE screen matrix is essentially a derivation of the Boston Consulting Group's **Boston growth matrix**. It was developed by McKinsey and Co. for General Electric as it had been recognized that the Boston Consulting Group matrix was not flexible enough to take broader issues into account.

The GE matrix cross-references market attractiveness and business position using three criteria for each – high, medium and low. The market attractiveness considers variables relating to the market itself, including the rate of market growth, market size, potential barriers to entering the market, the number and size of competitors, the actual profit margins currently enjoyed, and the technological implications of involvement in the market. The business position criteria look at the business's strengths and weaknesses in a variety of fields. These include its position in relation to its competitors, and the business's ability to handle product research, development and ultimate production. It also considers how well placed the management is to deploy these resources.

The matrix differs in its complexity compared with the Boston Consulting Group matrix. Superimposed on the basic diagram are a number of circles. These circles are of variable size (see Figure 22). The size of each represents the size of each market. Within each circle is a clearly defined segment which represents the business's market share within that market. The larger the circle, the larger the market, and the larger the segment, the larger the market share.

General environment

The term 'general environment' refers to the broad **macro-environment** in which a business operates. Broadly speaking, it can be identified as having four key elements, as outlined in Table 10.

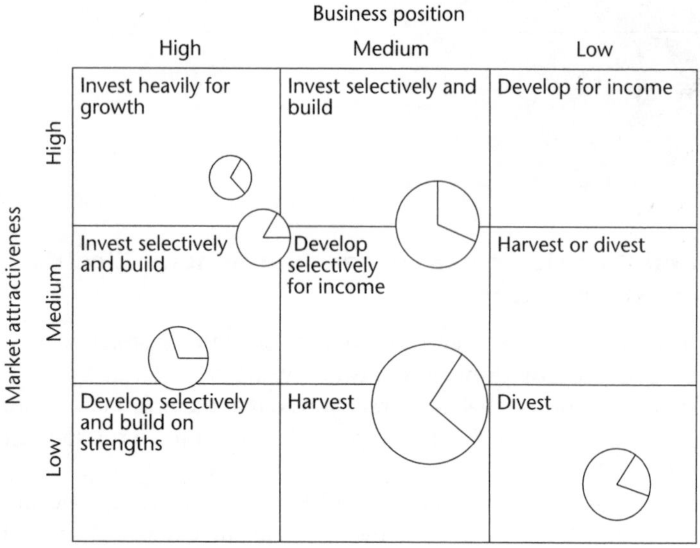

Figure 22 The General Electric (GE) matrix

Table 10 Elements of the general environment

Technological	Political/legal
New development inside and outside the industry	Potential/actual changes in regulations/legislation
New product development	Foreign trade regulations
Technological projects in the industry	Environmental protection
Industry (and government) spending on research and development	Changes in government (local/regional/national)

Economic	Socio-cultural
GNP growth	Population trends
Finance/market trends	Age distribution
Inflation	Regional movement of population
Interest rates	Demographics of the family
Money supply	Lifestyle
Employment/unemployment	Consumerism
Energy issues	

G

The most rapid of these trends in the general environment are technological and political/legal. The slowest moving are the economic and the socio-cultural.

Geographical structure

The **organizational structure** of a major business could be based purely on geographical regions. This could reflect the following possibilities:

- that the market is sufficiently remote to warrant a replication of the organizational structure in its geographical region;
- that the **factors of production** are sufficiently attractive to set up a geographically-based structure;
- that the market requires specific support that can only be delivered in the geographical region and not from the remote central headquarters of the organization.

Global area structure

A global area structure configures the organization along the main areas (geographically) in which it operates. Typically, the globe would be split up into a series of general areas such that the business can assume that all functions can be carried out by a centralized headquarters within each region. The configuration may take the form depicted in Figure 23.

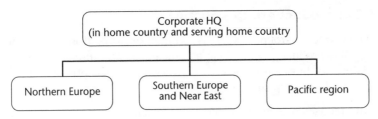

Figure 23   A global area structure

Global learning

Global learning is a process by which a multinational organization ensures that skills and knowledge flow freely between the different parts of the business across the world, regardless of national boundaries. Global learning can take the following routes:

- from the home country to an overseas division or subsidiary;
- from an overseas division or subsidiary to another overseas division or subsidiary;
- from an overseas division or subsidiary to the home country.

Global matrix structure

A global matrix structure is essentially a **horizontal differentiation** along product divisions and geographical divisions. In other words, to visualize the organization structure, product groups are placed on a vertical axis and the foreign divisions are placed on a horizontal axis. It allows businesses to reduce costs by increasing efficiency, and to differentiate their activities with innovation and responsiveness.

The feature of the global matrix structure is that there is dual decision-making responsibility, as there is both a divisional and an area hierarchy. The system is not without its problems, as many organizations consider this form of structure to be rather clumsy and bureaucratic. There is also the question of slow decision making and a lack of flexibility. Several international businesses have sought to overcome the problems by basing their organizational structure on wide networks with a shared culture and vision, and stressing that the informal structures are more important than the formal structure itself. These forms of organizational structure are known as flexible matrix structures.

Egelhoff, W. G., 'Strategy and Structure in Multinational Corporations: a Revision of the Stopford and Wells Model', *Strategic Management Journal*, vol. 9 (1988), pp. 1–14.

Global product group structure

A global product group structure is a variant **organizational structure** which has product groups along a vertical axis and foreign (overseas) **divisions**, or business units, on a horizontal axis. The primary purpose of the product group structure is:

- to reduce costs through increased efficiency;
- to differentiate the organization's areas of activity;
- to utilize any innovations or technologies;
- to improve customer service;
- to increase the speed of responses.

Typically, the structure would appear in the format shown in Figure 24.

Global strategic alliances

A global **strategic alliance** is usually formed by two or more organiza-

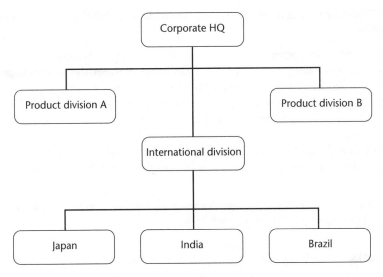

Figure 24 A global product group structure

tions from different countries. Typically, this involves the allocation of resources from these businesses based in different countries, to a new project or venture which they seek to undertake, using cooperative methods and the pooling of expertise and experience. The purpose of global strategic alliances is to:

- create **synergy**;
- accomplish more than could be achieved had the businesses been operating independently;
- coordinate effort;
- gain and share technologies;
- gain entry into an overseas market.

Major multinational businesses routinely enter into global strategic alliances as an integral part of their corporate strategy and the practice has become widespread in recent years.

See also **green-field investment.**

Global strategic planning

Global strategic planning aims to maximize global **economies of scale** and **economies of scope,** while at the same time incorporating the advantages of local responsiveness to customers in the countries in which the organization operates.

There are three main steps towards achieving global strategic planning:

- The development of a core business strategy – which forms the basis of attempts to create a sustainable **competitive advantage** (a replica of what has been achieved in the home market).
- The internationalization of this core strategy – the adaptation of the core strategy to overseas markets, along with expansion as necessary.
- The globalization of the international core strategy – which seeks to integrate the strategy in all of the countries in which the business operates.

Yip, G. S., *Total Global Strategy: Managing for Worldwide Competitive Advantage.* Englewood Cliffs, NJ: Prentice-Hall, 2002.

Global strategy

A global strategy is often adopted by an international business in order to increase its profitability by taking advantage not only of cost reductions that come from **experience curve** effects, but also of economies based on the location of parts of its operations. Typically a global strategy will consider the best alternative areas in which to concentrate research and development, marketing or production, choosing the most beneficial location for each of these key operations. In essence a global strategy can be called a **multi-domestic strategy**, in as much as the international business seeks to maximize its worldwide performance through maximizing any local **competitive advantages**, revenues or profits it can achieve. Equally, global strategies seek to maximize performance through integration and a sharing of resources.

Stonehouse, George, Hamill, Jim, Campbell, David and Purdie, Tony, *Global and Transnational Business: Strategy and Management.* New York: John Wiley, 2004.

Global web

The term 'global web' refers to the value creation undertaken by organizations at various points along the **value chain**.

In the case of multinational organizations, the global web is of supreme importance as it is the means by which they add value at the lowest cost. Typically, a business would select an overseas environment in which certain aspects of the value creation process can be undertaken at low cost, compared with other options they may have in choosing a location for these activities. Given that it is important for businesses to add value, whilst minimizing the cost of adding that value, they will seek locations where resources (human, natural, etc.) are available in sufficient numbers and quality. This means that a business will base its choice of location on quality and cost criteria which will contribute to generating the maximum profit.

Globalization of markets

The globalization of markets is in stark contrast to more familiar views of global marketing. The globalization of markets implies that many international businesses no longer consider individual national markets to be distinct entities. Although, until recently, many nations were closed by virtue of the fact that it was difficult to trade there, now that trade barriers have been removed, these national markets are merging and can be treated in a very similar manner. Concerns regarding transportation, distance to market, and even culture, are being subsumed as international businesses increasingly treat all national markets the same.

In May 1983 an article by Harvard Business School Professor Theodore Levitt prophesied the advent of globalization. Levitt predicted that as new technology extended the reach of global media and reduced the cost of communications, consumer tastes would converge, creating global markets for standardized products. His theory was considered somewhat outlandish at the time; a full third of the world's population still lived in communism countries. Levitt had failed to incorporate the role of technological change and its impact on production methodologies. Whilst globalization is a clear fact of life, standardization has given way to more varied and specialized products which are now produced as a result of improvements in production technology.

Levitt, Theodore, 'The Globalisation of Markets', *Harvard Business Review*, May–June (1983), pp. 92–102.

G

Globalization of production

The term 'globalization of production' refers to the trend among international businesses, notably multinationals, that have increasingly chosen to disperse their production processes across the world. In essence, these multinationals take full advantage of specific countries' factors of production in order to frame their global manufacturing policy.

Weiss, John, *Industrialisation and Globalisation: Theory and Evidence from Developing Countries*. London: Routledge, 2002.

Goals

Goals are targets, or states, which an organization seeks to achieve over a specified period of time. Goals need to be attainable, but challenging. The management of the process which delivers the achievement of these goals can be a key function of the strategic management process. The criteria or conditions that should be applied to the setting of goals are listed in Table 11.

Table 11 The setting of goals

Criteria or conditions	Goal description
Goals should be stable over time.	Continually changing the goals leads to problems of attainment and possible demotivation. Predetermined goals should be achieved, then amended.
Goals should be specific and clear.	Goals which are clearly spelled out can be judged more effectively in terms of attainment.
Goals should be linked to reality.	Impossible goals, plucked out of the air, require chance or good fortune to secure their attainment. Goals should be linked to a possible, and to the real, state or position of the organization.
Goals should be overarching.	Goals need to be central to the organization in the sense that all parts of the business can see their place in the attainment.
Goals should be unique and designed to differentiate.	Sharing similar goals with the competition is not an ideal way forward. They should be aimed at attaining some form of competitive advantage over the competition.
Goals should be linked to actions.	The interpretation of the goals at management and employee level should clearly indicate what has to be done in order to attain the goals. In other words, there needs to be a plan to attain the goals, by steps or actions over time.
Goals should suggest foresight.	Goals should be linked to cause and effect; by striving to attain the goals, the organization should be able to see where it is likely to be once those goals have been attained. Above all, it needs to be ready for that altered state and be prepared to set new goals from that point.

Goold, M. and Quinn, J. J., *Strategic Control: Milestones for Long-term Performance.* Harlow: Financial Times, Prentice-Hall, 1993.

Goal characteristics

'Goal characteristics' describes the ways in which goals should be meaningful to the organization. These characteristics are normally taken to be:

- They should have a precise nature.
- They should address key issues for the organization.
- They should be realistic, but challenge the organization as it strives to achieve them.
- They should have a definite time frame associated with them.

See also **goals**.

Goal congruence

Goal congruence occurs when the objectives of two **stakeholders** in an organization, such as the management and the shareholders, have been met. In other words, the goals or objectives of those two stakeholders have both been reached through the joint or several actions of the two parties.

Goal management

Goal management involves providing managers and employees with the tools they require to establish their individual goals, based on:

- objectives;
- directions.

The goal management process can be exemplified as in Figure 25.

Andersen, Erling S., Grude, Kristoffer V., Haug, Tor and Wiig, Roberta, *Goal Directed Project Management.* New York: Kogan Page, 1998.

G

Governance mechanisms

The three key aspects of governance mechanisms are:

- ownership structure;
- monitoring and controlling mechanisms;
- management performance.

Governance mechanisms deal with the ways in which the management structure, as determined by the ownership and overall structure of the

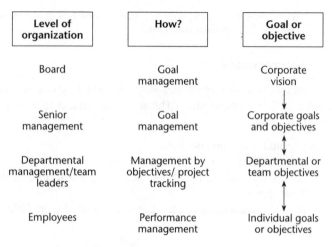

Figure 25 Goal management

business, both monitors and controls the business while at the same time it is monitored and controlled itself.

The governance mechanisms cover the board structure and composition, disclosure standards, financial accounting and standards, risk management, and the monitoring and control of information and transactions.

Monks, Robert and Minow, Nell, *Corporate Governance*. Oxford: Blackwell Publishing, 2003.

Green-field investment

When an international business considers foreign direct investment (FDI), it can choose to invest in the establishment of a completely new operation in a host country, which is known as a green-field investment, or it can merge with or acquire an existing operation. Many governments earmark specific areas of their country in which foreign green-field investment can be made. These restrictions, which were once rigid and widespread, are now far more relaxed. The primary advantage of green-field foreign direct investment is that it adds to the stock of domestic capital investment and, of course, it expands the productive capacity of the country.

Developing countries in particular are keen to attract green-field FDI as it brings new technology to the country, together with different organizational structures and management ability. This inflow of knowledge is far more limited in the case of acquisition. Green-field investment is also advantageous in the sense that it increases competition, whilst acquisitions concentrate ownership and reduce competition. Above all, green-field investments provide an inflow of foreign currency, whilst acquisitions may be funded by internally borrowed funds.

In the case both of green-field investment and of acquisitions and mergers, they are seen as a means by which international businesses can strengthen their market position in new countries.

Greenmail

The term 'greenmail' is most closely associated with the pursuing of shares in another business, and of the profits which can be achieved by re-selling these shares under certain circumstances. The process usually works in the following manner:

- A business secretly begins buying shares in another business.
- The purchasing business then announces the wish to take over control of the second business and acquire a majority shareholding.
- The board of directors of the business under threat, thinking that they will lose control of their business, invest or borrow money to purchase as many shares as they can from the market to protect their position.
- The business which originally purchased the shares is happy to sell back to the directors the shares they secretly purchased, at a profit.

Gross profit margin

The gross profit margin ratio is one of several ratios which help to assess the overall operating performance of a business. The ratio itself expresses the gross profit as a percentage of sales. The ratio is:

$$\frac{Gross\ profit\ margin \times 100}{Sales} = Gross\ profit$$

If a business generates some £700,000 in gross profit on a total sales revenue of £3,200,000, then the following calculation is made:

$$\frac{700,000 \times 100}{3,200,000} = 21.87\%$$

This indicates that the business earns £0.218 in gross profit for every £1 of sales.

Group-based bonus system

See **bonus plan reward system**.

Groups and teams

The definition of a group is two or more individuals who come into contact with one another in a work situation on a regular and continued basis. Within most organizations there are a number of groups who come together for a particular reason. Groups can be either formal in nature, or informal. The informal type of group often comes together to support activities, both within and outside the organization, and cooperate and collaborate with one another in order to carry out certain tasks and fulfil individual job roles.

Formal groups are often created in order to pass on and share information. Very often they assist in the decision-making process and are seen as an official function within the organization. Formal groups include **quality circles**, which tend to exist for a longer period of time than some of the other formal groups. Most formal groups consist of a variable number of representatives from different areas of the organization's activities. They are often given responsibility and authority to implement ideas and amend working practices, giving input regarding the possible impact of expected changes.

Many organizations have gradually come to the realization that teams represent a proven means by which productivity and performance can be assured. Various industry surveys, particularly in the manufacturing sector, seem to suggest that over two-thirds of all organizations actively encourage teams. The actual nature of the team is of prime importance and their creation is of particular relevance to human resources management. Essentially there are three different types of team, all of which have a degree of authority, autonomy or **empowerment**.

Empowered teams are usually given the authority to plan and implement improvements. Self-directed teams are virtually autonomous and are mainly responsible for supervisory issues. Cross-functional teams are more complex as they involve various individuals from different departments who are working towards a common end.

Training needs to be provided to teams both before and during their creation in order to assist the members in establishing relationships with one another and understanding their new responsibilities. It is also essential that teams are given clear instructions and, above all, support from management in order to carry out their tasks. Once a team has been established, and a degree of authority delegated to them, management and human resources departments need to step back and allow the team to develop and learn how their new working practices will operate.

The team itself, management, and the human resources despartment, retain the responsibility for monitoring and motivating the teams and their members. This requires effective communication skills and a feedback system which enables teams to request additional assistance should it be required.

Group think

The term 'group think' was coined by Irving Janis, who related the term to a phenomenon within groups. Janis considered that group think occurs when a group of individuals are so determined to make a decision that they ignore all major considerations and alternatives, as well as any disagreements within the group, in order to achieve this. Groups suffering from group think are often thought to be over-cautious and to lack necessary creativeness. They bond with each other, and the individuals see themselves as secure because they belong to the group. The group members have little doubt about the effectiveness or vulnerability of the group and consider the views of anyone not involved within the group to be those of insignificant outsiders. According to Janis the symptoms of group think are:

- invulnerability, in that they consider they cannot be touched;
- inappropriate rationale, in that they consider things are unlikely to happen to them;
- morality, in that they think they know what is best;
- stereotyping other groups, by considering them all to be less effective than they are;
- pressurizing other groups;
- exerting an element of self-censorship, by not communicating all, but selecting what they consider to be appropriate, information to other groups or relevant individuals;
- unanimity, by assuming a consensus when some individuals do not speak;
- mind-guards – referring to the fact that they do not allow any other thoughts to contradict what they have already decided.

Suffering from group think can make groups ineffective. Janis considered that management would have to encourage the individuals within the group to:

- consider and examine all alternatives;
- feel able to express their own doubts within the group;
- listen to criticisms from outside the group;
- challenge those who have firmly held beliefs;
- actively seek feedback, advice and information from outside the group;

G

- create sub-divisions within the group;
- avoid grapevine communication.

Group think can lead to ineffective decision making through insufficient attention to alternatives and risks.

Growth industry

A growth industry is an industry in which demand is increasing at a rapid pace. Growth industries are typified by first-time demand from consumers, as they enter the market for the first time. The potential of a growth industry is difficult to assess in the early stages as it is notoriously unpredictable in its longevity, as perhaps little is known about the overall dimensions of the market.

Growth strategy

Strategically, an organization has two major choices in terms of growth; either to expand within the existing industries in which it operates, or to undertake some form of **diversification** (in either products or services, or into another industry). The former course is often the most natural way forward, assuming of course that the industry offers, and will continue to offer, growth potential.

Concentration growth strategies tend to focus around either vertical integration or some form of horizontal growth. Diversification strategies involve either:

- concentric or related diversification;
- conglomerate or unrelated diversification.

Businesses have the option (depending upon circumstances) of being able to engage in growth strategies by:

- internally generated funds;
- investment and development;
- mergers;
- acquisitions;
- strategic alliances.

See also **horizontal growth, related diversification, unrelated (conglomerate) diversification** *and* **vertical integration**.

Guru concept

'Guru concept' refers to the influence which management gurus have had on all areas of business operations and management knowledge.

Management gurus propose management ideas in order to explain situations and to offer solutions to particular issues, perhaps anticipating the problematic nature of some of these issues before they are recognized by the organizations themselves. Systematically, management gurus have sought to understand the nature of managerial work and the needs of individuals in managerial positions. Management gurus develop these ideas, and either they themselves or other bodies seek to apply the ideas to organizations. Over the past century there have been at least six different waves of management gurus with their associated theories. These are:

- bureaucracy theories – as exemplified by **Max Weber**;
- scientific management – as represented by **Frederick Winslow Taylor**;
- classical management – such as **Henri Fayol**;
- human relations – as proposed by Elton Mayo and the **Hawthorne experiments**;
- neo-human relations – such as those of **Douglas McGregor**;
- the true gurus of the modern era – including **Tom Peters**, Michael Porter and **Rosabeth Moss Kanter**.

The take-up of the ideologies of these various gurus has been mixed and clearly any such theory has to strike a chord with either an organization or specific managers in order to gain any currency. Certainly many of the theories have found value as far as practical management is concerned, although few are sufficiently broad in their scope, or applicable in varied sets of circumstances, to be truly universal. Given the number of management guru texts which are produced each year, the guru concept continues to attempt to steer management in different directions, and this will continue over the coming years.

G

Hh

Hamel, Gary

The *Economist* describes Professor Hamel as 'the world's reigning strategy guru'. Professor Peter Senge of MIT describes him as 'the most influential thinker on strategy in the Western world'. Arguably, Hamel has changed the focus and language of strategy in many of the world's largest and leading organizations.

According to Hamel, the goal of organizations should be to accelerate change and embrace the new. In other words, organizations should not be frightened to re-configure themselves, adapt their processes and make other alterations in order to seize the opportunities presented to them and to take advantage of trends.

Change should be a continuous process, thus avoiding the chaos of sudden and major change. Major reorganizations are undesirable, suddenly closing or downsizing operations are avoidable, and writing-off subsidiaries or products unthinkable. Hamel believes that many organizations are simply not resilient enough, they allow too many defects, they miss opportunities, have outdated strategies, are more inclined towards retrenchment, and as a result both management and employees become dispirited.

In a recent article, Hamel said:

There are two core challenges to making innovation a deep capability in any organization. First, most companies have a very narrow idea of innovation, usually focusing just on products and services. We need to enlarge our view of innovation. Second, most companies devote much more energy to optimizing what is there than to imagining what could be. We need to create constituencies for 'What Could Be'.

('Innovation as a Deep Capability', no. 27, Winter 2003, Leader to Leader Institute, New York)

Hamel, Gary, *Leading the Revolution: How to Thrive in Turbulent Times by Making Innovation a Way of Life*. Watertown, MA: Harvard Business School Press, 2003.

Hard metrics

Hard metrics are measurement techniques which seek to base measurement purely on factual issues (such as input or output measurements). Usually, hard metrics are used as efficiency measurements. They are the opposite of **soft metrics**.

Harvest strategy

See **asset reduction strategy.**

Hawthorne experiments

Elton Mayo was employed by the Hawthorne Works during the 1920s and 1930s to attempt to improve the electrical company's productivity. As a result of this work he developed a theory which has since become known as the Hawthorne Effect.

Initially, Mayo adopted the scientific management theory of **Frederick Winslow Taylor** in his attempt to discover what environmental features of the workplace were affecting productivity. He made amendments to the lighting, the heating and the availability of refreshments, then went on to make changes to the length of the working day and week. Each time he made a change the rate of productivity increased. Puzzled by his findings, Mayo reversed his actions by removing tea-breaks and reducing the level of lighting, but productivity continued to increase. Mayo's conclusion was that the changes had been made in consultation with the employees and that this factor had been the determining influence on productivity, together with the fact that the employees had a good working relationship with their supervisors. This research became known as Mayo's Hawthorne experiments.

Further research was then undertaken in another department of the organization. Two different groups of employees were working on complex equipment; one group considered that their status was high because of the complexity of the job role. The second group considered themselves to be lower in status, and this resulted in a degree of competition between the two groups. Both groups had established their own sets of rules and code of behaviour and each had an established pace of work and degree of output. Individuals within the group who did not comply with these standards were put under pressure from the other members of the group.

Each group was given a target output for the day by the management of the organization. On some days these targets were exceeded but the groups would simply report that they had reached the target figures, and

H

include the excess in the target figure for the following day. Mayo's conclusions from this were that:

- The groups had been given a **benchmark**. Their benchmark had been the employer's output targets and they had been able to compare this with their own output totals.
- They had established for themselves a concept of a fair day's output and did not feel they needed to exceed these targets.

Mayo felt that lessons could be learned from this research in that a group's needs have to be in accord with organizational rules. Consultation was the key to achieving this, together with close monitoring of day-to-day organizational activities.

Mayo made three interesting discoveries from his research, which form the basis of his 'solidarity theory':

- Output and motivation improved when employees were being observed.
- Peer pressure contributed to the level of support by the individuals within the group.
- The group had strong feelings about what was possible and reasonable. This was as important to the group as their reaction to the demands of their managers.

Mayo, Elton, *The Social Problems of an Industrial Civilization*. London: Routledge, 1998.

Hierarchies of strategy

As far as strategic management is concerned, strategy itself can take place at three distinct levels:

- corporate;
- business unit (divisional);
- functional (departmental).

Given the fact that **corporate level strategy** takes place at the highest level of an organization, the other two levels should, theoretically speaking, contribute to that process. At the same time, however, they should be subservient to the corporate strategy.

At corporate level, the strategy is concerned with:

- *Reach* – which defines corporate responsibilities, and the overall **goals** of the corporation. It should indicate where and how the organization does business.
- *Competition* – which defines where the organization will compete for its **market share**.

- *Activities and relationships* – which seek to create **synergy** and coordination between managers and employees across the various business units of the organization.
- *Governance* – how the organization will be managed, where centralization will be used and where **decentralization** will be allowed.

At the business unit level, the primary focus is on achieving and maintaining a degree of **competitive advantage**. In this respect the strategy tends to involve:

- positioning (in the market and compared with rivals);
- change anticipation (demand, technology, etc.);
- competition (how the business can influence or have an impact upon competitors).

In essence, business unit level strategy deals with issues such as cost leadership, differentiation and business focus.

At the functional level, strategy is at the heart of the operating systems (departments, etc). Most of the strategy will therefore relate to the business process itself and, notably, the **value chain**. At the functional level strategies revolve around:

- marketing;
- finance;
- human resources;
- operations management;
- research and development.

Mintzberg, Henry, Ahlstrand, Bruce and Lampel, Joseph, *Strategy Safari: A Guided Tour through the Wilds of Strategic Management*. New York: Simon & Schuster, 2001.

Historical financial analysis

Historical financial analysis uses the historical cost principle, which makes the assumption that asset and liability measurements should be based on the amount that was given or received during the exchange transaction. Historical cost measurement is considered to be an important piece of **cash flow** information as it is verifiable. It is primarily used for accounting for plant assets. In this instance the recorded costs of the plant assets are equal to the cash equivalent price, the value of which does not change unless the asset has suffered impairment. In using the historical cost principle it is possible to value an asset over its lifespan on the more reliable basis of past transactions. The value of the plant asset is derived through its use and not its disposal at the end of its useful economic life.

H

Hold and maintain strategy

A hold and maintain strategy is exemplified by a business's attempts to protect its current **market share**, whilst not actively pursuing new customers in order to expand this market share. Since it is generally recognized that the bulk of profits are derived from existing customers, the hold and maintain strategy seeks to conserve the major customer base, effectively concentrating on efforts at fending off competitors.

The hold and maintain strategy should, theoretically, give the greatest return for the organization in terms of profitability and of dividends paid to the investors in the business. In effect, the business is maximizing returns on investment which have already been made.

The strategy is a sound one, providing that the environment retains a degree of consistency and that the competitors are not overly active in the market. The strategy does mean that the business runs the risk of being caught unprepared.

Horizontal differentiation

Horizontal differentiation involves the division of a multinational business into a series of sub-units, usually on a nation-by-nation basis.

Horizontal growth

'Horizontal growth' refers to the following forms of business expansion:

- The expansion of the organization's products and services into new markets or locations.
- An increase in the range of products or services offered to the same markets.
- A combination of the above two.

In effect, the business expands sideways into a part of the **value chain** which it already occupies. Businesses follow this form of expansion because it reduces the overall risks and costs.

H

Horizontal hierarchical structure

A horizontal hierarchical structure seeks to establish common objectives across departmental, divisional or business unit boundaries. Typically, processes will be shared in order for the different parts of the organization to recognize and utilize their common objectives. The primary purpose of the structure is to move together in the fulfilment of either customer or **stakeholder** demands or requirements.

Horizontal merger

Essentially a horizontal merger is the joining together of two businesses with similar product lines or range of services. Governments are concerned with the regulation of horizontal mergers as they may create a monopoly, either nationally or regionally. There are, therefore, rules and regulations governing horizontal mergers that may be considered against the interests of the country and of consumers. In actual fact, horizontal mergers can result in two radically different outcomes:

- Higher prices as a result of the newly merged business effectively controlling the market as a virtual monopoly.
- Lower prices as a result of lower future costs and/or better products. Less has to be spent on protecting market share through marketing and advertising.

www.dti.gov.uk/ccp/topics2/mergers.htm

www.usdoj.gov/atr/public/guidelines/horiz_book/hmg1.html

www.ftc.gov/bc/docs/horizmer.htm

Hubris hypothesis

In 1986 Richard Roll argued that bidding businesses have a tendency to overstate the value of economic benefits they would acquire as a result of a merger. In other words, the bid premium may be overstated as a result of a valuation error. This becomes all the more significant if the bidding business is dealing with a potential overseas acquisition. Managerial over-confidence, as exemplified in the hubris hypothesis, suggests a pursuit of the maximization of personal utility rather than the maximization of shareholder wealth.

Roll, Richard, 'The Hubris Hypothesis of Corporate Takeovers', *Journal of Business*, 59 (1986), pp. 197–216.

Human relations

Broadly speaking, the human relations strand of management theory is based on the individual and sentiment, rather than the individual as an economic unit, and notions of efficiency. The human relations school, which developed during the 1930s, arose out of a desire to provide alternative explanations to those proposed by scientific management. The key differences are:

- scientific management aimed to adjust the employees' actions in order to undertake a particular defined set of tasks;

H

- human relations aimed to adjust the tasks to suit the skills and expertise of the employees.

Both schools were concerned with improvements in efficiency and productivity. The human relations school in turn has given rise to other areas of approach, including:

- group dynamics;
- industrial relations;
- organizational humanism;
- individualism;
- systemic interdependence.

At present, the human relations school has several different sub-disciplines, which include:

- mutual accountability;
- self-managed teams;
- flexible working and flexible organizations.

See also **Follett, Mary Parker.**

Human resources

The role of management in the deployment and effectiveness of human resources within an organization is a vast concern, which has been much written about. Human resource management, as such, can be differentiated from personnel management in the sense that the latter has more to do with the practical aspects of recruitment, appraisal, training and other key issues. Human resource management itself is more strategic and is concerned with the overall deployment of the human resources that are available to the business.

Typically there are four main areas in which human resource management is concerned. These are:

- The aggregate size of the organization's labour force.
- The amount spent on training the workforce in order to achieve targets, such as quality, or production output.
- Relations with trade unions and other employee-based organizations.
- Human asset counting, which analyses the costs and financial benefits of different forms of personnel policy.

The broader approach to human resource management involves a number of concerns, which include the following:

- The implications of the management of change to encourage flexible attitudes to the acceptance of new work practices.
- Making a major input into organizational development.
- Being prescriptive and initiating new activities, as opposed to being responsive to employment law, which is the preserve of personnel management.
- Determining employee relationships by the establishment of a culture which is conducive to cooperation and commitment.
- To take a long-term view, to integrate the human resources of the organization into a coherent whole.
- To emphasize the need for direct communication.
- To develop **organizational culture**.
- To encourage employee participation in work groups.
- To enhance employees' capabilities in the longer term and not focus purely on their current duties and responsibilities.

Bernardin, H. J., *Human Resource Management: An Experiential Approach*. New York: McGraw-Hill, 2002.

Stroh, C. K. and Caliguiri, P. M., 'Strategic Human Resources: a New Source of Competitive Advantage in the Global Arena', *International Journal of Human Resource Management*, 9 (1) (1998), pp. 1–17.

Hypercompetitive industries

Hypercompetitive industries are those most closely associated with the rapid development of technology and the rapid development of innovations. Typical hypercompetitive industries include those producing computers, cars and other vehicles, and pharmaceuticals. Strategies adopted in hypercompetitive industries include:

- Those based on surprise, designed to gain a **competitive advantage** by effectively disrupting the market by the introduction of innovation.
- The manipulation of competitive conditions to create a competitive advantage in order to eliminate those advantages enjoyed by rivals. The business needs to have the ability to produce rapid innovation, and to have a superior short-term focus and, above all, market awareness.

These last three points perhaps need a little more explanation:

- The use of rapid innovation is critical. Hypercompetitive businesses need to innovate quickly and then follow up their innovation with equally rapid manufacturing, marketing and distribution. In this

H

way the business can shift the industry dynamics, thus gaining a market share which exceeds the reaction levels of the competitors.

- Superior short-term focus is essential for hypercompetitive businesses to gain a temporary advantage. They can achieve a short-term profit and then move again before the competitors react. Businesses which can manipulate the competition into making a long-term commitment in the area which they are about to leave are far more successful.

- Strong market awareness means that a hypercompetitive business needs to understand the consumer and deliver products which are superior in design, functionality and support. The identification of the customers is essential, as is the possibility of selling to a broader market, albeit temporarily.

D'Aveni, Richard A., *Hypercompetition: Managing the Dynamics of Strategic Maneuvering*. New York: Free Press, 1994.

D'Aveni, Richard A., *Strategic Supremacy: How Industry Leaders Create Growth, Wealth and Power through Spheres of Influence*. New York: Free Press, 2002.

H

Icarus paradox

The Icarus paradox is based on the tale of Icarus, the son of Daedalus. They had been imprisoned by King Minos of Crete. Daedalus' escape method was to build pairs of wings for himself and his son made of feathers, attached to a wooden frame by wax. Daedalus told his son not to fly too close to the sun, but in his joy at escaping Icarus ignored his father and the wax softened, the feathers loosened and he plunged to his death in the sea.

The Icarus paradox has been applied successfully to many businesses. It describes a situation where the business itself is extremely successful; so much so that it has become a specialized provider of products and services and is concerned more with the quality and the delivery of those products and services than with the market itself. In effect it becomes blinded to the need for change.

Because the business has been successful, when it moves into new markets it adopts the same business models which have proved effective in its core business. But it misses the point and finds itself losing sight of the reality of the market; it loses a grasp on its own **competitive advantage** and ultimately fails. This is known as a paradox because the success of the business in its core market ultimately leads to its failure. Many businesses, such as Wang, Xerox, Kodak and AT&T, continued to expand into new markets, continued doing what had made them successful, missed the market changes and were left in the wake of more flexible organizations.

Illusion of control

Clearly, this term suggests what could be considered an unrealistic optimism, in the sense that an individual believes that he or she has more control over events than is actually the case.

The illusion of control significantly limits performance and reduces the ability of a manager to be able to forecast with any clarity. The illusion of control leads to a simplification in the evaluation stage of strategic decision making in the following way:

- A process of partial representativeness leads to inaccurate predictions of the consequences of actions, by associating them with similar events in the past.
- Partially understood alternatives are rejected, even though they may be the best course of action.
- Inherent risks are inaccurately assessed.

If managers have misconceptions of their control on resources, for example, then it is possible that they will over-value the ratio of success for a task.

The illusion of control revolves around notions of personal efficiency and over-confidence. Any perceived efficiency corresponds to the manager's capabilities in mobilizing the **motivation**, resources and courses of action needed for specific situations. Over-confidence occurs when the manager believes that decisions are correct, when in actual fact they are not. Over-confidence leads to stress, ambiguity and more complex problems.

Bandura, A., 'Self-efficiency: Toward a Unifying Theory of Behavioural Change', *Psychological Review*, 84(2) (1977) pp. 191–215.

Starbucks, W. H. and Mezias, J., 'Opening Pandora's Box: Studying the Accuracy of Managers' Perceptions', *Journal of Organizational Behavior*, 17 (1996), pp. 99–117.

Implementation strategy

Oddly, the implementation strategy in respect of organizational change and strategic management is a much overlooked area of decision making. Many businesses, having made the decision to undertake organizational change, through a complex decision-making process, encounter problems with the implementation phase. Typically these problems include:

- The fact that implementation often takes longer than was anticipated.
- Major implementation problems being overlooked.
- There is insufficient coordination
- Other issues arise which take resources away from the implementation phase.
- Management and employees do not have sufficient capabilities to implement the changes.
- There is a lack of training for management and employees in order to implement the changes.
- External factors affect the implementation which were not anticipated.

- Management fails to take a lead.
- The key implementation criteria, as exemplified in the task and activities, are poorly defined.
- The implementation is not monitored well enough.

An implementation plan, ideally, should include a series of steps or actions.

- What needs to be done.
- How it needs to be done.
- Who needs to do it.
- When it needs to be done.
- Where it needs to be done.
- Why it needs to be done.

These steps need to be supported by human, physical, financial and perhaps technological resources. The steps also need to be supported by key **stakeholders** who will be affected by the changes, notably functional managers and employees. The steps also need to have a clear sequencing; in other words they need to be timed and monitored. The business's organizational structure may impede the changes and the implementation, so the structure may have to be amended in order to allow the implementation to take place.

Incremental innovation

Incremental innovation has been described as both familiar and reassuring. Effectively, it is the continual process of making small improvements in either efficiency or performance within the fixed parameters of a product, a business model or perhaps a practice. Incremental innovations tend to be year-on-year improvements, allowing the business to continue to function using recognizable systems or procedures without the huge upheaval of a truly radical innovation. 'Incremental innovation' therefore refers to slow, gradual refinements which improve performance in steady stages.

Tushman, M. L. and Moore, W. L., *Readings in the Management of Innovations*. New York: Harper Business, 1988.

Incumbent advantage

Businesses which have a competitive advantage over other businesses that wish to enter a specific overseas market, have an incumbent advantage. Incumbent advantage is a feature of businesses which are first movers into a new market, in as much as they have the opportunity to begin to erect **barriers to entry** against the competition.

Index/indexes/indices

An index, indexes or indices are effectively performance measures or metrics. Normally, a weighted value of a measure is used, based on its importance and relevance. Trends and measures are compared with an index, from which the organization can see movements from a specified point in the past. These figures can be used to provide a summary, in statistical form, which shows the movement of a measure, compared with the historical figure.

Industry life cycle model

The industry life cycle model consists of four distinct stages: fragmentation, shake-out, maturity and decline. The four stages effectively track the process, in a basic form, of the development, the dominance and eventual decline of any industry. A basic life cycle model can be seen in Figure 26.

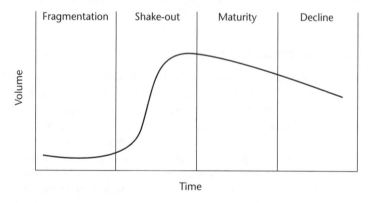

Figure 26 An industry life cycle model

The stages can be described in a variety of ways according to the exact nature of the industry itself; however, Table 12 summarizes the main aspects of each stage.

Frankl, Paolo and Rubik, Frieder, *Life Cycle Assessment in Industry and Business: Adoption Patterns, Applications and Implications*. Berlin and Heidelberg: Springer-Verlag, 2000.

Table 12   Stages of the industry life cycle model

Stages	Description
Fragmentation	Entrepreneurs are the prime catalysts in developing a new industry. New industries arise when an entrepreneur overcomes the twin problems of innovation and invention and works out how to bring the new product or service into the market. The entrepreneur must secure financial capital, obtain market feedback and overcome any barriers to innovation.
Shake-out	A dominant model of how to run the industry emerges, efficiencies begin to be realized and the value of the industry quickly rises. Businesses learn how to adapt and use any new technology.
Maturity	Technological advances yield only incremental improvements. The efficiencies of the dominant business model give these organizations a competitive advantage. Pricing, competition and cooperation take on complex forms.
Decline	Inertia may impede survival; wars of attrition between businesses may develop; and those with heavy bureaucracies may fail. Demand may be fully satisfied or supplies may be running out. Equally, new technologies may promise more value.

Inert cultures

If an organization has an inert culture it is considered to be inherently conservative, cautious and risk averse. An inert culture tends to impede an organization's ability to change, particularly when faced with a competitive threat.

In contrast, an organization with an **adaptive culture** tends to allow change in the strategy of the business in order to survive effectively in a changing environment.

Informal power

Whilst managers and supervisors have clear formal power to assert their authority over subordinates, others are given informal power to operate and to direct on behalf of those with formal authority. Informal power tends to occur in situations where an individual's job description does not explicitly convey authority or power. Usually, by virtue of their age, experience or understanding of the processes and tasks required, individuals are granted informal power as a form of **delegation**, to exercise authority over their peers.

Innovation-adoption model

The innovation-adoption model can be applied both to consumers and to businesses. When applying to consumers, the innovation-adoption model charts the process of gradual acceptance of a new product. The key stages are awareness, interest, evaluation, trial, and adoption.

The innovation-adoption process in relation to businesses was developed by Everett Rogers and details the five stages of the innovation process, together with the associated activities at each of these stages, as can be seen in Figure 27.

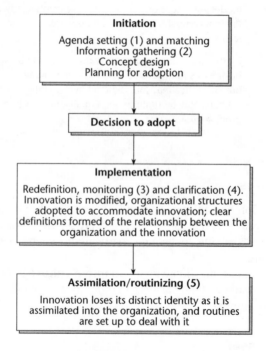

Figure 27 Innovation process stages

Rogers, Everett M., *Diffusion of Innovations*. New York: Simon & Schuster, 2003.

Innovation clusters

The innovation cluster is a theoretical model used to describe the relationship between the design of technology and science policy.

Innovation consists of the production and exchange of intangible inputs and outputs. Innovation studies suggest that knowledge-intensive business services (KIBS) have a key role in the creation and dissemination of up-to-date information and data, as shown in Figure 28.

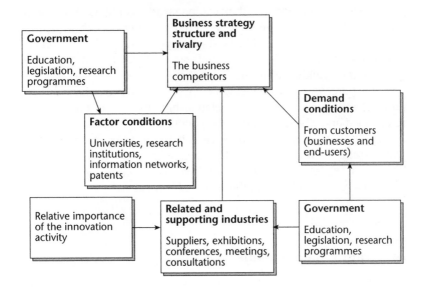

Figure 28   Knowledge-intensive business services

Roelandt, T. and den Hertog, P., 'Cluster Analysis and Cluster-based Policy Making in OECD Countries: Introduction to the Theme', in *Boosting Innovation: The Cluster Approach*. Paris: OECD Proceedings, 1999.

Input measure

An input measure is an estimation of the resources which need to be committed to a particular activity. A business will use input measures in order to assess and track the location of its available resources. Input measures, however, do not give an account of the effectiveness of deploying these resources in an activity.

Intangible assets

An intangible resource, or an intangible asset, is also known as an invisible asset. It is an asset which does not have a physical presence. In other words, intangible assets include goodwill, brand names, patents, trademarks, copyrights and franchises. Clearly, intangible resources are the opposite of **tangible resources**.

Interestingly, intangible resources can be more, or less, intangible. Brand names, trademarks or patents, for example, have, to some extent, a presence in the sense that they can be clearly identified as being an asset. Other intangible assets are rather more ethereal. Goodwill is probably one of the most intangible assets as it has no supporting documentation and is of variable commercial value. Goodwill can be a very valuable intangible asset in the sense that it can offer a business, or a potential purchaser of a business, the opportunity to capitalize on future profits based on the work and relationships that have already been established and which constitute the goodwill.

There is, however, a slight distinction between some forms of intangible assets. Goodwill could be described as either an intangible or an invisible asset, whereas insurance policies, for example, are invariably referred to as invisible rather than intangible assets.

Donaldson, T. H., *The Treatment of Intangibles: Banker's View*. Basingstoke: Palgrave Macmillan, 1992.

Integrating mechanisms

For international businesses a well-planned and considered means by which they can integrate their operations across several countries has become an essential strategy. Businesses that are involved in multi-domestic, international, global or trans-national business will seek to integrate their systems, usually through a more complex form of **organizational structure**. Of the various different forms of integrating mechanisms, perhaps the most obvious is to have individuals from the parent company in direct contact, or posted to, new overseas ventures in order to integrate the new business enterprise gradually into the overall organizational system. Some international businesses prefer inter-departmental liaison, in which selected individuals from key functional departments of the parent company are available to assist the new overseas enterprise in integrating its systems into the parent's mechanisms. Other international businesses choose to create temporary task forces to speed up the integration process. They may well choose to site permanent teams with the new overseas enterprise, with a view not only to integrating the overseas business, but to learn best practice from that overseas business, which can then be fed back to the parent company.

One of the most common forms of integrating mechanism is a **global matrix structure**, which effectively makes key functional departments in the parent company responsible for certain aspects of the overseas business activities and helps ensure clearer integration and permanent liaison.

Intended strategies

As the term implies, intended strategies are plans made for the future, with the intention of assisting the organization in fulfilling its objectives. By their very nature, intended strategies are proactive, having been made in advance, anticipating actions in the future.

Interface management

Interfaces are both the formal and the informal boundaries and relationships within an organization. The interfaces, therefore, include individuals, departments, functions or business units. Interfacing involves the establishment of satisfactory working boundaries between these facets of the organization.

Interface management can be defined as the communication and coordination and responsibilities across common boundaries. Alternatively, others prefer to describe interface management as dealing with problems which can occur between individuals, departments or functions within an organization.

Interface management takes place at various levels within the organization, typically:

- with superiors in the organization;
- with team members who have line or staff responsibility;
- with subordinates;
- with customers or product users;
- with suppliers, contractors or sub-contractors.

Internal governance

See **governance mechanisms.**

Internal marketing

At the centre of internal marketing is the desire to achieve change and have an impact upon attitudes and behaviours. Whilst external marketing seeks to assure customers of the value of the product and entice them to make regular purchases, internal marketing attempts to inform employees so that they understand, accept and adopt new processes.

In effect, internal marketing uses a modified communications plan, which features a fully functional flow of information, capable of amendment and revision as a result of feedback. The key stages are:

- Situation – determining the target audiences, and identifying channels of communication and the needs of each target audience.
- Objectives – generally using SMART (specific, measureable, achievable, relevant and timebound).
- Strategy – what are the short-, medium- and long-term issues and strategic goals?
- Targets – all must be identified and provided for within the system.
- Promotion – direct communications, where target audiences are encouraged to contribute.
- Training – referring to training needed both by those engaged in delivering the internal marketing and by those within each target group, as required.
- Control – in order to ensure that achievement is measurable and the budget justified.

Ahmed, Pervaiz K. and Rafiq, Mohammed, *Internal Marketing: Tools and Concepts for Customer Focussed Management*. Oxford: Butterworth-Heinemann, 2002.
Dunmore, Michael, *Inside-out Marketing: How to Create an Internal Marketing Strategy*. London: Kogan Page, 2003.

Internal stakeholders

Internal stakeholders are individuals who have a close functional, or ownership-related, relationship with the organization. Therefore internal stakeholders include:

- all levels of management;
- the board of directors;
- employees;
- stockholders or shareholders.

International business operations

'International business' is a generic term which is used to describe any form of business transaction, whether undertaken by an individual or a company, which involves two or more countries. The term suggests that the business world is no longer limited by national boundaries. The vast improvements in communication, transport and information technology have enabled businesses to operate in radically new environments, while simultaneously making many nations wholly interdependent on one another. Increasingly, businesses are as concerned with the international environment as they are with their local environments. Huge numbers of businesses carry out international operations and increase their opportunities through diversifying their markets and obtaining supplies of raw materials and components at lower cost. Alongside this, these international businesses are facing greater risks, in many cases, with an incomplete knowledge of the markets in which they are now operating. These new risks include political or economic instability together with volatile exchange rates.

International business is not simply concerned with the exporting of products or services to overseas markets. It has an equal relevance to the sourcing of goods and raw materials and, indeed, making direct foreign investments in countries which hitherto were rather closed and misunderstood.

Morrison, Janet, *The International Business Environment*. Basingstoke: Palgrave Macmillan, 2002.
Woods, Margaret, *International Business*. Basingstoke: Palgrave Macmillan, 2001.

International licensing

Licensing involves giving either legal or official permission for a third party to use, or own, the intellectual property of another business. This could include trademarks, technology, or the understanding of how to deliver a specific service. Innumerable international licence agreements exist between businesses in different countries, all of which are subject to laws applicable in each country, which often differ in their enforcement and the rights and liabilities of the parties that have entered into the agreement. In effect, licensing is a business arrangement whereby a manufacturer or owner of a product can grant permission to another business, or individual, to manufacture or offer that product (sometimes making use of proprietary material) in return for a payment, often in the form of royalties.

International strategy

Whilst strategy can be defined as being actions which the management of a business takes in order to meet the objectives of the organization, international strategy requires a more complex and holistic view. International businesses, which operate in different countries, need to be aware of the national differences, both in the markets in which they operate and in the potential advantages and disadvantages of establishing operations in those countries. They will often make a judgement as to the factors that could affect the performance of their activity in any given country. In each country the strategy needs to be adapted in order to match the economies in different locations.

One strategy could be the production, or the offering, of standardized products, but ultimately international expansion requires the business to attain specific competences in relation to each market. Multinational organizations can have a considerable advantage if they set up foreign subsidiaries and use the inherent skills in the marketplace in pursuit of their global strategy and objectives. Businesses will often look to find areas in which they can reduce costs and produce commodities where price is the main competitive weapon. Part of the success strategy revolves around being locally responsive and reflecting consumer tastes and preferences whilst working within the peculiarities of an overseas nation's infrastructure, and mirroring their traditional practices, using their distribution channels and being cognizant of the host government's policies and regulations.

Many multinational businesses will also consider that an integral part of their international strategy is the transference, into foreign markets, of skills and products which have been customized for local consumption. This means that the strategy aimed at customizing the products must include their overall business strategy in relation to that nation, and the framing of appropriate marketing strategies.

International businesses no longer consider simply replicating their domestic strategy in overseas markets. Indeed, to remain competitive and successful, they adopt a trans-national strategy which focuses upon cost reduction, the transference of skills and products, and stimulating local responsiveness.

Stonehouse, George, Hamill, Jim, Campbell, David and Purdie, Tony, *Global and Transnational Business: Strategy and Management.* New York: John Wiley, 2004.

Inter-organizational relations

In terms of strategic management, inter-organizational relationships, or the ways in which organizations establish and maintain relations with other organizations, have become increasingly important. Inter-organizational relationships provide access to resources which would otherwise not be available. The relationships are typified by increased information exchange, enhanced communications, exchanges of personnel and, above all, an increasing level of trust. Trends in inter-organizational theory focus on the processes of inter-relationships and coordination between organizations, and any factors which enable, or restrain, inter-organizational inter-reactions.

Intrepreneur

The term 'intrepreneur' was originally coined in the early 1980s and literally means an entrepreneur within an organization. The term is used to describe an individual with responsibility for developing new enterprises within the organization itself. Unlike standard start-up businesses, any such new enterprise can enjoy the protection and financial benefits of the existing organization, and usually has a far better opportunity to succeed.

Inventory turnover

Inventory turnover, or stock turnover, is equal to the cost of goods sold divided by the average investment in the inventory. Or, in other words, the cost of goods sold divided by the value of stock. The inventory turnover is the inverse of cycle time (which is the length of time required to compete a given product from the start time to the moment it rolls off the production line). Normally the inventory turnover increases in proportion to demand.

Investment strategy

Business investment strategy can be typified as having three primary exponents, namely exploration, exploitation and expansion. Investment strategy, be it internal or external, can involve strategic alliances, partnerships, acquisitions or mergers. Equally, investment strategy can move a business vertically, horizontally or laterally, in terms of its involvement in a specific market or markets. Investment strategy is not for the risk averse, as higher-risk investments often offer longer-term advantages, so long as the investment is a sound one. Clearly, any form of investment strategy requires the diversion of resources from the core business area to a new, or allied, area of operation. Investment strategy therefore requires a sound technical capability, a tacit knowledge of the market and, above all, an understanding of the rapidly changing markets themselves.

Business investment does not necessitate securing ownership of all of a partner's or subsidiary's assets. It can involve a cooperative arrangement which seeks to enhance both businesses' competitive positions.

Businesses will seek horizontal mergers and acquisitions in the hope that they will capture a larger proportion of the market. They may also create new entities in order to reduce costs through **synergy** effects.

Businesses will look for the optimum business investment, which will not only minimize their transactional costs, but will enhance their strategic objectives.

Bouchet, Michael Henry, Clark, Ephraim and Groslambert, Bertrand, *Country Risk Assessment: A Guide to Global Investment Strategy.* New York: John Wiley, 2003.

Invisible assets

See **intangible assets.**

Invisible hand

The concept of the invisible hand is essentially an economics-based notion, which suggests that ultimately businesses are guided to produce what consumers require. The invisible hand is, to all intents and purposes, related to the pursuit of profit. Therefore the invisible hand is simply the notion that businesses produce only what consumers need, because the provision of those products and services will produce a profit for the organization. Equally, they will not produce products or services which are ultimately harmful to the consumer, since the reaction would be adverse and cause the business to lose profits.

Irregular measures

'Irregular measures' means often random, demand-based organizational performance measures. These irregular measures may be required in specific formats, comparing criteria or conditions which are not, on a routine basis, measured or compared. Irregular measures can reveal specific relationships between different performance figures, and provide the organization with a different insight into these relationships.

Issue agenda building

Issue agenda building proposes a conceptual approach to decision making, particularly applicable to uncertain or ambiguous situations. A version of the model is outlined in Figure 29.

In this model, issues only attract attention if they conform to the strategy and the culture of the organization. Assuming the issue is simple, but of immediate interest, it will find itself on the agenda; otherwise

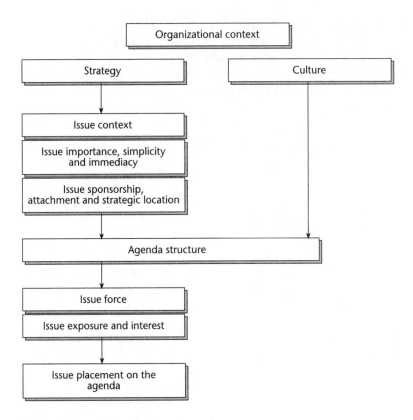

Figure 29 Formation of an issue agenda

there is a tendency to postpone deliberations until more information has been gathered.

In order for the issue to sustain attention, it must find a sponsor (an individual who is prepared to research and present the salient points of the issue). Equally, the issue may fail to reach the agenda if its context is not in line with the points in the diagram.

Pondy, L., Boland, R. and Thomas, H., *Managing Ambiguity and Change*. New York: John Wiley, 1988.

Ivory tower planning

'Ivory tower planning' is a term used to describe a process of planning which is restricted purely to the responsibility of senior management. This form of planning is considered to take place in a vacuum, with little understanding of the business's operations, realities and external environment. Typically, senior management would not elicit assistance or information from managers actually operating the business, and may well develop a short- to long-term planning strategy which pays little regard to the realities of running the business itself.

Japanese business strategy

Japanese business strategy tends to be formulated on the basis of industrial organization. Typically, this focuses around the factory, the business or the inter-business network. Around 100 years ago the Japanese business system was revolutionized by the creation of the corporation, yet the inter-business network remains strong within the Japanese system. Whilst sweeping economic and technical changes have wrought enormous impacts upon the economic environment, the Japanese business system is firmly rooted in robust organizations. They seek to be dynamic, and they continue to foster inter-relationships between the different businesses. Successive waves of manufacturing changes and associated strategies have changed the way in which Japanese businesses produce products or provide services. Not all Japanese businesses are concerned primarily with mass production. Newer businesses, which are known as 'knowledge works', adopt a totally different view from those of traditional Japanese businesses. These knowledge works aim to maximize both product innovation and process innovation. This is the primary objective as it not only integrates the organization, but also aims to minimize the time and the costs associated with bringing products and services onto the market.

Graham, Fiona, *Inside the Japanese Company*. London: Routledge Curzon, 2003.

Francks, Penelope, *Japanese Economic Development: Theory and Practice*. London: Routledge, 1999.

Joint venture

A joint venture implies a long-term agreement between two or more separate businesses to cooperate and jointly control a separate business entity. Typically, a joint venture would involve a manufacturer and, perhaps, a distributor, in developing a new business venture which affords both parties the potential for profit and a more secure share of the market. A contractual arrangement, setting out the terms of the joint venture, forms the basis of the association between the two separate founding businesses.

The term 'joint venture' is also applicable to international business deals which see collaboration between organizations based in two different countries. They will both contribute to a new business enterprise in which, in one way or another, ownership and control are shared.

Joint ventures may be characterized as being either populated or unpopulated. A populated joint venture is a legally independent business, with its own management and staff. An unpopulated joint venture is a shell company, in which the partner companies temporarily loan their management and staff to the joint venture.

> Vermeulen, Erik, *The Evolution of Legal Business Forms in Europe and the United States: Venture Capital, Joint Venture and Partnership Structures*. New York: Kluwer Law International, 2003.

Junk bond

Junk bonds are bonds issued by businesses that are in a comparatively weak financial condition. Typically, these businesses will have a high level of debt. The bonds themselves offer high yields as a result of the high risk associated with the investors involving themselves in the business.

Just-in-time (JIT)

JIT is a philosophy which was developed in Japan emphasizing the importance of deliveries in relation to the processing of small lot-sizes. The philosophy emphasizes the importance of reducing set-up costs, using small lot-sizes, pull systems, level production and, most importantly, the elimination of waste (*muda*).

JIT is designed to allow the achievement of high-volume production, whilst ensuring that minimal inventories of raw materials, work-in-process and finished goods are held by the business. Parts arrive at the manufacturing plant from suppliers just in time to be placed into the manufacturing process, and as the products progress along the line they arrive at the next work station just in time, thereby moving through the whole system very quickly.

JIT relies on the management ensuring that manufacturing waste is kept to a minimum and that nothing is made or brought onto the premises that is not required immediately. JIT requires precision, as the right part needs to be in the right place at the right time. Waste is described as being the results of any activity that adds cost without adding value (which includes moving and storing).

JIT is also known as 'lean production' or 'stockless production'. The theory is that it should improve profits and the returns on investment by the following means:

- reducing inventory levels;
- increasing the inventory turnover rate;
- improving product quality;
- reducing production and delivery lead times;
- reducing other costs (machine set-ups and equipment breakdown).

JIT also recognizes that any under-utilized capacity can be used to build up a small stock of products or components (buffer inventories) in order to ensure that in the event of a problem, the production process will not be interrupted.

JIT is primarily used in manufacturing processes which are repetitive in nature and where the same products and components are used and produced in relatively high volumes. Once the system has been set up, there should be a steady and even flow of materials, components and finished products passing through the facility. Each work station is linked in a similar way to an assembly-line (although the exact layout may be a jobbing or batch process layout). The goal is to eliminate queuing and to achieve the ideal lot-size per unit of production.

Delbridge, Rick, *Life on the Line in Contemporary Manufacturing: The Workplace Experience of Lean Production and the 'Japanese' Model.* Oxford: Oxford University Press, 2000.
Gross, John M. and McInnis, Kenneth R., *Kanban Made Simple: Demystifying and Applying Toyota's Legendary Manufacturing Process.* New York: Amacom, 2003.

J

Kk

Kanter, Rosabeth Moss

Rosabeth Moss Kanter has written a wide variety of books, primarily on management and management techniques. One of her main concepts brought together **empowerment**, organizational change management and bureaucracy. Kanter is a strong supporter of participative management and claims that management should use employees in order to achieve synergy within the organization. She is also a strong supporter of **flat structures**, with less hierarchical controls over the organization, which she feels would stifle empowerment and entrepreneurial opportunities.

Kanter, Rosabeth Moss, *Rosabeth Moss Kanter on the Frontiers of Management*. Boston, MA: Harvard Business School, 2003.

Keiretsu system

Keiretsu was formerly a unique Japanese type of corporate organization, but increasingly other countries have been moving towards this organizational typology.

The key aspect of a *keiretsu* is that a group or a family of affiliated trans-national organizations are operating together (both vertically and horizontally) in an integrated manner. Importantly, the *keiretsu* has its own trading entities and banks, thereby allowing it to control each part of the economic chain in a major industrial or service-based sector.

Therefore, not only can a *keiretsu* research and develop a technology and products, but it can also plan the production, secure the finance, cover the insurance implications and then find the resources (wherever they are) in order to process them. The purpose of the exercise is to maintain control and production in Japan, where the goods will be turned into finished products, packaged and then distributed across the world.

Keiretsu use **just-in-time (JIT)** and specific forms of supply chain management:

- They apply pressure to suppliers to reduce price.

- They encourage supplier involvement in *kaizen* (a Japanese term which infers the adoption of the concept of aspiring towards gradual, but orderly, continuous improvement).
- They involve suppliers at the earliest stage of the development of new products, in as much as they ask for comment on designs and do not merely supply the designs prior to the commencement of production.
- They commit suppliers to the notion that they will only supply quality parts and components.
- They use a two-vendor policy as a means of ensuring that suppliers remain competitive, as they risk losing a portion or all of their contracts to a better supplier.
- They encourage suppliers to use just-in-time.
- They use a monthly master schedule using *kanban* (a Japanese word meaning 'signal') as a signal for the adjustment of this schedule.
- They are commited to a levelled production.

Burt, David, *American Keiretsu: A Strategic Weapon for Global Competitiveness.* New York: Irwin Professional, 1993.

Miyashita, Kenichi and Russell, David, *Keiretsu: Inside the Hidden Japanese Conglomerates.* New York: McGraw-Hill Education, 1995.

K

Lag strategy

Capacity expansion can either lead demand, lag behind demand, or meet average demand. Of these three possibilities, a capacity lag strategy is said to produce a higher return on investment, although it can lose customers in the process. It is used in many industries which have standard products and weak competition.

A capacity lead strategy, on the other hand, is used to take customers away from competitors, on the basis that competitors have capacity constraints. Average capacity strategy is used when a business knows that it will be able to sell at least the majority of any additional output. The ideal solution is to consider an incremental expansion of capacity, which offers less risk although it can be more expensive.

In essence, a lag strategy seeks to satisfy demand for products once the increased demand has already been created.

Lagging indicator

A lagging indicator is an economic indicator that confirms but does not predict a change in the economy. Typically, lagging indicators include unemployment rates, the book value of inventories, labour costs, business spending and outstanding loans.

Latent conflict

See **conflict management.**

Lead strategy

Lead strategy involves the collection of foreign currency receivables before they are due, in cases where the foreign currency is expected to depreciate. It also involves the paying of foreign currency payables before they are due when a currency is expected to appreciate.

Leadership strategy

The precise leadership strategy of a business will very much depend on a number of priorities, but it is important to realize that there is a distinct difference between leadership and management. Beginning with the priorities, it is safe to assume that leadership strategy will be based on some, or all, of the following:

- the achievement of optimal performance;
- the acquisition of an overview rather than detail;
- the ability to become involved in detail if necessary;
- issues including development, continuity and improvement;
- the taking of remedial action;
- monitoring and evaluating work, and those involved in work;
- ensuring that those with the right skills and capacities are matched to the right jobs;
- continuous improvement through systems such as **total quality management (TQM)**;
- **motivation** and the promotion of a harmonious workplace;
- general operational management activities.

It is generally thought that leadership requires a number of different and often mutually supporting skills. These are:

- the ability to show measurable results;
- the ability to inspire;
- the actuality, or the illusion, of hard work;
- the receiving and giving of respect;
- the ability to add value to the organization, its processes, products and services;
- a degree of apparent honesty;
- the ability to take and give responsibility, accepting and giving the rewards associated with this responsibility.

It is also believed that any leadership role should effectively represent a specifically named role, so that the organization and its employees understand the precise nature of that leader's function. These leadership roles can be typified as any of the following:

- A figurehead – who effectively represents the organization or a part of the organization to the external environment.
- An ambassador – where the leader acts as an advocate or a problem solver.
- A servant – which is based on the premise that the manager is a

L

servant of the business, its customers, its employees, its products and services.

- A maintenance leader – who attends to problem solving, continuous improvement, procedures and practices, and may handle crises.
- A role model – who sets standards and attitudes and tries to influence the behaviour of those who work in the organization.
- A ringmaster – who may adopt several different roles, as outlined above, and may have to shift the emphasis as needs arise.

Pettinger, Richard, *Introduction to Management*. Basingstoke: Palgrave Macmillan, 2002.

Leading indicator

Leading indicators are economic indicators which tend to change shortly before an economy is about to change. Leading indicators can include the money supply, stocks or share prices, changes in inventories, the number of building permits granted, and a falling level of employment. Governments can seek to react to these leading indicators by making adjustments to the interest rates, although in many cases this is now the reserve of independent central banks. Leading indicators are seen as useful predictive tools in assessing how an economy may change in the near future. They are differentiated in this respect from either coincidence indicators or **lagging indicators**.

Lean production

Lean production/manufacturing is an approach based on the Toyota production system. An organization takes a number of steps to assist in ensuring that its manufacturing activities focus on threee key concepts:

- Value centred on customer needs, by creating activities as and when customers demand them.
- Value creation – which occurs along a series of steps, and is known as the value stream. This is achieved through a closely synchronized flow of the organization's activities.
- Continually making improvements within the production process in order to maintain customer service and strive for perfection.

Central to an organization adopting the lean production/manufacturing approach is the question of waste reduction and a high level of engagement of all company personnel in implementing and improving the manufacturing process.

The benefits available to an organization adopting the lean production/manufacturing process are high. It is claimed that organizations have achieved an 80% reduction in cycle time, a 50% reduction in lead times, a 50% reduction in the levels of their inventory, and an increase in customer response rates, as well as an increase in quality.

Lean Enterprise Institute www.lean.org/

Learning effects

'Learning effects' refers to cost savings which are achieved as an international business moves along an **experience curve**. By continuing to operate and learning from experience, the business will be able to make considerable cost savings by adjusting its operating procedures.

Legitimate power

Legitimate power derives from the authority which a manager has in a chain of command. Legitimate power is used on a daily basis and the manager's legitimate power will increase as his or her responsibilities increase.

Greenleaf, Robert K., Spears, Larry C. and Covey, Stephen, *Servant Leadership: A Journey into the Nature of Legitimate Power and Greatness.* Mahwah, NJ: Paulist Press, 2002.

Leveraged buy-out (LBO)

Leveraged buy-outs are an alternative means by which a business can seek to acquire another company. The business which is buying another company borrows money to pay the majority of the purchase price. The debt incurred is secured against the assets of the business being purchased. Interest payable on the loan will be paid from the acquired company's future **cash flow**.

During the 1980s, leveraged buy-outs became very much a trend, and businesses were able to raise loans of millions of dollars to purchase other businesses, which were often unwilling to sell. Many of these purchases ended in disaster, with the borrowers being declared bankrupt, as they could not meet the interest demands. However, many other businesses recognized that once having purchased another business on this basis they would need to run the acquired business far more efficiently than the previous owners, in order to ensure that sufficient funds were available to pay the interest.

Theoretically, of course, leveraged buy-outs can be, and are, used by international businesses to acquire overseas companies. In practice the approach is dependent upon the prevailing regulations which apply to the different nations.

L

Liquidation

Liquidation means turning a business's assets into readily available cash. This process normally begins when the business ceases to trade in its current form as a result of insolvency. Liquidation, often described as 'winding-up', is usually the result of a creditor finally taking the business to court for non-payment of debts. In these cases an individual known as a receiver or liquidator will be appointed to raise enough cash to satisfy the creditors. This is achieved by disposing of the business's assets or by selling the business, as a going concern, to a third party.

In many cases businesses will choose to go into voluntary liquidation, deciding to cease trading as they are currently organized. In these cases the business appoints a liquidator, who then calls a meeting of creditors to endorse the liquidator's powers. The liquidator assumes control of the business and collects assets, pays debts and if there is surplus, distributes it to the company's members according to their rights.

The liquidation value is equal to the current realistic and realizable amount of money which either an asset or a business is worth if it needs to be sold immediately. The liquidation value represents the true market value of any assets or businesses, taking into account an evaluation of the business's liabilities. Technically, should the liquidation value of a business be less than the cumulative value of its shares, then the business should no longer be trading and the share price does not accurately reflect the true value of the business itself.

In the majority of cases the liquidation value is only ever a useful measure if a business is on the verge of collapse. In reality, the liquidation value, when compared with the current share price, often reveals that the business is indeed worth less than the cumulative value of all of the shares available.

Liquidity

The liquidity ratio, which is also known as the 'acid-test ratio', compares a business's liquid or current assets with its current liabilities. Under the majority of circumstances a business's liquid assets are considered to be cash, trade debts and any other assets which can readily be sold. The ratio is normally configured in the following manner:

Current assets
―――――――――
Current liabilities

The ratio seeks to indicate whether the business is capable of paying its debts without having to make further sales. It is a prime measure of a business's solvency. The majority of accountants recommend that the ratio should produce a figure of around 1.5, and that values below 1.0 indicate that there is a severe problem with the business. Equally, values greater than 2.0 indicate that the business has invested too much money in short-term assets.

A variation known primarily as the 'acid-test ratio' presents a slightly different version of the liquidity ratio. The acid-test ratio is:

$$\frac{Current\ assets - stock}{Current\ liabilities}$$

Again, most accountants would recommend that the figure should be equal to 1, indicating that the business has $1's worth of liquid assets for every $1's short-term debt. If the business has an acid-test ratio result of less than 1, then it has a low liquidity and may be unable to find sufficient funds to cover its short-term debt commitments.

Chorafas, Dimitris N., *Liabilities, Liquidity and Cash Management: Balancing Financial Risk.* New York: John Wiley, 2002.

Local demand conditions

Local demand conditions have a direct impact upon a business's opportunity to create **economies of scale**, and shape the rate at which it can develop and innovate. Typically, local demand conditions comprise:

- the composition or nature of the demand (in other words the nature of the buyers' needs);
- the size and pattern of growth of the demand;
- the way in which the domestic preferences of the market are transmitted to foreign markets.

The reason nations themselves gain **competitive advantages** in certain industries or segments is usually that home demand will give home businesses a clearer picture of what the buyer requires than could possibly be hoped for in the case of a foreign rival. The composition of local demand conditions can be affected by three factors. These are:

- The segment structure of demand – where a business can gain a competitive advantage in a global segment which has not hitherto been brought to the attention of domestic businesses.
- Sophisticated and demanding buyers – local businesses may not be able to meet high standards unlike overseas businesses that are able to offer quality or additional service features.
- Anticipatory buyer needs – a business that has proved to be

successful in supplying products and services to its home market may be able to anticipate a demand that is about to occur in an overseas market, before the domestic businesses in that market realize the possibilities.

Location economies

Location economies are achieved by businesses that can locate any value creation activities in an optimum location. Businesses seek to discover the ideal location for value creation, in order to lower the costs of that value creation. Location economies can also be employed by a business in differentiating its product offering and then being in a position to charge a premium price for those products or services.

Locked in

The term 'locked in' can refer to either managers or employees in general. It tends to be used to imply that, despite wanting to find alternative employment, the individual is somehow tied financially, or contractually, to the organization. Typically, managers and employees can be locked into an organization in the sense that their future pension benefits, or ongoing share-ownership schemes, require them to continue to work for the organization for years to come. They may also have signed a caveat to their contract of employment in which they undertook to remain with the organization for a specified period of time, probably following the business's funding of their education or training.

Logical incrementalism

James Quinn suggested that real business strategy should develop as a result of a consensus of action. He further suggested:

- that planning systems should produce strategy;
- that strategy formulation is inherently a political act;
- that strategy formulation is neither behavioural nor formal;
- that strategies should emerge incrementally on an opportunistic basis;
- that incrementalism is the ideal policy for large organizations;
- that incrementalism must be carefully managed.

Strategy is seen as an evolving process between the environment and the intentions of the decision makers. Strategy is clarified and defined incrementally as events unfold.

Quinn, James Brian, *Strategies for Change: Logical Incrementalism*. Homewood, IL: Richard D. Irwin, 1980.

Logistics

Logistics incorporates the planning and control of all materials and products across the entire production and supply chain system. Logistics is, in effect, a managerial function which deals with the flow of materials, including purchasing, shipping and distribution issues before, during and after the completion of a finished product.

In international business, logistics can be far more complex as it may require that particular elements needed in the manufacture of products are coordinated in shipment and delivery terms from various parts of the world. Increasingly, raw materials and components are sourced from overseas locations and delivered either to a single country, or to a series of manufacturers within a multinational, for onward processing. Logistics therefore includes the shipment of raw materials, components, finished goods, machinery, packaging materials and innumerable other inputs into a manufacturing and packaging service.

Clearly it is advantageous for multinational businesses to reduce the movement of heavy or bulky raw materials and components, but often the associated transportation costs are offset by the fact that these materials can be sourced at significantly lower prices then could be achieved in the domestic market. This means that the logistical task of multinationals has become increasingly complex, particularly in cases where the business has chosen to locate parts of the manufacturing process across the world. Increasingly, multinationals have sought to acquire businesses which hitherto were their suppliers, in order to have a firmer grasp and control of the logistics chain.

Christopher, Martin, *Logistics and Supply Chain Management*. London: Financial Times, Prentice-Hall, 1999.

Long-term contracts

Long-term contracts are, in effect, **strategic alliances**. The long-term contracts cement long-term cooperative relationships between two or more businesses.

Loose–tight principle

'Loose–tight principle' refers to the concept of tight central control of an organization by its headquarters' senior management; simultaneously it

allows certain managers, and specifically subsidiaries, a loose autonomy. This allows these individuals and subsidiaries to use a degree of
initiative within clearly defined managerial limitations.

The loose–tight principle is considered to be one of the major contra-
dictions of strategic management and is exemplified by other forms of
autonomy, such as:

- **quality circles**;
- flexitime;
- job enrichment.

Whilst the bureaucratic, hierarchical principles remain, responsible
autonomy is promoted.

L

Macro-environment

The term 'macro-environment' refers to all the external activities, or influences which may have an impact upon the operations of a business or organization. Some do not have a direct impact, but may influence how the business operates over a period of time. In the vast majority of cases organizations have little or no possibility of affecting these macro-environmental factors. Typically, the macro-environment would include society in general, politics, economics, socio-political change, technology, or socio-cultural changes and trends.

Most businesses develop a means by which they can assess, or analyse, the macro-environment and identify strategic issues which may affect their operations. Typically this would include:

- an identification of the principal phenomena that will have an impact on the organization;
- a determination of the trends of each of those phenomena;
- classification of the phenomena, determining whether they are opportunities or threats;
- an evaluation of the importance of the phenomena as opportunities or threats.

Once the opportunities and threats have been prioritized, the organization can then identify their strategic impacts upon the business.

See also **Five Forces model.**

Make or buy strategy

Given the premise that an organization should never outsource a product or service for which it has a **core competence**, the decision still remains as to the merits and demerits of **outsourcing** as opposed to producing parts or components in-house. Clearly, buying in more parts and components than the company actually produces itself does add to the overheads and complications arising out of inventory or stock control. It is generally the case that the more a manufacturer outsources, the more it has to outsource in order to continue operations, as it will have reorganized its internal production routines to take account of the fact that it does not need to produce those parts or components.

Management buy-out (MBO)

A management buy-out involves the acquisition of a business by its existing management. In many cases the management group will establish a new holding company, which then effectively purchases the shares of the target company. There are variations of management buy-outs, notably the 'management buy-in', where external management buys the business, and 'buy-in management buy-out', which is a combination of the two.

Management buy-outs may arise as a result of any of the following:

- A group may decide to sell a business that has become a non-core activity.
- A business may find itself in difficulties and need to sell part of its business.
- The owner of a business may choose to retire.
- A receiver or administrator may sell the business as a going concern.

The normal sequences of events in a management buy-out are:

- an agreement of the management team as to who will become the managing director;
- appointment of financial advisors;
- assessment of the suitability of the buy-out;
- attaining approval to pursue the management buy-out;
- evaluation of the vendor's asking price;
- formulation of business plans;
- selection of suitable equity investors and obtaining written offers;
- appointing legal advisors;
- selection of a lead investor;
- negotiating the best equity deal available;
- negotiating the purchase of the business;
- carrying out a due diligence test with the aid of an auditor;
- obtaining finance and other equity investments;
- preparation of legal documents;
- achieving legal ownership.

Andrews, Phildrew, *Management Buy-Out.* New York: Kogan Page, 1999.

Management by objectives

The concept of management by objectives (MBO) was developed by Peter Drucker in the 1950s. The management concept relies on the defining of objectives for each employee and then comparing their performance, and directing that performance, against the objectives which have already been set. MBO requires that clear objectives are set, and that every employee is aware of what is expected of them, a factor which often means that the employees themselves have a considerable input into the setting of the objectives. Also at MBO's heart is **delegation**, as it requires employees to take some responsibility for the achievement of objectives. It is recognized that employees are much more able and willing to seek to achieve their objectives if they have some degree of independence in how those objectives are achieved, rather than being led or directed overtly by management.

MBO has at least one fatal flaw, in as much as the objectives of individuals within different departments can be different. When they are required to act together collaboratively, the objectives of one of the individuals may override those of another individual, who has a different set of priorities and a different set of objectives. Inevitably, conflict or inertia may occur, which will clearly have an impact on productivity. Provided the business has thought the whole process through, objectives need not be mutually exclusive, but can be compatible, seeking to impel all collaborative projects forward, and facilitating inter-disciplinary cooperation.

Managerial behaviour

Managerial behaviour is an area of study and research which has a venerable heritage stretching back over fifty years. Successive waves of academics, researchers and management gurus have sought to understand the complexities of managerial behaviour, and define the true nature of managerial work or roles, hoping to create generalizations which will allow comparability studies to take place. The study of managerial behaviour, which began back in the early 1950s, has sought to develop a general understanding of the role of management.

M

The study of managerial behaviour has distinct strategic management implications, as in the past it was widely believed that there was little generalization relevant to managers who were operating in different cultures and had been socialized within a particular culture. Generalized theories, it was felt, could not be applied universally across national boundaries. Increasingly, however, with the globalization of business, strategic managerial behaviour is beginning to reveal similar working patterns regardless of cultural divides.

Clearly, managers have a social function, as an organization itself is a social system. Managers, regardless of their cultural background, inevitably involve themselves in networking, talking and listening, information exchange, and negotiations. It is notoriously difficult, however, to extend the generalizations and suggest that managers in similar jobs carry out similar functions. The vast majority of the research work so far carried out on management behaviour at a strategic level has been carried out either in the US or in the English-speaking world.

The key complex questions with regard to the study of managerial behaviour are:

- What is distinctive about managerial work that makes the role managerial?
- What do managers do? Do they operate for their own interest or the organizational interest?
- Do managers have an overriding ideology of management?
- What is a manager's perception of managerial tasks and what is the researcher's perception of those tasks?
- What is the context in which managers work?
- What are the implications arising from the study of managerial behaviour that can improve an organization's ability to first select and then train managers?

Managerial culture

'Managerial culture' refers to the organization and professional stance which the managerial structure of a business represents. Typical managerial cultures may be based on innovation, the value of human resources, quality, or a number of other different issues. These managerial cultures determine the climate in which all interpersonal and group interactions take place.

Whilst there may be an overriding, organization-wide, managerial culture, the exact nature of each individual manager's own stance, or ways of carrying out work, and, indeed, how they deal with employees, make decisions and solve problems, varies.

Watson, Tony J., *In Search of Management: Culture, Chaos and Control in Managerial Work*. London: Thomson Learning, 2000.

Manifest conflict

See **conflict management**.

Manufacturing strategy

Whilst there is no ideal or prescribed manufacturing strategy, there are standardized models of manufacturing strategy processes which seek to define the basic steps. One such version of the model can be seen in the diagram in Figure 30.

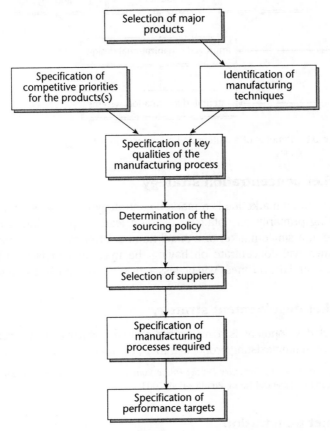

Figure 30 A manufacturing strategy model

In incorporating the manufacturing strategy into the overall strategy of the business, the organization is able to attain considerable advantages. An integrated manufacturing strategy leads to **synergy** in other associated areas of operations, as can be seen in Figure 31.

Hill, Terry, *Manufacturing Strategy: Text and Cases*. Basingstoke: Palgrave Macmillan, 2000.

Wu, Bin, *Handbook of Manufacturing and Supply Systems Design: From Strategy Formulation to System Operation*. London: Taylor & Francis, 2001.

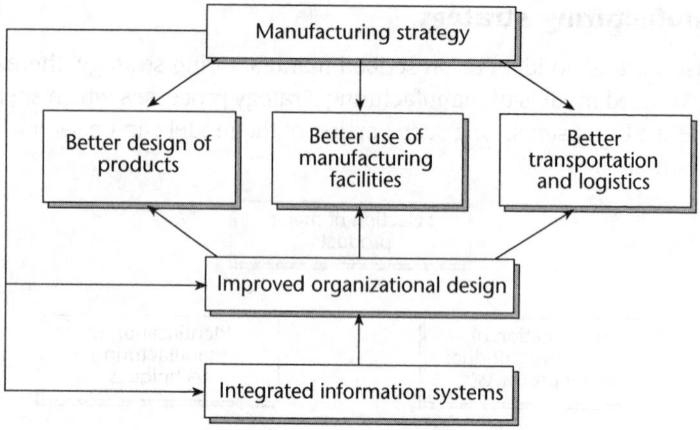

Figure 31   Benefits of an integrated manufacturing strategy

Market concentration strategy

Concentrated marketing is a marketing strategy which sees a business focusing primarily on obtaining a brand leadership or market dominance in a single market or a small number of markets. All marketing activities will concentrate on having the maximum impact on these markets and the business will be less active in other markets as a result.

Market development strategy

Market development is a marketing strategy which aims to increase sales by selling existing products into a new market.

> Raymond, Martin, *Tomorrow People: Future Consumers and How to Read them Today*. London: Financial Times, Prentice-Hall, 2003.

Market penetration

This is a marketing strategy adopted by businesses in order to increase their sales of existing products in markets in which they already operate. Market penetration is usually achieved by an aggressive use of the marketing mix, which uses a balance of price cutting, sales promotions and advertising, enhanced distribution, and new product development.

Market segmentation

Market segmentation involves the identification of specific target markets for broader-based products and services, in order to enable a business to develop suitable marketing mixes for each of its target segments.

Market segmentation probably came into existence in the 1950s when product differentiation was a primary **marketing strategy**. By the 1970s, however, market segmentation had begun to be seen as a means of increasing sales and obtaining a **competitive advantage**. In recent years more sophisticated techniques have been developed to reach potential buyers in ever more specific target markets.

Businesses will tend to segment the market for the following reasons:

- to make marketing easier in the sense that segmentation allows the business to address the needs of smaller groups of customers which have the same characteristics;
- to find niches, typically unserved or under-served markets, and to be able to target these buyers in a less competitive environment;
- to increase efficiency in being able to apply resources directly towards the best segments identified by the business.

There are some common rules regarding market segmentation which determine whether the identified segments are significant enough or measurable. These are described in Table 13.

In effect, there are two ways of segmenting a market. These are described either as *a priori* or as *post hoc*. These two approaches are typified in the following manner:

- The *a priori* approach is effectively based on a mixture of intuition, use of secondary data and analysis of existing customer database information. *A priori* segmentation takes place without the benefit of primary market research and may well produce relatively simplistic segmentation, such as 'male or female', 'young or old', regional segments or 'buyers and non-buyers'.
- *Post-hoc* segmentation uses primary market research to classify and describe individuals within the target market, but segments are not defined themselves until after the collection and analysis period. The definition of each segment requires the placing of all members of the target market into specific segments.

There are a number of different types of information which are used extensively in market segmentation. These can best be described by category as in Table 14.

M

Table 13 Market segments

Segmentation criteria	Description
Size	The market itself needs to be large enough to warrant segmentation. Once a market has been segmented, it may be revealed that each of the segments is too small to consider.
Differentiation	There must be measurable differences between the members of the segment and the market in general.
Responsiveness	Having segmented the market, the business needs to develop marketing communications to address the needs of that segment. If a business cannot develop marketing communications which can contact this segment and have an impact upon it, there is little value in knowing about the segment in the first place.
Reachability	Marketing communications need to be able to get through to the segment in order to be effective. There may well be a single best advertising medium or promotional device which can reach the segment and convey the business's message.
Interest	Having established what benefits the segment is looking for, the business needs to be assured that this is precisely what the potential customers require and that the product or service matches these needs.
Profitability	A decision needs to be reached as to whether it is cost effective to reach these segments, considering the cost which may be incurred in running varied marketing programmes alongside one another. Existing products or services may need to be redesigned in order to match the specific needs of the segment.

McDonald, Malcolm and Dunbar, Ian, *Market Segmentation*. Basingstoke: Palgrave Macmillan, 1998.
Wedel, Michel and Kamakura, Wagner A., *Market Segmentation: Conceptual and Methodological Foundations*. Dordrecht: Kluwer Academic Publishers, 1999.

Market share

Sales figures do not necessarily indicate how a business is performing in relation to its competitors. Changes in sales may simply reflect changes

Table 14   Information used in market segmentation

Measured variable	Description
Classification	Broadly speaking, classification actually encompasses demographic, geographic, psychographic and behavioural. It requires a system of classifying individuals and placing them into segments by using a mixture of these variables.
Demographic	Demographic features age, gender, income, ethnicity, marital status, education, occupation, household size, type of residence and length of residence, amongst many other demographically based measures.
Geographic	This broad range of variables includes population density, climate, zip or postcode, city, state or county, region or metropolitan/rural.
Psychographic	Another broad range of variables which include attitudes, hobbies, leadership traits, lifestyle, magazines and newspapers read, personality traits, risk aversion, and television or radio programmes watched or listened to.
Behavioural	These variables encompass the current ways in which the target market views, buys and responds to products, services and marketing. The category includes brand loyalty, benefits sought, distribution channels used and level of usage.
Descriptor	Descriptor variables actually describe each segment in order to distinguish it from other groups. The descriptors need to be measurable and are usually derived solely from primary research, rather than secondary sources of information. Descriptors will typically explain in shorthand the key characteristics of each segment and the members of that segment, so that these characteristics can be exploited more readily by subtle changes in the marketing mix. A descriptor variable may be featured as 'under 30, single, urban dweller, rented accommodation, medium to high income', etc.

M

in the market size or changes in economic conditions. The business's performance relative to competitors can be measured by the proportion of the market that the firm is able to capture. This proportion is referred to as the business's market share and is calculated as follows:

$$Market\ share\ =\ \frac{Business's\ sales}{Total\ market\ sales}$$

Sales may be determined on a value basis (sales price multiplied by volume) or on a unit basis (number of units shipped, or number of customers served). While the business's own sales figures are readily available, total market sales are more difficult to determine. Usually, this information is available from trade associations and market research firms.

Market share is often associated with profitability, which is why many businesses seek to increase their sales relative to competitors. Businesses may seek to increase their market share in the following ways:

- Economies of scale – higher volume can be instrumental in developing a cost advantage.
- Sales growth in a stagnant industry – when the industry is not growing, the business can still increase its sales by increasing its market share.
- Reputation – market leaders have power, which they can use to their advantage.
- Increased bargaining power – a larger market share gives an advantage in negotiations with suppliers and distribution channel members.

The market share of a product can be modelled as:

$$\frac{Share\ of}{market}\ =\ \frac{Share\ of}{preference}\ \times\ \frac{Share\ of}{voice}\ \times\ \frac{Share\ of}{distribution}$$

According to this model, there are three drivers of market share:

- Share of preference – can be increased through product, pricing, and promotional changes.
- Share of voice – the business's proportion of total promotional expenditures in the market. Thus, share of voice can be increased by increasing advertising expenditures.
- Share of distribution – can be increased through more intensive distribution.

From these drivers, market share can be increased by changing the variables of the marketing mix.

M

- Product – the product attributes can be changed to provide more value to the customer, for example, by improving product quality.

- Price – if the price can be varied, a decrease in price will increase sales revenue. This tactic may not succeed if competitors are willing and able to meet any price cuts.
- Distribution – adding new distribution channels or increasing the intensity of distribution in each channel.
- Promotion – increasing advertising expenditures can increase market share, unless competitors respond with similar increases.

Miniter, Richard, *The Myth of Market Share*. London: Nicholas Brealey Publishing Ltd, 2002.

Market to book value

Market to book value is considered to be a good indicator of a business's ability to create value above and beyond its physical and financial assets. The term is usually used to describe the difference in value between the actual total value of all a business's assets and the prevailing stock or share price.

It is therefore possible to calculate the market to book value by expressing it as a business performance in the form of value creation. Any capital investment should create value for an investor, which results in a higher valuation of the business than the book value of its assets. The book value itself is the amount of investment capital which is recorded on a balance sheet (or stockholder's equity, as reported as historical value). The market value, therefore, is the bid price for a share, based on current stock market exchanges. Typically the following ratio or formula is used:

$$Market\ to\ book\ value = \frac{Stock\ price\ per\ share}{Book\ value\ per\ share}$$

Marketing strategy

The term 'marketing strategy' refers to specific processes adopted by the marketing function of a business in order to achieve specific goals or objectives. Marketing strategy also encompasses the deployment of resources in order to develop and maintain the business's market opportunities. At its core, marketing strategies seek to deploy a marketing mix in the most effective manner, not only to achieve the business's goals and objectives, but also to satisfy the customers' needs and wants.

M

Doyle, Peter, *Markeing, Management and Strategy*. New York: Financial Times, Prentice Hall, 2001.
Fill, Chris, *Marketing Communications: Contexts, Strategies and Applications*. London: Financial Times, Prentice-Hall, 2001.

Mass customization

Mass customization is an increasing trend and of considerable importance to marketers. Mass customization involves the production of mass produced, standard products, with slight variations or customizations for particular market or customer segments. As the manufacturing process has developed technologically and become more flexible, it is possible to produce these personalized products without any detrimental effect on profit margins. Indeed, these customized products can often warrant a premium price, providing a margin in excess of what had previously been enjoyed by the manufacturer. Manufacturers have therefore realized that mass customization is a means by which they can improve their profitability without the attendant loss of production or productivity.

See also **customization.**

Materials management

Materials management involves the planning, organization and control of all aspects of a business's physical inventory, including shipping, distribution, warehousing and dealing with work in progress. For international businesses the essential problem is to minimize the total costs involved and to maximize savings where those savings can be identified. This requires an integrated materials management or logistics organization, which takes full responsibility for supply, production and distribution. Clearly any reduction in cost can contribute to profit.

Arnold, J. R. and Chapman, Stephen, *Introduction to Materials Management*. New York: Prentice Hall, 2003.

Matrix and matrix structure

The use of a matrix organizational structure allows the opportunity for teams to be developed in order that particular tasks can be undertaken. Matrix structures often develop in stages, with the first being the establishment of temporary teams, who, having studied a particular problem and suggested recommendations, might be considered significant enough to be retained on a more permanent basis. These teams will consist of a number of different individuals from the different functions of the organization (see Figure 32).

As can be seen in Table 15, a matrix structure has some advantages and disadvantages.

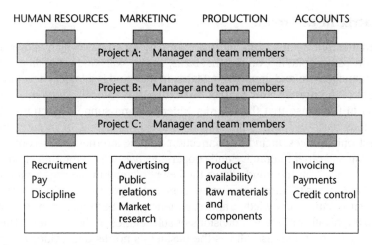

Figure 32 A matrix organizational structure

Table 15 Advantages and disadvantages of a matrix structure

Advantages	Disadvantages
Good use can be made of specialist and functional knowledge from within the organization.	Because there is not a clear line of command and authority, this may affect a manager's ability to understand requirements and make changes.
Enhanced communication can be facilitated between departments, providing a greater level of consistency and efficiency of policies.	There is often a higher level of stress and a feeling of constant competition with added responsibility.
The availability of multiple sources of power allows the establishment of recognized mechanisms to deal with different forms of culture.	Demand on individuals and departments may be inconsistent, resulting in a high demand on some areas and only a limited demand on others.
The structure enables the organization to adapt to environmental changes by moving its main emphasis from a functional one to a project-based one.	There may also be inconsistency between individuals with the ability to flourish and those who are more technically-minded. This could cause exclusion for some employees by those who are competitive enough to wish to manage the project teams.

M

Sutherland, Jon and Canwell, Diane, *Organisation Structures and Processes*. London: Financial Times, Prentice-Hall, 1997.

Weiss, Joseph, *HND/HNC Business: Core Module 5, Organisational Structure and Processes*. Cheltenham: Nelson-Thornes, 1999.

Matrix in the mind

A matrix in the mind is an internal information network which allows a business to capitalize, on a global basis, on the skills and capabilities of its management and employees. Matrix in the mind is a logical development of the **matrix and matrix structure**. It is radically different, but only in the sense that the interdependencies and support functions of various parts of the organization are virtual, by means of integrating electronic devices, including connections via the internet, video-conferencing and other interactive and cooperative two-way communications.

The matrix in the mind allows the key personnel in the organization to have access to information, managers and employees at a local level. All information, knowledge and experience can be transferred, either geographically or between divisions or subsidiaries of the business. The matrix in the mind also allows the business's norms and values to be transmitted to geographically remote parts of the organization.

Mature industry

See **industry life cycle model.**

McGregor, Douglas (1906–64)

He was a management consultant theorist and a social psychologist and in 1954 he became Professor of Management at the Massachusetts Institute of Technology and later taught at Harvard where he helped establish the Industrial Relations section. Douglas McGregor's book *The Human Side of Enterprise* was published in 1960, examining the behaviour of individuals at work. He formulated two models which he called Theory X and Theory Y.

Theory X assumes that the average human has an inherent dislike of work and will do all that is necessary to avoid it. This assumes the following:

- because people dislike work they have to be controlled by management and often threatened in order to work hard;
- most people avoid responsibility, need to be directed by management, but seek security within work as a primary concern;
- managers who adhere to the Theory X approach rarely give their subordinates any opportunity to show traits other than those associated with Theory X.

Theory X has given rise to what is often known as tough or hard management, typified by tight control and punishment. Soft management adopts the opposite view, aiming to create a degree of harmony in the workplace.

Theory Y assumes the following:

- most people expend the same amount of energy or effort at work as in other spheres of their lives;
- providing individuals are committed, or made to be committed, to the aims of the organization in which they work, they will be self-directing;
- job satisfaction is the key to involving and engaging the individual and ensuring his or her commitment;
- an average individual, given the opportunity and encouragement, will naturally seek responsibility;
- in ensuring commitment and responsibility, employees will be able to use their imagination, ingenuity and creativity to solve work problems with less direct supervision.

Management which follows Theory Y is often considered to be soft management, and recognizes that the intellectual potential of the employees is vital to the success of the business. In many cases, it is argued, businesses ignore the benefits of Theory Y and under-utilize their employees.

McGregor saw his two theories as being very separate attitudes. He believed that it was difficult to use Theory Y for large-scale operations, particularly those involved in mass production. It was an ideal choice for the management of professionals. For McGregor, Theory Y was essential in helping to encourage participative problem solving and the development of effective management.

McGregor, Douglas, *The Human Side of Enterprise*. New York: McGraw-Hill Education, 1995.

Micro-environment

M

The micro-environment is that of a business's external **stakeholders** who are in direct contact with the organization. These are the groups which significantly influence the actions of the organization, and may include partners, providers of finance, regulators, government and competitors. Some of the micro-environmental external stakeholders will have a positive effect on the business, such as creating demand or supplying the business with resources. Others, such as regulators or the government, for example, may impose constraints on the business which can affect its development. Typically, a business will attempt to analyse its micro-environment and may carry out the following steps:

- an identification of the key stakeholders as far as the organization is concerned;
- an assessment of the influence of each of these key stakeholders;
- a classification of the stakeholders as representing either opportunities or threats (in some cases a stakeholder may be classified as both an opportunity and a threat);
- an evaluation of the importance of each of these opportunities and threats.

On the basis of the opportunities and threats identified the organization can now establish its strategic objectives.

See also **macro-environment.**

Minimum efficient scale

The minimum efficient scale is taken to be the level of output at which the economies that a manufacturer achieves by an optimum level of production, have been eliminated by a scaling down of the output. The minimum efficient scale is the lowest output level which is economically viable for the business to sustain, albeit for a short period of time.

Mintzberg, Henry

Mintzberg (born 1939) has written more than 10 books and 120 articles about managerial work, strategy formation and forms of business organizations.

Mintzberg offers us the suggestion that the managerial role is split into three distinct areas of endeavour (see Figure 33). Certainly, the interpersonal skills area is an important one as this will determine the following:

- the ability of the manager to be seen as the one who is in charge;
- the ability of the manager to motivate and lead;
- the ability of the manager to be able to co-ordinate and co-operate.

As for the information-based roles that need to be performed by the manager, Mintzberg identifies the following as being important:

- the fact that the manager has to control and monitor the ways in which the work is being carried out by the subordinates;
- the way in which the manager is able to operate as an effective conduit of information, passing on what is needed by others and amending other information as and when required;

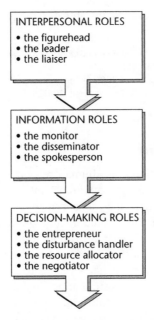

INTERPERSONAL ROLES
• the figurehead
• the leader
• the liaiser

INFORMATION ROLES
• the monitor
• the disseminator
• the spokesperson

DECISION-MAKING ROLES
• the entrepreneur
• the disturbance handler
• the resource allocator
• the negotiator

Figure 33 Mintzberg's model of the managerial role

● the fact that the manager has to also operate as a spokesperson for the department or group of individuals to whom s/he is responsible.

Finally, Mintzberg suggests that the third area of interest is the most complex. It involves the decision-making abilities of the manager, and more closely accords with what we have already discussed in terms of the style and the approach of the manager. To this end, he suggests the following:

● that the manager needs to have entrepreneurial skills in order to be able to notice an opportunity as well as being able to cope with changes that are thrust upon the organization or the department;

● that the manager needs to be able to operate as a 'disturbance handler'. This means that the manager has to be able to cope with the unexpected without unduly affecting the overall operations of the department whilst doing so;

● the means by which a manager allocates the resources of the department maybe one of the major indicators as to the style and approach preferred – theoretically, this should be achieved in an objective manner;

● finally, Mintzberg was concerned with the ways in which the manager handles disagreements and other differences of option –

again, this gives valuable insights into the style and approach of the manager.

Mintzberg, Henry, *Power In and Around Organizations: The Theory of Management Policy*, New York: Prentice Hall, 1983.

Mintzberg, Henry, Lampel, Joseph B., Quinn, James Brian and Ghoshal, Sumantra, *The Strategy Process*. New York: Prentice Hall, 2003.

www.henrymintzberg.com

Mission statement

In many cases indications of a human resource management's fundamental policy will be contained within a mission statement. A mission statement essentially describes, as succinctly as possible, the organization's business vision. This would include the fundamental values and the essential purpose of the organization. It will also make allusions to its future or its pursuit for the future, as a mission statement tends to be a statement of where a businesses wishes to be rather than a description of where it is at the current time. In this respect, although the fundamental ethos may remain the same, mission statements are subject to periodic change. A business may choose to incorporate within its mission statement a vision of how it wishes its employees and systems to respond, react and fulfil the needs of its customers or clients. Human resources departments will, therefore, seek to match these aspirations by instituting employee development programmes and associated training, in order to fulfil the espoused desires and commitments made in the mission statement.

Moore, Geoffrey

Geoffrey Moore is the co-founder of the Chasm Group, a consultancy which provides business and marketing strategy services to businesses. He has written several books, primarily addressing his key interest, market capitalization.

Moore suggests that strategy issues can be addressed by considering and analysing his core-versus-concept model. He defines 'core' as being anything which contributes to the organization's competitive differentiation and leads directly to customers making a positive choice to purchase from that business. 'Concept' covers all issues which make the organization function, and the product appear fit for its purpose.

Moore, Geoffrey A., *Crossing the Chasm: Marketing and Selling Technology Products to Mainstream Customers*. Oxford: Capstone Publishing, 1999.

Moore, Geoffrey A., *Living on the Fault Line: Managing for Shareholder Value in the Age of the Internet*. Oxford: Capstone Publishing, 2000.

Motivation

Motivation implies the instilling in employees of a drive to take action. In human resource terms this means inducing, or providing an incentive to, employees to perform to the best of their abilities. The subject of motivation has been at the heart of a large number of theories over a number of years, including those of Abraham Maslow and Frederick Hertzberg. Both theorists recognized that there were a series of actions or circumstances which could be initiated by an employer in order to achieve a degree of motivation. Both recognized, too, that simply providing pay and a degree of security were insufficient in the long term to motivate employees. Motivation needed to be longer lasting and reinforced by concrete rewards and praise. At its most basic, motivation needs to be sustained by employers in order not only to ensure continued high performance and productivity, but also to create a situation where employees have a positive attitude towards work, a commitment to the organization and, above all, a belief that their individual roles are not only valued but of crucial interest to the organization.

Multi-dimensional measure

A multi-dimensional measure seeks to express a relationship between two different units of performance measurement. Typical examples would include:

- number of units produced per hour;
- number of customer calls taken per shift;
- number of orders fulfilled per week;
- number of distributors visited per month.

In other words, a multi-dimensional measure incorporates two measurements, both related to performance, but usually in either a time frame or a quantity frame.

Multi-divisional structure

A multi-divisional structure, also known as an 'm-form' is an organizational configuration based around quasi-autonomous operating divisions. Usually these operating divisions are organized around product lines or brands. In some cases the organization is based on geographical or functional divisions. The key advantages of adopting a multidivisional structure are:

- Operating decisions can be delegated to individual sub-units.

- The corporate headquarters, or executive staff, can provide advisory and auditing functions in order to control the sub-units.
- The corporate headquarters, or executive staff, can undertake the control and planning functions and allocate resources to the sub-units.
- The functional units and the headquarters staff have separated functions so that the executive staff can focus on overall corporate goals.
- Multi-divisional structures are often more effective and efficient than they would have been had the organization remained fully integrated.

The m-form can be considered to be something of a market in itself, or a system which is loosely controlled by a holding company. This analogy of the relationships between a holding company and subsidiary businesses holds true in most multi-divisional structures.

Riahi-Belkaoui, Ahmed, *The Nature and Consequences of the Multi-divisional Structure.* Westport, CT: Greenwood Press, 1995.

Multi-domestic strategy

A multi-domestic strategy tends to lead a business with international operations to allow the operations in one country to be relatively independent of those in other countries. In essence, a multi-domestic strategy emphasizes the unique conditions which apply to each country in which the multinational organization operates. This may involve separate design, production and sales operations.

In using a multi-domestic strategy the business focuses upon local responsiveness to specific strategies wholly designed to suit that nation's market.

Mutual dependence

The term 'mutual dependence' can refer either to internal relationships and needs within an organization or to the dependencies which may develop over time between businesses.

Mutual dependence implies a symbiotic relationship in as much as both parties need, require and desire something from the relationship. Mutual dependence goes somewhat further than simple needs for support and circumstance and may well suggest that the two parties in question are dependent upon each other to be able to carry out specific tasks, roles or operations.

Naisbitt, John

John Naisbitt describes himself as a futurist, and made his first mark in 1982 when his book *Megatrends* remained on the bestseller lists for two years and sold over 8 million copies. His first book suggested that in order to understand the future, it is necessary to understand the present. He effectively predicted the information society and the trends and implications for business:

- technology would come into use provided it was appealing to customers;
- the national economies would transform into a global economy;
- businesses would have to shift from short-termism to long-termism;
- organizations would decentralize;
- governments would step back from supporting and regulating businesses;
- there would be a shift from representation to participation;
- hierarchies would give way to networks;
- corporate dominance in the US and Europe would be replaced with Asian dominance.

Naisbitt further predicted that computers would 'smash the pyramid'; in other words, computers and the exchange of information and ideas would render traditional organizational structures obsolete.

Naisbitt, John, *Megatrends: Ten New Directions Transforming Our Lives*. New York: Warner Books, 1984.
Naisbitt, John and Aburdene, Patricia, *Re-inventing the Corporation*. New York: Warner Books, 1985.
Naisbitt, John, *High Tech/High Touch: Technology and Our Accelerated Search for Meaning*. London: Nicholas Brealey Publishing, 2001.

Negative sum game

A negative sum game occurs when two parties engage in actions which ultimately are to the detriment of both sides. There are many examples of negative sum games which are actively pursued, both within an organization and between organizations. Primarily, negative sum games occur when both sides assume that their overall gain will be greater if they continue to pursue their lines of action. Equally, they believe that the losses the other side will suffer will be greater if they continue to pursue that action. In the final analysis, however, both sides risk losing more and both lose, comparatively speaking, as a result of their joint actions and inability to change their course of direction. A negative sum game is therefore a lose–lose situation and is the opposite of a **positive sum game**.

Net profit margin

The net profit margin is often referred to as the 'net margin' and is calculated by deploying the net profit margin ratio. This divides a business's net profit by its net revenues and then expresses this relationship as a percentage. A business's net profit margin serves as a means by which the cost control functions can be assessed. If a business has a high net profit margin then it is seen to be able to convert revenue into profit. Net profit margins are often used to compare businesses in the same industries, since they are under the same pressures and have similar opportunities.

Net profit margins are also useful in the comparison of unlike businesses in unlike markets, as the net profit margin reveals to potential investors the comparative profitability of different types of businesses.

The net profit margin ratio differs from the gross profit margin ratio in as much as it expresses the net profit as a percentage of the sales generated. In effect, it measures the percentage return on sales after expenses, such as tax, have been taken into account. The ratio is:

$$Net\ profit\ margin\ =\ \frac{Net\ profit\ after\ tax}{Sales} \times 100$$

Therefore, if a business with a total sales revenue of some $3,200,000 has a net profit after tax of $200,000, the calculation is:

$$\frac{200,000}{3,200,000} \times 100\ =\ 6.25\%$$

Typically, the business would then compare this figure with the industry standard to assess its overall ability to produce a net profit from its generated sales.

Network economics

Network economics has considerable importance as far as strategic management is concerned, as it describes a condition in which the availability of complementary products is a prime determinant of the demand for an industry's primary products. In other words, the primary industry and its associated demand is linked not only to the availability of complementary products, but also to their quality and use in relation to the primary products.

Network structure

Although a network structure can be examined and identified by network analysis, the term 'network structure' is a broader one which refers to the overall structure in terms of relationships and hierarchy in an organization. Traditional organizations will adopt a network which is task-structured in order to achieve predictable performances. Increasingly, however, network structures have become more complex, notably as a result of organizations adopting decentralized, team-based or distributed structures. Others have taken the concept of network structures further and have adopted virtual networks or cluster organizations. The network structure, however it may be configured, is designed to provide a supportive coordination between individuals who work in different locations.

The network structure should also reflect both formal and informal communications within the organization. In this respect the network structure reflects formal rules, procedures, reporting, norms and, increasingly, the various forms of informal communication which occur without reference to the normal network procedures. Most network structures reflect the hierarchy, however, and provide a means by which the legitimate power and authority vested in individuals within the organization are exemplified in the business's organizational chart.

Many network structures actually fail to recognize the importance of informal communication. Much of this is at a personal level, is interactive and peer orientated. When researchers investigate the patterns of communication within an organization they often refer to them as the 'network structure' and suggest that these network structures explain organizational behaviour in a far more precise manner than any organizational chart or formal structure could hope to achieve.

In the case of **virtual corporations**, which tend to be non-hierarchical and decentralized, the network structure is, perhaps, the only true means by which the inter-relationships of the individuals involved can possibly be explained.

N

Birkinshaw, Julian and Hagsrom, Peter (eds), *The Flexible Firm: Capability Management in Network Organizations*. Oxford: Oxford University Press, 2000.

New venture division

New venture divisions have become a primary means by which organizations facilitate their corporate entrepreneurship. In effect, new venture divisions are allowed to act rather like an autonomous business, supported by the financial resources of the main business.

The new venture division can be defined as an organization unit which has three primary functions:

- the investigation of potential new business opportunities;
- the development of business plans for these new ventures;
- the management of the early stages of the commercialization of these ventures.

A high proportion of new venture divisions are short-lived. Indeed the majority of them only have a lifespan of some four years. There are three reasons for this:

- They mature, by retaining the ventures which they began and effectively transform into an operating division.
- They are redefined, and management and employees within the division are given staff functions.
- They are either eliminated or disbanded, either having successfully concluded their work, or having failed.

Burgelman, R. A., 'Managing the New Venture Division: Research Findings and Implications for Strategic Management', *Strategic Management Journal*, 6(10) (1985) pp. 39–54.

New ventures

N

New ventures can be described as either literally new businesses or new sub-divisions or subsidiaries created by existing businesses to exploit a new business opportunity. In the case of wholly new ventures, there is a tendency for the majority of the businesses to fail. In many cases this is largely as a result of poor strategic planning. Indeed, many new ventures have less than a 1 in 8 chance of success. Key issues regarding the failure rate of these new ventures include:

- insufficient technical, marketing or financial competences;
- inadequate management skills;
- inability to manage the business on a strategic level;

• use of an inappropriate business plan, or not adhering to the business plan.

There are, of course, factors outside the competences of the business, or indeed its plan or strategic management, which can conspire to cause failure. However, there are several reasons why new businesses and existing business are attracted to new ventures, including:

• changes in the underlying industry or market structure;
• changes in society or consumers' attitudes, beliefs or priorities;
• the availability of new knowledge or technology that can be applied;
• changes in demographics;
• addressing a problem or a need in an existing process.

Various environmental factors can improve the chances of a new venture's success. These include:

• a rapidly changing industry;
• a high-growth stage in the industry.

Niche strategy

Businesses using niche strategy approaches seek to concentrate attention on a narrow segment of the total market. Having achieved this, they seek to provide for niche buyers more effectively than their rivals. The key success factors involved in dealing with niche markets are:

• to choose a market niche where buyers can be distinctively identified by their preferences, special requirements or unique needs;
• to then develop unique capabilities to serve the needs of the segment.

There are two ways in which businesses seek to achieve this:

• by achieving lower costs than competitors serving that market niche (low-cost strategy);
• by offering the buyers in that market something different (differentiation strategy).

Niches are attractive to businesses for the following reasons:

• They are big enough to produce a profit and may offer growth potential.
• They are often overlooked by the industry leaders.
• Competitors involved in a more multi-segment approach may consider them too expensive in terms of meeting the buyers' needs.

- Few competitors will be specializing in that niche.
- The business may be able to deploy most of its resources into that niche.
- Once established, the niche can effectively be defended from rivals by the provision of a superior service.

Non-price competition

Non-price competition, as one would expect, is competition that is based on factors other than price. The primary task is initially to establish differentiating criteria which mark the product or service as being sufficiently unlike those offered by competitors. Normally, non-price competition would mean convenience, taste, or a degree of prestige. Businesses have recognized that in the medium to long term, pricing-based competition does little to benefit either organization. Competition based on pricing can temporarily increase **market share**, but in the longer term, customers begin to expect lower prices, and alternative measures need to be sought in order to maintain the market share. All price-cutting achieves is a cut in the contribution of each unit, and it may detrimentally affect profitability.

Non-price competition has, therefore, become an important battle-field for many markets. It is typified by the concept of adding a degree of value to whatever the business is offering its customers. Typically these would include some or all of the following:

- customer loyalty cards;
- additional services;
- home delivery systems;
- discounts in allied product areas;
- extended opening hours;
- self-scanning of products by customers;
- incentives to purchase off-peak or out of season;
- internet shopping.

Metwally, M. M., *Price and Non-price Competition: Dynamics of Marketing.* Bombay: Asia Publishing House.

Not-for-profit organizations

Not-for-profit organizations are often ignored in any analysis of strategic management issues. There are vast numbers of not-for-profit organizations, which include:

- special interest organizations;

- government entities;
- educational or medical organizations;
- charities;
- religious foundations;
- political groups;
- social groups.

It is undoubtedly the case that many of these not-for-profit organizations compete openly with profit-based organizations and provide similar products and services. This is particularly the case in the medical and educational field.

Broadly speaking, the revenues obtained by not-for-profit organizations come from two different areas:

- customers or clients who receive products or services from the organization;
- sponsors, government agencies, providers of funds in the form of grants and donations

On the one extreme there are organizations, such as private schools or hospitals, that derive the bulk of their revenue from their customers or clients. On the other hand there are organizations that derive the bulk of their revenue from sponsors, which is undoubtedly the case in situations such as charities. The vast majority of organizations can be found somewhere between these two radically different forms of not-for-profit organization as they combine both types of funding.

The primary ways in which not-for-profit organizations differ from profit-based organizations are:

- Their outputs and results are often intangible and therefore difficult to measure.
- They may not be unduly influenced by their clients or customers.
- Financial contributors may well have different priorities from those of the customers or clients which the organizations actually serve.
- Many of the employees are such in name only, as they are volunteers.
- These volunteers may be subject to external influences and other commitments which could affect their commitment to the organization itself.
- There are more constraints on finances as not-for-profit organizations tend not to have access to credit facilities. They cannot offer shares on the market and therefore have fewer debt options.

In terms of strategic management, there are a number of considerations with regard to not-for-profit organizations. These are:

- Goal conflicts – as they often lack unifying central goals (such as profitability).
- The management and planning has to take into account inputs of resources, as they have a direct impact upon what the organization is able to output.
- There is considerable political infighting in many organizations as a result of either conflicting or ambiguous objectives.
- Many of the organizations are controlled by professionals, who may not have managerial expertise, but are recognized as being experts in their field.
- Many not-for-profit organizations are centralized to ensure that maximum value is achieved from the inputs

N

Objectives

The objectives of an organization often derive from, or are the catalyst which creates, a business's **mission statement**. Objectives are broad **goals** or strategies which the organization seeks to adopt in order to achieve its primary aims. Objectives, by their very nature, are broad and often somewhat ill-defined. They merely represent a broad outline, or guideline, which suggests the direction in which the organization intends to move. Broad objectives could include a considerable increase in output, the desire to launch new products, or a determination to provide higher-quality customer service. As with many concerns of organizations, the detail becomes an operational issue and there may be little time spent on identifying how the objectives themselves will actually be achieved.

Occupational psychology

Occupational psychology is essentially a UK or European term which is a broad descriptor for the study of the behaviour of individuals at work. As occupational psychology clearly takes a psychological perspective, it attempts to provide insights and perspectives on various areas of behaviour in the workplace. Typically, occupational psychology includes the following:

- the selection process;
- counselling;
- training and development;
- work design;
- the work environment;
- motivation;
- performance management;
- linkages between employees and the organization;
- employees' well-being;
- the quality of working life;
- impacts on the individual from change and transition.

Arnold, John, Cooper, Cary and Robertson, Ivan, *Work Psychology*. London: Financial Times, Prentice-Hall. 1998.

Fincham, Robin and Rhodes, Peter, *Principles of Organizational Behaviour*. Oxford: Oxford University Press, 1999.

On-the-job consumption

'On-the-job consumption' refers to management participation in activities which effectively diminish shareholder value. The term refers to time and resources that may be expended by managers in order to pursue their own goals at the expense of the overall profitability or efficiency of the business itself. More generally, on-the-job consumption involves the behaviour of managers who choose to use their authority and control over the financial resources of the business in order to secure their own job security, income, power or status. This is often exemplified by individuals at director level who create elaborate or expensive perks for themselves which are not necessarily linked to performance.

Operating budget

A business's operating budget is, essentially, a forecast of its future financial needs. The operating budget may cover a range of different periods in the future, but typically the forthcoming years.

The operating budget will include estimates not only of the financial requirements, but also of the expected revenue streaming into the business, which will (ultimately) fund the operations. The operating budget will, therefore, incorporate sales, production and **cash flow**.

It is the function of managers and accountancy personnel to monitor the relationship between the operating budget and the actual figures being produced, as they occur. Changes or divergent figures are monitored, assessed and adjusted as required.

O

Operating responsibility

'Operating responsibility' is a term used to describe the function or role of the divisional management in a **multi-divisional structure**. The divisional management has the responsibility of handling the operations of the division on a day-to-day basis.

Operations management

Formerly, operations management was known as 'production management', and was applied almost exclusively to the manufacturing sector.

For many organizations this term is still used rather than 'operations management'. However, the management function in manufacturing has broadened to incorporate many other aspects related to the supply chain. It has therefore become common to use the term 'operations management' to describe activities related both to manufacturing and increasingly to the service sector. At its heart, operations management deals with the design of products and services, the buying of components or services from suppliers, the processing of those products and services and the selling of the finished goods. Across all of these disparate areas of business, operations management can be seen as an overarching discipline which seeks to quantify and organize the whole process. None the less, there is still a considerable emphasis placed on issues directly related to manufacturing, stock control and, to a lesser extent, the management of the distribution systems.

As Figure 34 illustrates, a large manufacturing organization will include aspects of operations management under a wide variety of different, but closely related, managerial disciplines. Primarily, human resources, marketing, administration and finance and, of course, the research and development department of an organization, support and are mutually dependent upon the operations division.

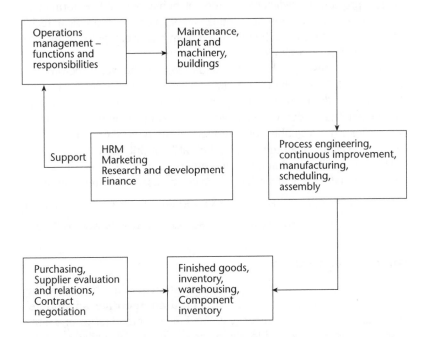

Figure 34 Aspects of operations management

Given the wide spread of different job roles and tasks within operations management, it is notoriously difficult to give a perfect definition of what operations managers actually do. Certainly they would be responsible for a wide range of different functions, but the functions themselves will often be determined by the nature of the business itself, whether it is a service-based industry or an organization primarily concerned with manufacturing.

Hill, Terry, *Operations Management: Strategic Context and Managerial Analysis*. Basingstoke: Palgrave Macmillan, 2000.

Operations research

Operations research is concerned with the development and application of various quantitative techniques which can be used to solve problems. Methodologies and theories which are used primarily in mathematics and statistics are adapted and used to identify, formulate, solve, validate, implement and control decision making. Effectively, it is a scientific approach to the analysis of problems and the making of decisions. Operations research aims to provide rational foundations for the understanding of decision making, particularly in complex situations, and thereby provide a predictable system of behaviour and performance. Typically, operations research utilizes analytical or numerical techniques, which have often been derived from either computer or mathematical models of systems.

Operations research has its foundations in the years before the Second World War, when it was known as 'operational research'. The UK used operational research to prepare for an anticipated air war and the impact that radar would have on tracking incoming streams of enemy aircraft. Arguably, operational research was one of the key elements which helped the UK win the Battle of Britain in 1940.

The field has evolved and is now primarily concerned with the development of mathematical models which can be used to optimize systems.

The Institute for Operations Research and Management Sciences is at www.informs.org

Taha, Hamdy A., *Operations Research: An Introduction*. New York: Prentice-Hall, 2002.

Operations strategy

Essentially, an organization's operations strategy aims to deploy the organization's resources in order to gain a **competitive advantage**. The operations strategy is usually defined in very broad terms and hints at aspirations in respect of levels of service, quality, flexibility and cost control. In many cases an organization will identify a key objective which will give it a competitive advantage, but this may mean that other objectives may need to be sacrificed in order to achieve the primary goal.

Organization bonus system

See **bonus plan reward system.**

Organization environment

See **external environment, external stakeholders, general environment** *and* **internal stakeholders.**

Organization networks

See **network structure.**

Organization types

There are many different forms of organization, which can be typified as being primarily related to the way in which they coordinate themselves, the degree of their centralization or decentralization, and the aspect which the organization considers to be of primary importance. Table 16 illustrates the different forms of configuration, although any such treatment or coverage of organization types cannot hope to incorporate all of the variants which exist.

Organizational behaviour

The study of organizational behaviour incorporates both an academic and a practical approach. Any such investigation begins with the primary definition of the word 'organization', or 'organizational'. Clearly it refers to a form of social collectivity, or in the organizational sense, a series of collectivities. The study of organizational behaviour can be a highly specialized area of investigation. Typically, researchers and theorists will tackle many of the different aspects of organizational life, including performance, **goals**, product- or service-related issues and general performance.

The dominant approaches to the study of organizational behaviour tend to revolve around culturalist, institutionalist or utilitarian explanations. Undoubtedly the study of organizational behaviour began with a simple study of organizational structure and functions. This moved further into the field of the behaviour of groups and individuals. The

Table 16 Types of organization

Configuration	Prime coordinating mechanism	Key part of organization	Type of Decentralization
Entrepreneurial organization	Direct supervision	Strategic apex	Vertical and horizontal centralization
Machine organization	Standardization of work processes	Techno-structure	Limited horizontal decentralization
Professional organization	Standardization of skills	Operating core	Horizontal decentralization
Diversified organization	Standardization of outputs	Middle line	Limited vertical decentralization
Innovative organization	Mutual adjustment	Support staff	Selected decentralization
Missionary organization	Standardization of norms	Ideology	Decentralization
Political organization	None	None	Varies

study draws heavily on psychology and sociology, but later studies have begun to incorporate industrial relations, political science, economics and engineering.

The study of organizational behaviour does derive elements from both the theoretical and the empirical. It attempts to understand how and why organizations develop their ways of regulating their operations and their employees and management. The studies of **Frederick Winslow Taylor** could be considered to be a scientific management approach to organizational behaviour. Much of the structural theory is derived from **Max Weber**, the group theory from Elton Mayo and his **Hawthorne experiments**.

Cole, G. A., *Organizational Behaviour*. London: Thomson Learning, 2000.
Mullins, Laurie, *Management and Organizational Behaviour*. London: Financial Times, Prentice-Hall, 2001.

Organizational conflict

See **conflict management**.

Organizational convergence

Organizational convergence is the centralization primarily of information systems, networks, telecommunications and computing services under a single authority within a business. The organizational convergence provides the necessary managerial framework to bring together the various strands of the organization. In effect it allows a fuller integration, from all areas of the organization to the core of the business. Inevitably, of course, convergence is seen as being the way forward, as a means of facilitating improved internal communication and coordination.

Whilst organizational convergence is a theoretical concept it is also a practical reality as networked telecommunications and computer systems bring hitherto disparate groups within the organization closer together for collaboration, the sharing of ideas, and greater overall control.

Organizational culture

There are a number of ways in which an organization's culture can be classified. The main classifications were suggested by a number of researchers, including R. Harrison, Charles Handy, Terrence Deal and Allan Kennedy, and R. E. Quinn and M. R. McGrath. As years have passed, so these classifications have become more developed, making it possible generally only to approach them in broad terms.

In 1972 Harrison suggested four main categories of organizational culture – power, role, task and person. Charles Handy reworked Harrison's theory and identified the categories as described in Table 17.

During the 1980s Deal and Kennedy developed their own set of theories about organizational culture and the way it affected how managers made decisions and formed their strategies. Their conclusions are shown in Table 18.

Quinn and McGrath also identified four different organizational cultures, as shown in Table 19.

It should be remembered that no one organization fits neatly into any one of the categories mentioned and the majority are too complex to be categorized generally. The classifications should be regarded only as a reference point for the comparison of extremes.

Handy, C. B., *Understanding Organizations*. Harmondsworth: Penguin, 1985.
Harrison, R., 'Understanding your Organization's Character', *Harvard Business Review*, May–June, 1972.
Quinn, R. E. and McGrath, M. R., *The Transformation of Organizational Cultures: A Competing Values Perspective in Organizational Culture*, edited by C. C. Lundberg and J. Martin. New York: Sage Publications, 1985.
Schein, E. H., *Organizational Culture and Leadership*. New York: Jossey-Bass Wiley, 1997.

Table 17 Organizational culture according to Charles Handy

Culture	Description
Power	This type of culture is based on trust and good personal communication. There is little need for rigid bureaucratic procedures since power and authority are based on only a few individuals. The power culture is dynamic in that change can take place quickly, but is dependent on a small number of key, powerful individuals. This culture tends to be tough on employees because the key focus is the success of the organization, often resulting in higher labour turnover.
Role	This type of culture tends to be bureaucratic in nature, thus requiring logical, coordinated and rational processes with a heavy emphasis on rules and procedures. Control lies with a small number of employees who have a high degree of authority. These tend to be stable organizations, operating in a predictable environment with products and services that have a long lifespan. Not considered to be innovative organizations, they can adapt to gradual, minor change, but not to radical ones.
Task	This type of organizational culture relies on employee expertise. The matrix structure tends to prevail in these organizations, with teams of individuals specializing. They need and tend to be flexible organizations with individual employees working with autonomy, allowing fast reaction to changes in the external environment and having set procedures in place to address this aspect.
Person	This type of culture relies on collective decision making, often associated with partnerships. Compromise is important and individuals will tend to work within their own specialist area, coordinating all aspects and working with autonomy without the need to report to other employees.

Organizational design

The way in which an organization decides to configure its activities can be depicted in terms of organizational design. The primary objective of any organizational design is to ensure that the structure conforms to the following:

- the business objectives;
- the business resources;
- the environment in which the business operates.

Table 18 Organizational culture viewed by Deal and Kennedy

Culture	Description
Macho	These types of organization have to make decisions quickly and adopt a tough attitude towards employees and their managers. There is a high degree of internal competition and the operations tend to be high risk. The majority of these organizations do not form strategies or plan for the long term, but are considered short-termist, with a low level of cooperation within the organization itself. There is a high labour turnover resulting in a weak organizational culture.
Work hard/ play hard	This type of culture tends to be associated with sales. The majority of individual employees are sales-orientated but the level of risk is low. It is the employees' ability to accumulate sales that is important and the culture tends to encourage team building and social activities for employees. The organization encourages competition and offers rewards for success, but does not necessarily rate quality as highly as volume.
Company	These types of organization are often in high-risk areas and operate on the basis that decisions take a long time to come to fruition. Decision making takes place at the top of this hierarchical organization and the overall approach can often be old-fashioned. Each new invention or technical breakthrough will pose a threat to the business.
Process	This type of culture operates in a low-risk, slow-feedback environment where employees are encouraged to focus on how they do things rather than what they do. They tend to be systems- and procedures-based, requiring employees to work in an orderly and detailed fashion, attending meetings and work groups. There will be rigid levels of management in the hierarchical structure, but because the organization operates in a predictable environment, reactions from management are often slow.

It is the structure, or the design, that describes the relationship between the different parts of the organization and those who work within it. The design also specifies the following:

- the divisions of work;
- the hierarchical structure;
- the authority structure;
- formal links within the organization.

Table 19 Organizational culture by Quinn and McGrath

Culture	Description
Rational	The rational culture is firmly based on the needs of a market. The organization places emphasis on productivity and efficiency and encourages management to be goal-orientated and decisive. All activities are focused on tangible performance and employees are rewarded for achievement.
Adhocracy	This type of culture is an adaptive, creative and autonomous one where authority is largely based on the abilities and charismatic nature of leaders. These organizations tend to be risk-orientated, and emphasis is placed on employees' adherence to the values of the organization itself.
Consensual	These types of organization are often concerned with equality, integrity and fairness and much of the authority is based on informal acceptance of power. Decisions are made by collective agreements or consensus and dominant leaders are not often present. Morale is important, as is cooperation and support between employees in order to reach organizational objectives. Employee loyalty is high.
Hierarchical	This type of culture relies on stability and control through the setting of rigid regulations and procedures. Decisions are made logically on facts alone with the management tending to be cautious and conservative. The employees are strictly controlled, with management expecting obedience.

Organizational design therefore is the process of actually configuring the organization in relation to its strategies to attain optimum performance. Organizational design has to be reactive and flexible in the sense that changes may have to be made if discontinuity occurs. The net effect of not changing the design is to create a gap between the way in which the organization works and its strategy objectives. It is therefore imperative that the organizational design does not affect the performance of the business. The following problems may be encountered and strategies adopted:

- As the organization grows, the design is amended to decentralize decision making, making it easier for experts in certain areas to take control.
- Changes in strategy must be matched with changes in design.
- Changes in priorities must be matched with changes in design.

- Technological changes may mean changes in information, communication and decision making; all need to be reflected in the organizational design.

Harvey-Jones, John, *Managing to Survive*. London: Heinemann, 1993.

Organizational development

Organizational development (OD) is a planned process of change. Organizational development is about performance improvement, in which a business will seek to align more closely to the environment and markets in which it operates in order to achieve strategies efficiently and effectively. OD can involve development in the areas of culture, values, people, structures, processes and resources.

OD is a complex issue and often specific in terms of process, timing, and those involved. There are, however, some overarching processes and elements that can be identified as being common to many OD situations. OD tends to begin with research into the current situation to assess all the issues. This research will inevitably involve the following aspects:

- clarifying the impact obligations, which have to be honoured;
- the availability of appropriate resources such as skills, facilities and finances;
- the desires and career aspirations of those who will be affected;
- the proposed plan's overall fit with future business strategy.

Once the research process is completed, the organization should have a better view of how the OD will work in practice. This begins with planning the change programme, which may involve the design of the new organizational structure, job descriptions and evaluation, salary and benefits provision, physical resources, the phasing in of the overall project, and the management of impacts on existing employees.

Throughout the process, the organization needs to ensure that it conducts communication, development and counselling events to help establish the new organizational structure. It may also be necessary to reshape or re-profile certain areas of the organization, with the intention of improving employee retention and making the best use of skills and expertise in order to make the intended developments in efficiency.

Hamlin, Bob, Keep, Jane and Ash, Ken (eds), *Organizational Change and Development: A Reflective Guide for Managers, Trainers and Developers*. London: Financial Times, Prentice-Hall, 2000.
Mello, Jeffrey, *Strategic Human Resource Management*. Mason, OH: South Western College Publishing, 2001.

Organizational evolution

It was inevitable that the general theories of evolution would eventually be applied to organizations. The theory of organizational evolution revolves around the following concepts:

- Human practices and norms are a direct result of human action.
- Therefore management theory and organizational theory are a direct result of human actions.

See also **evolutionary theory**.

Organizational learning

A learning environment occurs in an organization which is deemed to be a learning organization. In other words, the organization has put in place both facilities and a culture for learning. An exact definition of the term 'learning organization' is somewhat problematic since there are a number of different categories of learning organization. The essential encompassing concept is that the organizations learn from external stimuli and, as a result, alter or amend their internal framework to match those opportunities. This requires a re-evaluation of **goals** and, in extreme circumstances, a change in **organizational culture**, organizational structure and the patterns of work, in order to take advantage of the new opportunities.

The main recognized categories of learning organizations are:

- Knowing organizations – which tend to be businesses in static or mature markets.
- Understanding and thinking organizations – which are prepared to adapt their culture and structure within certain parameters.
- Learning organizations – which accept change as being both necessary and desirable, and are ultimately the businesses which drive their competitors to mimic them.

Clearly, a human resource department which operates in a learning organization, of whatever type, has to be adaptable and flexible, as well as effective and efficient, in driving changes within the organization. It has been recognized that there are two stages of evolution in a learning organization, of which human resources are an integral part. The first is known as a single-loop or adaptive learning organization, where new techniques and ideas are assimilated. The second type of learning organization is known as a double-loop or generative learning organization. In this case the business continually evaluates its **goals** and objectives, as well as its organizational culture, to suit any emerging external opportunities. Both forms of learning organization offer considerable challenges to those managing human resources, who have to quickly learn that they are in an ever-shifting and adaptive organization.

Chawla, Sarita and Renesch, L. (eds), *Learning Organizations: Developing Cultures for Tomorrow's Workplace.* Shelton, CT: Productivity Press, 1995.

Kline, Peter and Saunders, Bernhard, *Ten Steps to a Learning Organization.* Arlington, VA: Great Ocean Publishers, 1998.

Organizational mapping

Organizational mapping seeks to identify the tasks and functions carried out by each individual employee to act as a means by which under- or over-commitment of individuals can be identified. The process begins with assigning a number to each task that needs to be performed. It also requires the name of the individual responsible and the projected time required to perform that task, usually expressed as either hours or weeks. Once this has been carried out, it is possible to total up the projected time for the completion of all necessary tasks for each individual, which will produce either a negative or a positive number. The process should then reveal where key employees are over- or under-committed. Typically, the organizational mapping is displayed as a traditional organizational chart, which details the over- or under-commitment.

Organizational norms

Organizational norms reinforce the socialization process of individuals within a business. The norms and the socialization work together in order to instil in the management and employees the **goals** of the organization as a whole. Organizational norms seek to identify the ways in which individuals spend their time, manage information, communicate, take responsibility and make decisions. In other words, organizational norms involve the moulding of attitudes and behaviours in order to achieve collaboration and performance.

Organizational performance

Organizational effectiveness is measured in various ways by different businesses. Essentially, organizational effectiveness is a measure of performance against set standards, such as profitability, efficiency, earnings per employee, or a variety of other means. More generally, organizational effectiveness can be typified as being the business's ability to achieve predetermined outcomes or targets within a given time frame.

Organizational politics

Organizations are essentially political systems and power is used on a day-to-day basis to determine organizational relationships. Within the organizational context, politics is a means of recognizing and ultimately reconciling various competing interests. Whilst, in the past, business organizations were controlled rigidly by management, they have increasingly developed into various forms of democratic working environments, which are no longer based on coercion. Clearly, in their politics, organizations can range from the autocratic to the democratic. Within these two extremes there are bureaucratic organizations, which run their politics on a very formalized basis, or technocratic systems, in which the politics are based on skills and abilities.

Politics involves what can often be non-rational influences on decision making. It is widely believed, however, that successful organizational politics can lead its practitioners to higher levels of power, and ultimately result in a more reasoned organization, which can adapt and change, as well as being more effective in its decision making. In order to understand organizational political behaviour, Table 20 may prove to be a useful starting point in as much as it identifies three key dimensions:

- where the political activity takes place – whether internal (inside) or external (outside the organization);
- the direction of the influence – either vertical or lateral;
- the legitimacy of the political action.

Table 20 Defining organizational politics

Dimensions		
Internal/external	Internal examples: Exchange of favours, reprisals, obstruction, symbolic protests.	External examples: Whistle-blowing, legal action, information leaks.
Vertical/lateral	Vertical examples: By-passing chains of command, complaining to managers, interaction between peers.	Lateral examples: Exchanges of favours, formation of coalitions or groups.
Legitimate/illegitimate	Legitimate examples: Any actions taken with the overall organizational procedures and policies	Illegitimate threats

O

Organizational populations

Undoubtedly the study of organizational populations was inspired by **evolutionary theory**. Organizational population looks at the dynamic processes which affect the development of those populations over a period of time. It focuses on selection as being the main mechanism of change. Initially organizational populations considered selection to be more important than adaptation as a means by which an organization developed. Selection, as far as organizational theory is concerned, tends to focus on the advantages some organizations have in their competition for scarce resources.

Organizational population theory, therefore, suggests that organizational types and populations are a result of variation, selection or retention. In effect there are three levels of examination. These are:

- The demography of organizations – which looks at the processes organizations go through in order to deal with variations in their environment.
- Population ecology – which looks at organizational population growth and decline as a result of competition, which can have an impact on the population of organizations over a period of time.
- The community ecology of organizations – which considers the various groups within an organization, such as unions, employer associations and perhaps agencies which regulate the industry, and regards them as interacting populations.

The study of organizational populations is an evolutionary approach which investigates the emergence and ultimate disappearance of different organizational forms.

Organizational socialization

Organizational socialization is said to begin at the very point when an individual starts his or her career in an organization. The individual needs to understand and analyse the particular **organizational culture** in which they are now placed. Whilst formal training programmes are important in developing any technical knowledge or skills, a more discreet and subconscious form of socialization begins to take place in order to bring the individual into the organization, both physically and mentally. Individuals may need to be re-socialized, as they may bring with them views and ways of carrying out work which are not expressly acceptable to the organization.

O

Organizational strategy

'Organizational strategy' can refer to either a functional-level, a business-level or a corporate-level strategy. The organizational strategy is the specific pattern of any decisions or actions which managers will undertake in order to use the business's **core competences** in the achievement of a **competitive advantage**. Organizational strategy, therefore, means that the business will seek to mobilize its resources in the form of the functional skills of employees and management and/or the attributes of the organization itself in order to achieve specific goals. Clearly, organizational strategy involves a coordination of both the functional and the organizational resources in order to achieve any objectives.

Normally, organizational strategy is formulated at three distinct levels in an organization. These are:

- Functional level – which is carried out by functional managers with the aim of strengthening the business's functional and organizational resources, to coordinate and to create and maintain core competences.
- Business level – which is carried out by the senior management and aims to mobilize functional core competences in order to gain a competitive advantage.
- Corporate level – which may be derived from the key stakeholders in the business, notably the senior executives, and will seek to ensure that the business finds ways in which to create value and to compete, perhaps through **diversification**, or through some form of acquisition, intergration or merger with another organization.

Stacey, Ralph D., *Strategic Management and Organizational Dynamics: The Challenge of Complexity.* London: Financial Times, Prentice-Hall, 2002.

Organizational structure

Organizational structure is a crucial consideration for all international businesses. Efficient organizational structure requires three main criteria. These are:

- The way in which the organization is divided into sub-units. This is known as 'horizontal differentiation'.
- The location of the decision-making responsibilities within the structure. This is known as 'vertical differentiation'.
- How the business has established integrating mechanisms.

Arguably, there is a fourth consideration, which is known as 'control systems'. This is taken to mean how the performance of sub-units within the organization is assessed and how well the managers of those sub-units control the activities within their area of responsibility.

It is essential for organizations which are pursuing a variety of different strategies as part of their international business activities to choose and then adopt appropriate organizational architecture which is responsive enough to implement the identified strategies. The organizational structure or architecture of a multinational business will very much depend on whether it is a multi-domestic business, global, or transnational in its nature. As multinationals spread their interests across the globe they inherently become more complex. In addition to this, they also become less able to change. None the less, the move towards increased globalization has meant that businesses trading internationally must be able to adapt or amend their organizational structure to incorporate new strategies and operations in new markets.

Organizational values

An organization's values are standards which the business regards highly and holds as its ideal. Values may be ethical standards, but essentially they guide the organization as to how to carry out its business. Organizational values can derive from senior management, line management or even teams and employees. Often organizational values are incorporated into the business's **mission statement**. In effect, the organizational values seek to establish role models for these aspirations.

Outcome measure

An outcome measure can be defined as a means by which an intervention in a certain issue can be assessed. There are two ways of calculating the outcome: either as an efficacy outcome (when the intervention was successful and produced the intended result) or as an adverse outcome, which was not successful.

Output control

The term 'output controls' has a specific reference to international businesses in as much as it suggests the inherent difficulties in setting **goals** for subsidiaries and then expressing those goals in terms of objective criteria. The more complex an international business becomes, perhaps with a series of subsidiaries in different nations, the more difficult it becomes for the parent company to judge the performance of those subsidiaries. There is no simple solution, yet output controls seek to provide an objective means by which the goals can be expressed. The objectivity needs to be applied equally to all subsidiary organizations; only then can it be used as a true performance measurement and a means by which the subsidiaries' ability to meet those goals can be judged.

Output measure

The output measure is an alternative means of describing the capacity of a business over a given period of time.

Outsourcing

The outsourcing of human resources is gradually gaining ground as a primary means by which the functions related to employees are handled by a business. There have been significant changes in policy, where a shift has been in progress from providing human resources in-house to using external organizations. In effect, outsourcing is the use of another organization or an agency for some, or all, of the human resource functions.

Outsourcing is not merely restricted to the smaller business. It is notable that businesses which have grown significantly over recent years have a greater tendency to consider outsourcing, largely as it prefers to focus on the operations of the core business, and there is a culture of outsourcing which has enhanced this growth.

In the US, the human resource industry as a whole was worth an estimated $13.9 billion in 1999 and, according to research businesses such as Dataquest, it is expected to have reached $37.7 billion in 2003.

Outsourcing human resources falls into four broad categories:

- Professional Employer Organizations (PEO) take on all of the responsibilities of the human resource administration for a business, including the legal responsibilities, the hiring of staff and the termination of employment. Typically, the relationship is cooperative, with the PEO handling human resources and the business itself dealing with all other aspects of operations. Not all PEOs take the full responsibility for human resources; some merely handle payroll and benefits systems.
- Business Process Outsourcing (BPO), although a general term used to describe outsourcing in the broadest sense, refers to human resources in respect of supporting the human resource functions with technology and software (including data warehousing and other services).
- Application Service Providers (ASPs) restrict their relationship with a business to providing either web-based or customized software to

help manage human resource functions such as payroll and benefits.

● E-services can be either ASPs or BPOs, which again are restricted to web-based services such as recruitment, software and data warehousing, or other forms of data storage and access provision for human resources.

Incomes Data Services, *Outsourcing HR Administration*. London: Incomes Data Services, 2000.

Vanson, Sally, *The Challenge of Outsourcing Human Resources*. Oxford: Chandos Publishing, 2001.

O

Pp

Parallel sourcing

Parallel sourcing is used by organizations in order to ensure that they have a guaranteed supply of vital resources, components or parts. For many years organizations such as Japanese car manufacturers have used parallel or network sourcing. This allows them to have a variety of sources for each type of component, although each of these components arrives at the manufacturing unit with a single product or code number. In effect, parallel sourcing is an expansion of dual sourcing, which also uses more than one supplier for each part. This ensures that in cases where a particular supplier is unable to cope with a particular volume, or the variety of parts required differs, or they cannot deliver by a specified time, the manufacturing process is protected by sourcing elsewhere.

Parenting advantage

The parenting advantage refers to multi-business organizations which have two elements:

- business units, which are often independent businesses operating in specific markets;
- one or more layers of other line and staff managers above or outside these businesses.

The latter group is known as the parent. The businesses themselves are directly involved in activities related to the value chain, in as much as they create products and services and sell those on to customers. The parents make a contribution in terms of the support and influence they provide or offer to the businesses.

The business level management should be concerned with more than just the creation of profit. They need to appraise continually the value chain and seek solutions to possible problems. Parents, at the corporate decision-making level, need to concentrate on the fact that rival parents exist and that they are supporting and influencing their own businesses.

The key element of the parenting advantage is that the parents of one set of businesses manage to achieve more value from their portfolio of businesses than other rival parents. If they are unable to do this, the stakeholders at least would be better served by a change in the parents of the businesses. Figure 35 illustrates the major concerns and influences of the parenting advantage:

Judgements regarding the 'fit' (the appropriateness or closeness of the parents to the businesses) are therefore relative. Parents must examine whether they are more fit as a parent for the businesses compared to other rival parents. In doing this, the parents can identify and then implement decisions regarding the businesses by adopting the style and approach of the rival businesses had they been parents of the businesses in question.

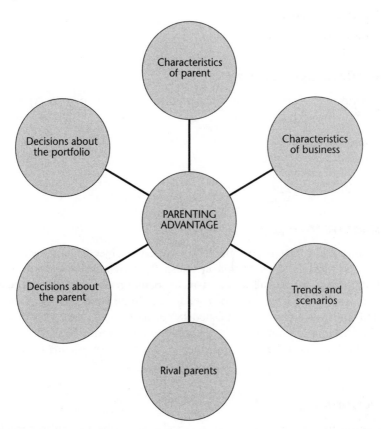

Figure 35 Parenting advantage model

Source: Adapted from Marcus Alexander, Andrew Campbell and Michael Goold, *Parenting Advantage: The Key to Corporate-Level Strategy* (1995).

Ongoing audits of the fit, the changing business environment and an examination of what may or may not occur in the market (trends and scenarios) all assist the parent in structuring and restructuring their support and influence mechanisms. In doing this, the parents can seek to maintain and improve their parenting advantage. Whilst the parents examine the approach of rival parents, they are also able to identify and perhaps target businesses belonging to other parents which would be more effective under their own parenting arrangements.

A full copy of *Parenting Advantage: The Key to Corporate-Level Strategy* by Marcus Alexander, Andrew Campbell and Michael Goold can be found at: www.adl.com/prism/pdf/1995-Q2_08-12.pdf

Perceived conflict

See **conflict management**.

Performance drivers

A performance driver is a quantitative measurement of output. Typically, performance drivers include:

- cycle time;
- defect rate;
- quality rate;
- financial metrics.

Performance gap

A performance gap is the difference between an objective and the actual results. Most businesses will establish their own key **performance indicators**, which will allow them to focus on the **critical success factors**. The indicators can be used to determine the degree of change, and are invariably an established target associated with a particular date. The performance gap is, therefore, the difference between where the business is at that date and where it had hoped or assumed it would be.

Performance goal

Central to the concept of performance goals is the setting of specific measurable goals. In reaching all the conditions of a measurable goal, a business can be confident and comfortable in its achievement. However, if it consistently fails to meet the measurable goals, these will need to be adjusted or an analysis needs to take place to find out the reason(s) for the failure. Businesses will often set unrealistically high goals for various reasons, including:

- Setting the goals in accordance with an external party's over-optimistic appraisal, which may not take into account the actual abilities of the business.
- Insufficient information – the business will often not have a clear, realistic understanding of what it is trying to achieve or the skills and knowledge that are required.
- Expecting that the business will always perform well and at its optimum. This is unrealistic, as many factors can affect performance and it is often better to set goals based on average performance, which could be consistent.

Alternatively, goals can be set too low for the following reasons:

- Fear of failure – businesses which lack self-confidence will not consider it wise to set goals which are risky. They will ignore the fact that failure can be positive, as it shows where skills and performance need to be improved.
- Taking the easy option – this is an attractive basis for goal-setting as it does not require the business to stretch itself; but the achievement of these goals would probably be worth very little.

Goal-setting needs to be at the correct level and this is a skill that can only be acquired by practice. Unrealistic goals are self-defeating because the business will quickly realize that there is little point in putting serious effort into goals which cannot be reached. Goals should not be set in stone; they need to be continually measured and adjusted.

Performance importance grid

A performance importance grid can be used by an organization in order to identify its priorities, as well as its current strengths and weaknesses. In effect, the performance importance grid is a variant form of a SWOT analysis. Its direct application is to identify current priorities and current success in specific areas of the business's operations. The grid enables the organization to identify the ideal strategies in relation to these two criteria which are categorized as being either high or low (see Figure 36).

Performance indicator

Performance indicators are the key measurement of performance in a

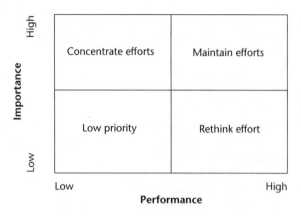

Figure 36 A performance importance grid

business, needing to be continually monitored and assessed. They aim to identify particular strengths and weaknesses. Whilst many businesses may adopt a series of key performance indicators (KPIs), measuring efficiency (input versus output), adaptability (reconfiguring time), financial status (return on equity) and effectiveness (non-defects produced), others divide them into the following key areas:

- Behavioural – relating to the management of staff, including labour turnover, absenteeism, accidents, etc.
- Confidence – examining the relationship between the organization and its broader environment, specifically its **stakeholders**.
- Ethical – considering the standards of behaviour of the organization against set criteria.
- Operational – which considers profitability, product mixes, portfolios, productivity and output.
- Specific issues – such as profit per employee, returns on investment, delivery speed and quality targets.
- Strategic – considering the overall effectiveness of the organization.

Businesses will attempt to identify leading indicators which will help them quickly respond to conditions just as the situation is beginning to have an effect. They can then make adjustments to their processes before unexpected outcomes affect them.

Performance management

Performance management can be seen as a systematic and data-oriented approach to managing employees, based on positive reinforcement as the primary driver to maximize their performance. Performance management assumes that there is a disparity between what an employee is currently achieving (on the basis that they have to do this work and perform to this standard) and the possibly that they might desire to perform better (based on the assumption that they will have desires to perform more effectively if given the opportunity and the encouragement). In many respects, the concept behind performance management is a recognition of this potential performance gap between actual performance and desired performance. This can be illustrated in the graph in Figure 37, which identifies the discretionary effort of an individual. This discretionary effort is applied according to circumstances, and is variable. Performance management seeks to identify the gap between 'having to' and 'wanting to', and to push the performance up to the 'want to' level.

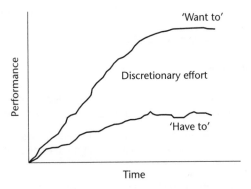

Figure 37   Discretionary effort

Performance management has been used in its various forms since the mid-1970s and is believed to be applicable to almost every area of a business. Its primary focus is, of course, employees. The first major step in implementing a performance management system is to move away from negative reinforcement of standards, which seeks to punish individuals for not performing to (often) unspoken levels of performance. Performance management uses positive reinforcement to generate effort beyond what is normally (minimally) exhibited by the employees. In this way, the discretionary effort is encouraged and the organization as a whole can move towards a maximization of performance.

Kotter, John P. and Heskett, James L., *Corporate Culture and Performance*. New York: Free Press, 1992.

Porter, Michael, *The Competitive Advantage: Creating and Sustaining Superior Performance*. New York: Simon & Schuster, 1998.

Performance measurement

Performance measurement is a means by which a business can monitor its key **performance indicators**. Typically these may include output, costs and asset utilization, and other measures. Performance measurement is an important tool in business improvement.

PEST analysis

This concept originally began with just four criteria, with the acronym PEST (Political, Economic, Social and Technological). These forces are seen as being the principal external determinants of the environment in which a business operates. In later years the Four Forces became five, under the acronym SLEPT (Social, Legal, Economic, Political and Technological). The concept has now been extended to include seven

Table 21 The main areas of STEEPLE

Letter	Description
S	Social and cultural influences, including language, culture, attitudes and behaviour which affect future strategies and markets.
T	Technological and product innovations, which suggest how the market is developing as well as the future developments in research and opportunities arising.
E (E1)	Economics and market competition, which considers factors such as the business cycle, inflation, energy costs and investments; an assessment is made as to how they will affect the level of economic activity in each market.
E (E2)	Education, training and employment, primarily the trends in these areas which may have an impact upon the availability of trained labour as well as the potential demands of new generations, and probable expectations.
P	Political factors, which focus on current and proposed policies that will affect the business and the workforce.
L	Legal aspects, focusing on current and proposed legislation, of equal importance is the business's adherence to current laws and regulations.
E (E3)	Environmental protection, which addresses the business's current and future impact on the environment, working on the basis that environmental protection will continue to be a major issue in restricting and amending the ways in which a business operates.

P

forces, using the acronym STEEPLE (Social, Technological, Economic, Educational, Political, Legal and Environmental protection).

The purpose of the Five Forces, or its variants, is to examine or audit where threats originate and where opportunities can be found. In other words, the broader STEEPLE acronym applies to the **macro-environment** (factors outside the organization). The main areas of interest within each letter are outlined in Table 21.

Porter, Michael, *Competitive Advantage*. New York: Free Press, 1985.

Peters, Tom

Although Tom Peters has written extensively on broader issues regarding the success of businesses, his central message is the use of leadership, or rather the habits of leaders. He prefers to use the term 'leadership' rather than 'management' as he suggests that managers should focus on leadership qualities, specifically motivating and facilitating their employees. He therefore places leadership at the centre of all aspects of the business (as can be seen in Figure 38), including creating new ideas through innovation, satisfying customers and, above all, deploying people (employees) in the most effective manner.

Although Tom Peters is probably best known for his theories on customer orientation, having identified 12 attributes or traits of the most successful US businesses, many of these theories have human resource implications (as can be seen in Table 22).

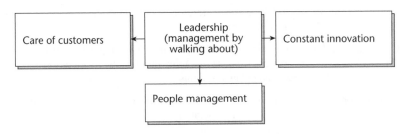

Figure 38   Position of leadership in business organization

Peters, Tom and Waterman, Robert H., *In Search of Excellence: Lessons from America's Best-running Companies*. London: Profile Business, 2004.

Pettigrew, Andrew

Andrew Pettigrew is the Dean of the University of Bath's School of Management. Pettigrew has written or edited 16 books, and in 1995 he

Table 22   Attributes of successful businesses

Trait or quality	Description
Quality obsession	Given the assumption that quality is of paramount importance, leaders should tackle quality issues the moment they arise.
Passionate systems	The drive for quality should not just be a system; it should be an ideology with a system.
Measurement of quality	Everyone in the organization should understand how quality is measured.
Quality rewards	Incentives should be given to those who consistently provide quality.
Quality training	All employees should receive training on quality.
Multi-function teams	**Quality circles** should be established, with the power to drive change.
Small improvements	Any quality improvement, however small, should be celebrated and rewarded.
Continuous **Hawthorne effect**	Employees should always be given new goals, and leaders should be seen to be seen.
Quality teams and structures	A structure of quality teams should be established to closely examine all aspects and processes of the business.
Total involvement	Suppliers and distributors should be included in any quality drive or vision.
Quality and cost	There is a direct relationship between quality (which reduces wastage, etc.) and profitability. All employees should be aware of this.
Quality utopia	Having achieved specific quality goals, new ones should be set to strive towards.

P

was elected Distinguished Scholar of the Organization and Management Theory Division of the Academy of Management (the first non-Northern American to achieve this). He is a Fellow of both the Academy of Management and the British Academy of Management.

In his latest work Pettigrew suggests that there is a convergence of economic, technological, informational and political models which is driving the creation of innovative organizations. He suggests that international competition, cost-cutting and efficiency and the concentration of manufacturing resources have simplified organizational structures.

Technological change has shortened product life cycles, in his view, meaning that businesses need to be more flexible in responding to change. Increased information flows suggest that both qualitatively and quantitatively senior management and decision-makers have access to knowledge and the means by which they can disseminate information to others. Knowledge which had been difficult to share in the past is now much easier to share, and more creative effort can now be spent on achieving greater organizational flexibility.

The traditional complex planning departments are now no longer required, but rigorous planning still needs to be incorporated. The planning processes are now more rooted in the reality of the organization's situation and current opportunities and threats. Strategic decisions can be filtered out of the decisions being made by increasing numbers of decentralized business units within the organization, so that the organization can concentrate on shaping the overall direction.

Pettigrew, Andrew and Fenton, Evelyn (eds), *Innovating New Forms of Organizing*. New York: Sage Publications, 2000.

Piece-work plan

Piece-work means that employees are not paid according to the hours they work; instead, they are paid for the number of items produced. A worker should, theoretically, not get less than the minimum wage if paid on a piece-work basis.

Many factories pay staff a flat rate per hour plus 'piece'-work (so much extra per piece of work), which allows experienced staff the opportunity to increase their wages.

Pioneering costs

The term 'pioneering costs' is associated with the costs and risks facing an international business entering a new overseas market for the first time. In many respects these are trail-blazing organizations; they do not have the benefits of knowing how to deal with that overseas country, either from experience or by learning lessons from other international businesses that have come before. Pioneering costs include the time and effort required to learn how the market operates and how the country's government, rules and regulations can have an impact upon the business's ability to succeed. Pioneering costs are borne alone by the first entrant into the market. Later entrants into the market can benefit from lessons and mistakes learned by the pioneer. However, assuming the pioneer has been successful, later arrivals may find it as difficult, if not more so, to establish themselves in the new marketplace.

Planning

See **strategic planning**.

Politics of strategy

The politics of strategy has become a growing area in the study of management theory and practice, primarily as it has a direct impact upon corporate decision making and all forms of strategic management. The politics of strategy is primarily concerned with the ways in which power, both internally and externally, affects the decision-making processes of the organization. Notably, the studies have revealed that many of the decision-makers within organizations actually feel powerless, in the sense that they are overwhelmed by other, more powerful and competing power bases, from both inside and outside the organization.

Dixit, Avinash K. and Nalebuff, Barry J., *Thinking Strategically: The Competitive Edge in Business, Politics and Everyday Life*. New York: W. W. Norton, 1991.

Poor commercialization

Poor commercialization refers to situations where there is a clear demand for new technology, or a new innovation, yet businesses have failed to convert these new technologies or innovations into saleable products and services. Many such products and services are rushed out by organizations wishing to capitalize on the commercial potentials afforded them by being first in the field. None the less, many of these products suffer from poor quality manufacture and less than adequate design features. They are simply unable to provide the functionality which the consumers assumed the new technology or innovation could offer.

Porter's four generic competitive strategies

P

Porter's initial argument with regard to competitive strategies suggests that organizations have two basic decisions to make in order to establish a **competitive advantage**: (1) whether to compete on price or on differentiation (which justifies higher prices); (2) whether to target a narrow or a broad market. He suggests that the decision behind these two choices leads to four generic competitive strategies (although there is a fifth, which he does not mention). In essence, the choices of strategy are listed in Table 23.

Day, George S. and Reibstein, David J., *Wharton on Dynamic Competitive Strategies*. New York: John Wiley, 1997.

Porter, Michael, *The Competitive Advantage: Creating and Sustaining Superior Performance*. New York: Simon & Schuster, 1998.

Porter, Michael, *Competitive Strategy: Techniques for Analyzing Industries and Competitors*. New York: Simon & Schuster, 1998.

Table 23 Competitive strategies

Strategy	Description
Overall price or cost leadership	Theoretically this strategy seeks to appeal to the widest possible market, as products and services are offered at the lowest price. This form of strategy requires ongoing efforts to reduce costs without detrimentally affecting the product or service offered to the consumer. This tends to be an attractive strategy if the products generally on offer in the industry are much the same, or if the market is dominated by price competition. It is also the case that this is a good way forward in cases when product differentiation is difficult and most buyers purchase through the same channels.
Differentiation	This strategy rests on being able to offer differentiating features to consumers, who are then prepared to pay premium prices, on the basis of concepts such as quality, prestige, superior technology or special features. Ultimately any sustainable differentiation is derived from the **core competences** of the organization. The organization has to have unique resources or capabilities, or some form of better management of **value chain** activities. Differentiation tends to take place when there are many ways in which products and services can be differentiated and the needs of the consumers are diverse. It is also the case that differentiation is useful when competitors are not using this strategy and the market, or industry, experiences rapid, technological change or product innovation.
Price or cost focus	This is essentially a market **niche strategy** which aims to sell into a comparatively narrow segment of the competition, where lower prices are attractive to the consumer. This form of strategy tends to be used when the business lacks either resources, or the capabilities to offer their products or services to a wider market. It is ideal in situations where the consumers' needs are diverse and there are many niches, or segments, within the market. To some extent this is a trial-and-error strategy as the segments will differ in size, growth, intensity and profitability. It is also true to state that major industry leaders will not see the niche as being critical to their success and will therefore not focus upon it. Generally the strategy only works if few competitors are targeting the same segment.

$\Rightarrow$

Table 23 Competitive strategies (*continued*)

Strategy	Description
Differentiation focus	In essence, this is a variant form of market niche strategy, but instead of highlighting low prices, the organization concentrates on creating differentiating features.
Best cost provider	Theoretically at least, this strategy gives consumers a blend of cost and value, as the organization is offering them products or services which have relatively high-value characteristics and quality at a lower cost than most of the competitors. In essence, this strategy has two elements: low cost and differentiation, and can be successfully used to target value-conscious buyers. Normally businesses operating this form of strategy do not target the broader market, but niches larger than segments. In order to be successful with this strategy the business has to have sufficient resources and capabilities and must have the facility to be able to scale up production and their fulfilment whilst maintaining low costs.

Portfolio planning matrix

See **Boston growth matrix.**

Portfolio strategy

Portfolio strategy is a corporate level analysis of the portfolios of a business, or its strategic business units, but not an investigation of individual products themselves. In essence, two models are used: either the **Boston growth matrix** or the **General Electric screen matrix** or business screen. The purpose of these portfolio matrix models is to understand the portfolio of the business and to consider whether any changes are necessary.

Typically, any portfolio strategy investigation will suggest a number of questions related to the overall growth and profitability of the business and how the portfolio may, or may not, allow the business to attain its performance objectives. Typical questions which would need to be answered include:

- Does the portfolio contain enough operations in attractive industries?
- Are there any marginal business operations or question marks?
- What is the proportion of business operations in either mature or declining markets?

- Are there any business operations which should be divested?
- Are any of the business operations considered to be leaders in their area?
- Do core businesses provide a predictable **cash flow** and profit?
- Are areas of the business producing cash, which can finance areas which require cash?
- Are any areas of the business seasonal or subject to the detrimental impact of recession?

Positioning strategy

Positioning is most commonly associated with the term 'product positioning'. In this sense positioning strategies attempt to establish an image or a view of a product or service in the mind of the target customer. Positioning may also be applied to the business as an entity. Marketing may be used to establish in the minds of customers, competitors and the industry in general, the overall stance, identity and image of the business, based on criteria such as quality, service, innovation or price.

The basic positioning map can be seen in Figure 39. A completed positioning map may appear in the form shown in Figure 40.

Ries, Al and Trout, Jack, *Positioning: The Battle for Your Mind – How to be Seen and Heard in the Overcrowded Marketplace.* New York: McGraw-Hill, 2001.

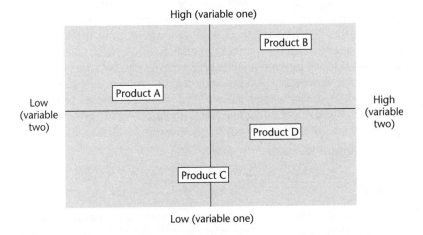

Figure 39   Basic positioning map

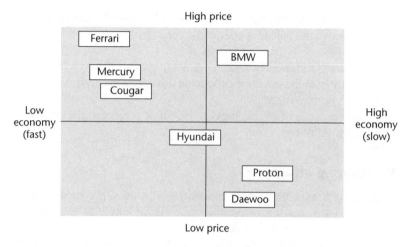

Figure 40   Example of a completed positioning map

Positive sum game

The term 'positive sum game' in the context of international trade suggests that all the countries involved benefit, even though some may benefit more than others. Indeed, international trade only occurs because both parties benefit from the exchange. International trade is considered to enhance world prosperity, therefore economic integration or globalization is a positive sum game and not, as some suggest, a process of exclusion and marginalization. Adopting the positive sum game viewpoint, the inference is that all countries, both the developed and the lesser developed nations, achieve material gains from international trade, regardless of whether the trade is imbalanced. By removing any restrictions to international trade, resources can be, to a greater or lesser extent, more fairly distributed throughout the world. Any increase in the transfer of technology, skills or competition increases productivity, which in every nation should bring about economic growth and a rise in real incomes. This is a positive sum game for all countries.

See also **negative sum game.**

Power

Power equates to the ability to command. Power is an essential element of any consideration in strategic management, since it not only conveys the ability to direct operations, but also allows those with power to delegate to those at lower levels of the organizational structure to exercise power on their behalf. Clearly power can also be exemplified through the hierarchical structure of an organization. This reflects the power structure within the organization, notwithstanding any functional inter-dependencies between those with power and those with the ability to control the business operations.

The actual power structure is a system which continually evolves and changes. In many respects, close examination of the organization chart fails to disclose where actual power lies, and the relative position of an individual in the organizational structure does not necessarily reveal the true extent of the power of that individual at a particular level.

Prahalad, C. K.

C. K. Prahalad is concerned with how organizations operate the nature of the management role and the potato. This last word needs some explanation before moving on. Some years ago Prahalad read a book about the history of the potato. It explained how its eventual spread transformed the world. For Prahalad, the history and the impact of the potato reminded him of the internet. International trade had facilitated the spread of the potato, and the internet would ultimately allow the global diffusion of individual power. This he believed would ultimately change the world and business.

Prahalad also believes that when times are difficult for a business, it is leadership that matters. He says on the issue: 'Leaders must behave like emotional and intellectual anchors. There are no external cues now. The critical issue is about faith, passion, and, most importantly, authen-ticity – so that people know you are not pretending. People can see a sham.' Prahalad also believes that managers should not be frightened of difficult situations when they may have to make unpopular decisions that may affect others. Above all, he believes that all decisions revolve around strategy and that the concept of strategic thinking should never be far from the minds of managers. He says, 'I spend a lot of time talking about what we're doing in terms of strategy. You have to give the same message over and over again.'

Prahalad likens a pack of wolves to the board of directors of a busi-ness. Wolves exchange roles when they are hunting; they have a combi-nation of leadership and teamwork that works. This is a lesson to be learned from nature and an organization should not rely on a single visionary figure or an innovator to always lead the way and come up with the solution to problems.

On planning and decision making, Prahalad could not be clearer. He co-owns a small business and says, 'In a company like ours, if we want

P

to do something, we can just call a meeting. But in a small company, you have to exercise caution and build your own personal dampers so that you don't act on everything. Sometimes not acting may be smart. But if I get the feeling that everybody's becoming so thoughtful that nobody's doing anything, I want to go and light some fires somewhere.'

Hamel, Gary and Prahalad, C. K., *Competing for the Future*. Watertown, MA: Harvard Business School Press, 1996.

Price to earnings ratio

The price to earnings ratio has the following structure:

$$\frac{Current\ market\ price\ of\ shares}{Earnings\ per\ share}$$

The price to earnings ratio is usually calculated on an annual basis and expresses the relationship between the actual share prices, as a multiple of the earnings which each share provides in the form of a dividend. In the following example, a business has a share price of some £10 and has paid a dividend of £0.50. Therefore:

$$\frac{10}{0.50} = 20$$

This reveals that the current market price for the share is 20 times its earnings. Technically, this means that on current earnings performance it would take 20 years to justify the current value of the share price. In fact, however, a high multiple suggests that the business is growing fast, as low yields are most closely associated with high multiples. Other investors may take the opposite view and consider that high multiples simply reflect the fact that the business's share price is grossly over-inflated.

The price to earnings ratio, therefore, is used as a fundamental investment appraisal tool in making a judgement as to whether the shares of a business represent good value compared with the market as a whole.

Pricing strategies/policies

There are innumerable pricing strategies which can be adopted by a business in order to fulfil specific marketing objectives. The most common are summarized in Table 24.

Nagle, Thomas and Holden, Reed, *The Strategy and Tactics of Pricing: A Guide to Profitable Decision-Making*. New York: Prentice Hall, 2001.

Table 24 Pricing strategies

Pricing strategy	Explanation
Market penetration pricing	Low prices, particularly when a product is first launched, in order to obtain a significant penetration into the market.
Market skimming	High prices to support heavy advertising and sales promotion. Involves a higher than usual profit margin on each unit sold.
Average price	Basing pricing on the average for the industry.
Product mix	A pricing strategy associated with setting prices along a product line, which successively offers more features or higher quality for a higher price.
Optional	The practice of setting price according to optional or accessory products which are offered together with the main product.
Captive	Setting a premium price on products that must be used with a popular main product.
Product bundle	Combining several products and offering the whole bundle at a discounted or reduced price.
Discount	Offering a variation in price for those who settle their account quickly, or offering seasonal discounts to encourage customers to buy at times when demand is low.
Discriminatory	Setting the price within a set of parameters, negotiated with each individual customer, dependent upon quantity purchased, location, time-scales or product type.
Psychological	Setting prices which appear to be fundamentally better or more appealing to the customer.
Promotional	Offering temporary pricing structures to increase short-term sales, such as loss leaders or prices attached to special events, cash discounts for frequent purchasing, or reduced prices for local stockists.
Cost-plus	Setting the price at a set proportion or percentage above the cost of production and all other associated costs.

P

Prior hypothesis bias

Prior hypothesis bias refers to decision-making situations where a cognitive bias occurs. In these situations, managers tend to base their decisions on prior beliefs, which are strongly held despite the fact that empirical evidence suggests they are wrong or unfounded. In these cases, the manager believes that knowledge already exists as to the relationship between certain disparate variables, when in fact there may be no relationship, or the interaction between those variables is misunderstood. Decisions are therefore made on an ambiguous basis rather than through logical processes.

Procedural justice

Procedural justice represents both managers' and employees' access to legitimate channels within the organization in order to deal with problems and disputes. Procedural justice puts a detailed mechanism in place which the organization applies, either through management or human resources, to deal with specific problems which may arise from the interaction between different managers and employees. The existence of procedural justice also implies that there is a standard procedure, a set of standards and ethics, which are applied to the handling of any of these situations. Procedural justice should not be confused with any form of civil or criminal procedure, and it may not be precisely in accordance with any governmental rules or regulations regarding the handling of disputes, complaints, arbitration or grievances.

Process management

Process management involves investigating the activities of a business which contribute towards the total activity of the organization. Typically this would include the procurement of materials and equipment, the development of products and services, the production or creation of those products and services, delivery, distribution, and customer support. A key aspect of process management is to break down each of the steps and see where improvements need to be implemented. To do this, a process orientated model needs to be developed, an example of which can be seen in Figure 41.

Building models such as these requires an intimate knowledge of all the functions of the business, as a full model would include specific activities, steps in the process, functions of different parts of the organization, and available information and materials. Models can also contain information regarding potential problems and ideas for future improvement.

Process mapping

There are four major steps in process mapping:

Activity	Benefit	Potential

- Manage: • Manage performance and continuous improvements.
- Improve: • Execute actions to improve lead times, optimize resources, etc.
- Measure & simulate: • Identify costs, lead time, quality, cost for non-value-adding activities, improvement potential, problem areas.
- Document: • Improved routines, securing of quality.
- Identify: • Increased understanding, involvement, ideas.

Figure 41 A process orientated model of process management

1 *Process identification* – which entails a full appreciation of all of the steps of a process.
2 *Information gathering* – which seeks to identify objectives, risks and controls within that process.
3 *Interviewing and mapping* – collating the views of all individuals involved in the process, and then the designing of the actual process maps.
4 *Analysis* – a careful analysis of the process map in order to ensure that the process operates efficiently and effectively.

Two of the most important documents which underpin the process mapping are the process profile worksheet and the workflow survey. The process profile worksheet looks at the trigger events, the inputs and the outputs, the risks, key controls and other measures of success. The workflow surveys are carried out by employees working on the process and include a detailed list of all the tasks carried out. Business process mapping should enable the business to understand what it is trying to achieve and highlight ideas which could streamline those operations.

Jacka, J. Mike, and Keller, Paulette J., *Business Process Mapping: Improving Customer Satisfaction.* New York: John Wiley, 2001.

Process paradox

The process paradox suggests that a business can decline, or even fail, at the very point when changes in its processes have dramatically improved its efficiency, and saved time and money whilst improving quality. The concept, which was put forward by Peter Keen, suggests that this paradoxical situation can occur because the immense benefits are not translated into business value.

Streatfield, Philip J., *A Paradox of Control in Organizations (Complexity and Emergence in Organizations)*. London: Routledge, 2001.

Process planning

Process planning involves the development of a set of instructions which describe a sequence of tasks to be carried out in order to achieve a particular goal. Typically they will specify raw materials and components required to produce a product, and what tasks are required to transform these into a finished product. Process planning, therefore, specifies in the most precise terms how a business manufactures a particular product, in line with its technical specifications. Process planning is essential in order to make the link between product design and product manufacturing.

Product development

Product development is a complex procedure which involves considerable interaction between different elements of an organization. Product development begins with the idea, at strategic level, to produce a new product or service in line with the possibility of its offering successful potential and furthering the overall objectives of the business. In effect, the process involved in developing products from an idea to the fulfilment stage (where the product or service reaches the end-user or consumer) involves four connected sequences of events.

Planning for new products begins at strategic level, where perhaps an opportunity has been identified, but this must now be translated into a form of reality which specifies the product design and requirements. Clearly this needs to be in line with any of the organization's business plans or product strategies. Having successfully negotiated this area of product planning the product now moves into the development stage, where it is transformed from a concept seeking to identify the solutions it will provide and the functions it will require, to a detailed design which will act as a precursor to any manufacturing or processing of the product or service in the future.

Assuming that the product is still a viable concern, it can then move into manufacturing and processing, where further teething problems in actually producing the product are ironed out before the product goes into full production.

As the product reaches this stage, the marketing department of the business will roll into action and begin obtaining as much pre-publicity as possible for the new product or service. As soon as the product or service is available, deals which have been struck with distributors and re-sellers will be fulfilled. Normally this fulfilment process will coincide with advertising in selected media in order to further raise awareness of the product or service on the part of the end-user. Once the products or services are available to the business, distributors or re-sellers, it can be delivered directly to the consumer or end-user. Figure 42 illustrates the processes through which product development takes place.

Fitzsimmons, James and Fitzsimmons, Mona J. (eds), *New Service Development: Creating Memorable Experiences.* New York: Sage Publications, 1999.

Ulrich, Karl T. and Eppinger, Steven D., *Product Design and Development.* New York: McGraw-Hill, 2003.

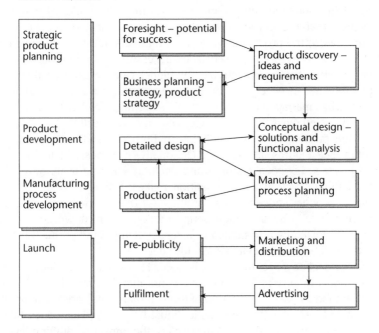

Figure 42 The process of product development

Product differentiation

Product differentiation is also known as 'brand differentiation'. Brand differentiation involves the identification of tangible and intangible benefits or features that can be used to differentiate the brand from competing products or services.

Tangible features or benefits tend to be conscious and rational benefits such as the precise function of the brand and what it achieves or provides to the customer. The intangible benefits tend to be emotional or subconscious features that the business wishes to attach to the brand, such as providing warmth or nourishing food to the family, and safety or other physiological needs.

Differentiation strategies include featuring: low prices; larger selections; convenient, efficient and rapid service; the latest or most trendy product; prestige; best value overall; and reliability.

Product life cycle analysis

The product life cycle is a widely accepted model which describes the stages that a product or service, or indeed a category, passes through from its introduction until its final removal from the market. The model suggests that the introduction stage, or the launch, of the product, during which the product sells in small numbers and marketing activities are expensive, is superseded, if successful, by three other stages. The growth stage is characterized by higher sales, greater profitability, but crucially, more competition. At the maturity stage, providing a product has managed to survive, stable sales and a higher level of profitability are enjoyed. The final stage, known as the decline stage, shows that the product is finally declining in both demand and associated profits (see Figures 43 and 44). Optionally, it is possible to insert a further stage between maturity and decline, denoting a period of the product's life cycle when competition makes it difficult to sustain the original product. Indeed, it may be the case that the product is already growing stale. This saturation period marks a slight downturn, which can be adjusted by a re-launch or a repackaging of the product; otherwise it will begin its inevitable slip into decline.

At the decline stage, the business needs to consider its policy towards the product or service carefully, as it is not merely a question of letting the item fade away over a period of time (perhaps until stocks are finally exhausted). An abandonment policy must be put in place which takes into account the ramifications in terms of the impact on staffing levels, the deployment of human and other resources, as well as its impact on the market, suppliers and distributors.

D. Rink and J. Swan (1979) presented product life cycle patterns (see Figure 45), which afford an opportunity to consider whether a business is able to influence or manage the shape of the curve. Specifically, the implicit ideas of the various shapes offer the following conclusions:

1 The most critical problem for a multi-product business is to deter-

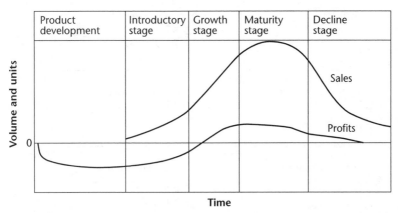

Figure 43   The standard product life cycle graph showing the phases of the life cycle and the association between profits and sales over the cycle

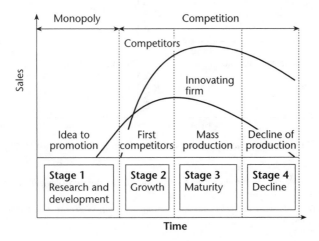

Figure 44   This is a more complex view of the product life cycle, which illustrates the dangers often faced by product innovators in developing new product ideas only to lose the potential of sales as a result of the actions of competitors

mine how its limited resources can best be allocated to the various products. In this respect, the product life cycle concept is an ideal basis for optimizing the allocation of the resources.

2 The multi-dimensional approach is useful in conceptualizing the product life cycle of future products.

3 The use of product life cycles is ideal when brought into the equation, as far as business planning is concerned.

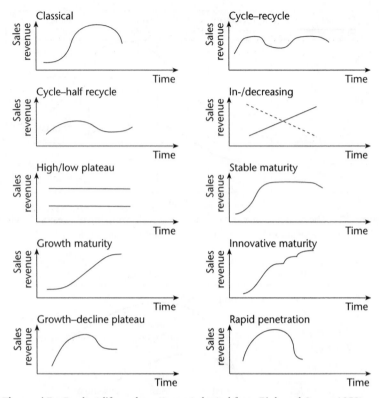

Figure 45   Product life cycle patterns (adapted from Rink and Swan, 1979)

Rink, D. and Swan, J., 'Product Life Cycle Research: a Literature Review', *Journal of Business Research*, vol. 40 (1979), pp. 219–43.
Shaw, John J., *Product Lifecycles and Product Management*. Westport, CT: Greenwood Press, 1989.

Product proliferation

'Product proliferation' is a description given to the vast numbers of new products and services released by businesses. It can also refer to the variety of products and services.

Businesses continue to pursue policies of product proliferation on the following series of assumptions:

- A broader product line adds to the general demand for products offered by the business.
- Broader product lines do add to the supply costs.
- Broader product lines can act as a deterrent to competitors (effectively acting as a **barrier to entry**).

Clearly, product proliferation has both supply and demand implications. The strategy does not tend to deter competitors, whilst the costs associated with supporting a broad produce line are a significant concern.

Bayus, Barry L. and Putsis, William J., Jr, *Product Proliferation: An Empirical Analysis of Product Line Determinants and Market Outcomes*. Gainesville, FL: Marketing Science, vol. 18, no. 2 (1999).

Product team structure

In product team structures tasks are divided along product (or project) lines (see Figure 46). The team will be supported by functional specialists who are an integral part of cross-functional teams. In essence, product team structures are similar to the **matrix and matrix structures** but are easier to control and less costly to operate.

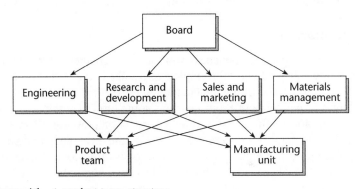

Figure 46   A product team structure

Productivity

Productivity is a measure of an organization's outputs divided by its inputs. In other words, the value of products and services produced and offered by the business compared with the costs of employees, capital and materials, and other associated costs.

Profit ratio

At its simplest, profit can be described as the difference, or excess, between the selling price of components, products or services when they are provided to a third party, and the costs associated with producing them. Profit can be expressed as either gross profit (before tax, expenses, etc.) or net profit (after taxes and expenses, etc.). Profits can be calculated using the following simple formula:

P

Revenue – costs (before or after tax and expenses) = profit

The term 'profit' equally applies to a surplus of net assets at the end of a trading period, compared with the net assets which were available to the business at the start of the trading period. The profit figure, clearly, has to be adjusted to take into account the fact that capital may have been added or taken out of the business during that period.

Despite profit's importance, it remains one of the most difficult figures to calculate objectively. A business's true profits can be measured in a variety of ways; it is not just a simple task of identifying the figure which is ultimately taxed and then, perhaps, distributed in the form of dividends to shareholders. Profit can be, of course, and often is, reinvested in the business in order to produce greater profits in the future. Profit, as recorded by the business in whatever form, can be found most clearly in the profit and loss statement (account).

Profit sharing

This is a term which is applied to a number of schemes offered by an employer which aim to give the employees a stake in the business; many were prompted in the UK by the Finance Acts (1978, 1980 and 1984).

Around 20 per cent of UK business has some form of employee share ownership, and the move is seen as a form of employee participation and industrial democracy. In reality, however, the level of share ownership is low and the employees have little or no real control over the business (mainly because the shares tend to have non-voting rights).

The three most common forms of profit sharing are:

- Employee Share Ownership Plans (ESOP), which were brought to the UK from the US and provide a means by which employees can gain equity in the business. A trust is formed and the dividends on the preference shares pay off the loans used to purchase the shares on behalf of the employees. The shares are held in trust, but employees have the right to sell them.
- Profit sharing schemes (PSS) usually take the form of Approved Profit Sharing (APS) schemes, which involve the distribution of shares to employees free of charge. Shares are purchased through a trust, which is financed from the profits of the business. Alternatively, employees can become involved in SAYE (save-as-you-earn), where employees sign a savings contract, with the option to purchase shares at the end of a contract period at a predetermined price. Both of these methods are popular as they have tax benefits attached to them.

P

- Profit-related pay (PRP) schemes are present in around 20 per cent of private sector businesses and are, essentially, an element in the total employee pay package. Profit-related pay is variable according to the profits made by the business, making a direct link between the activities of the employees, their productivity, and the extra pay that they ultimately receive in the form of PRP.

Profit sharing is seen as an effective means by which a business can encourage individual performance and motivation. Employees have a direct interest in the success of the business and therefore greater commitment and profit-consciousness.

The obvious downside as far as employees are concerned is that they are tying both their jobs and their savings to the success or failure of the business. As far as the business is concerned there is also a worry that increasing staff involvement (particularly in share ownership) may mean that the employees will make increasing demands on the business to give them a greater role in the decision making. Management may be unwilling to concede in the areas of strategic decision making which can affect profitability and employees' pay, as they may be considering longer-term issues.

Profit strategy

A business's profit strategy is, to a large extent, wholly dependent upon many external factors which relate to the demand generated as a result of the growth or distribution of national and, increasingly, international income. The relative profit potential is determined by the demand for products and services, the availability of funding and the extent to which the business can attract suitable employees. The relationship between these factors and a business's profit strategy can be seen in Figure 47.

These, then, are the external factors which have an impact upon the business's formulation of its profit strategy. However, internally there are other factors to take into consideration. A business must configure its offerings of products and services in line with the demands for such products and services and also, to a large extent, the availability of supplies, which determines its ability to offer these products or services. The profit strategy is also influenced by the strategies related to each individual product and service, the way in which these are manufactured, the human relations strategies, and the way the business itself is run and what motives it may have.

Gundling, Ernest, *The 3M Way to Innovation: Balancing People and Profit*. London: Kodansha Europe, 2000.

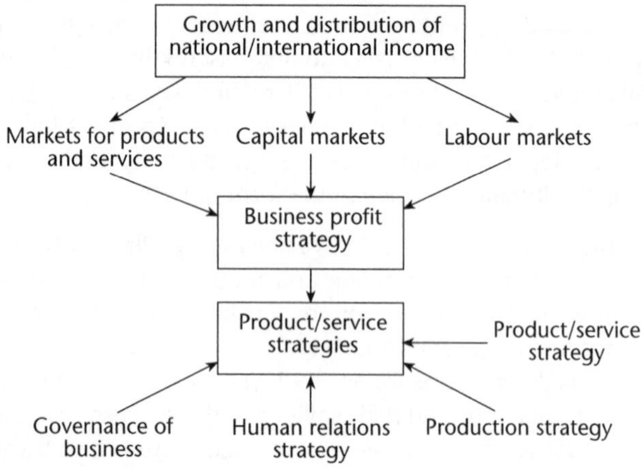

Figure 47   External factors influencing profit strategies

Project boss/manager

Project management involves the planning, organizing, controlling and directing of usually one-off activities. Typically, a team will be assigned to manage a specific project and will use a project evaluation and review technique (PERT) or critical path analysis (CPM) in order to structure the management of the activities related to the project.

Project planning is concerned with organizing the implementation of a project in order to meet its objectives in terms of costs, functionality, quality, reliability and scheduling. A project plan serves five main functions:

- It defines the scope of the project and states the end products that will be delivered, taking into account any assumptions or constraints.
- It details the project activities and how they will be performed.
- It details the inter-dependence between the activities and a schedule of when these activities will be accomplished.
- It identifies the resources required in order to develop the project to meet its end results.
- It describes all the procedures and processes which will be managed during the project in terms of scheduling, cost, procurement, risk and quality.

Figure 48 illustrates the inter-relationship between the activities. The core processes are those required to implement the project, whilst the facilitating processes ensure that the project meets the **goals** and will be managed in a successful manner.

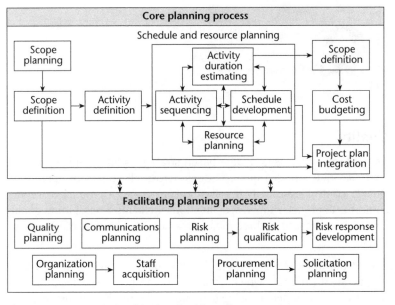

Figure 48   Inter-relationships involved in project management

A project portfolio is simply a collection of projects. The projects will be at various stages in their progress and some will, at different times, need more attention than others. The art of project portfolio management is to balance the needs of each of the projects throughout its life cycle and ensure that each of them remains consistent with the project management process, that progress reports are provided and that systems are consistently applied to the projects across the organization. This will enable the business to allocate resources efficiently, with a clearer understanding of forthcoming requirements.

Lester, Albert, *Project Planning and Control*. Oxford: Butterworth-Heinemann, 2003.

Punctuated equilibrium

Punctuated equilibrium takes the view that the majority of industries and markets experience relatively long periods of equilibrium in which the industry itself and demand are fairly stable. This stability is rudely interrupted by flurries of activity which take place in the wake of innovation or the introduction of new products onto the market. During these periods the industry and the market experience a period of rapid change. After a time the industry and the market begin to settle down once more and return to a degree of stability, albeit at a different level from that prior to the rapid change.

Quality

As the term suggests, a quality-based strategy is an organization-wide approach that stresses quality issues across all phases of operations. Quality control essentially involves ensuring that a product or service conforms to predetermined specifications. In its most basic form, quality control is addressed in three major areas of the manufacturing process. These are:

- At the input stage – where only the parts, components and part-finished products which conform to the given specifications are used or identified as being suitable for the production process.
- During the production process itself – when parts, components and other items are converted into finished products. All systems and control procedures need to be in place to continue to check that specifications are conformed to on a consistent basis.
- At the output stage – only products which are seen to conform to the specifications are allowed to exit the system and become available to customers.

The conclusion of this holistic system therefore incorporates input, process and output control.

Typically, input control would incorporate an inspection of raw materials, and of any subcontracted or purchased parts, and a periodic review and rating of suppliers. During the control process, inspection is a key issue of work in progress, along with swift correction or rectification of problems, usually using control charts. At the output stage inspections are again crucial, as are performance tests. Customers will provide a genuine assessment of the products being used as they were designed to be used. Therefore, interaction with customers and a swift response to any problems they encounter are essential, the findings of which will then be passed down for action at the input and process stage.

See also **total quality management (TQM).**

Wild, Ray, *Essentials of Production and Operations Management: Text and Cases.* London: Continuum, 1995.

Quality assurance

Quality assurance is the attempt by a business to make sure that agreed quality standards are met throughout the organization, primarily to ensure customer satisfaction. There has been a degree of international agreement about quality, consistency and satisfaction, which are enshrined in the International Standards Organization (ISO) 9000 series of quality systems standards. If a business meets these standards, it is normally assumed to have achieved quality assurance.

Quality circles

A quality circle is a discussion group which meets on a regular basis to identify quality problems, investigate solutions and make recommendations as to the most suitable course of action. The members of quality circles are employees and may include individuals with specific skills or expertise, such as engineers, quality inspectors or salespersons. Quality circles were first created in the 1950s in the Toyota motor company. In the 1980s this Japanese form of employee participation and consultation was adopted on a large scale in both Europe and the US. Quality circles aim to use untapped knowledge from the employees, as well as providing them with the opportunity to show their knowledge and talents in their problem-solving skills.

Quantum innovation

A quantum innovation is far more than a simple improvement. It is a considerable change and transformation of a product, a service or a manufacturing or service delivery procedure. In the past, organizations have gone through a four-stage process with regard to innovation:

- They have concentrated on problem solving related to crises as they arise.
- They then moved towards being more proactive and engaging in cost-cutting exercises.
- They adapted to **total quality management (TQM)** or other **quality** improvement programmes.
- They then realized that TQM is simply not enough.

Quantum innovation requires businesses to look beyond **benchmarking** and even beyond their most successful competitors and the top performers in their industry. Quantum innovation requires a radically different way of doing things; in effect, it intends to break the mould. Potentially, of course, a quantum innovation can provide significantly better returns on investment, but it is risky.

It has been estimated that whilst incremental growth or **incremental innovation** provides a year-on-year 10–20% increase in returns, a quantum innovation has the potential of returning a growth of 60–70% per annum.

Quick ratio

This is a fundamental business health test or formula. The quick ratio, or the 'acid-test ratio' measures current assets less stock, against total current liabilities. This ratio shows how well a business is able to cover its short-term obligation – in other words, its liquidity. This is considered to be one of the most stringent tests, as it simply considers current assets which can be turned into cash immediately; it does not consider stock as being immediately convertible into cash. The ratio shows creditors or potential investors what proportion of the business's short-term debts can be met by selling liquid assets. A satisfactory result is where:

Current assets – stock = current liabilities

An alternative way of working out a business's ability to turn assets into cash in order that sufficient money will be available to pay creditors is:

Debtors + cash balances = current liabilities

Quinn, R. E.

Quinn has written extensively with a number of other authors on strategic processes, organizational culture and organizational structure. Together with M. R. McGrath he wrote about mechanic versus organic systems of **organizational design**. But it was his work with J. Rohrbaugh in 1981 which provided a useful model to describe competing values within an organization. The general thrust of their theory is illustrated in Figure 49.

The theorists suggested that the primary thrust of an organization, be it people-orientated, task-orientated, or by virtue of the fact that it is inherently an organic or a mechanic system, will determine the ways in which it can seek to balance what appear to be four radically different and competing sets of values.

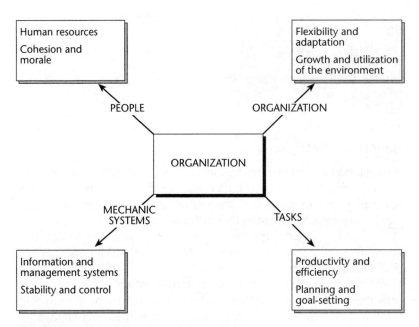

Figure 49 Competing values within organizations

Quinn, R. E. and McGrath,. M. R., 'Moving Beyond the Single-Solution Perspective: The Competing Values as a Diagnostic Tool', *Journal of Applied Behavioral Science*, 18, (1982), pp. 463–82.

Quinn, R. E. and Rohrbaugh, J., 'Competing Values Approach to Organizational Effectiveness', *Public Productivity Review*, 5, (1981) pp. 122–40.

Q

Reactive strategies

Reactive human resource management adopts the contrary position to that of proactive human resource management. A reactive human resource stance relies on the ability to respond to problems and make rapid decisions about them as they arise. Adopting this approach means that human resources can concentrate on current issues rather than attempting to put in place policies and procedures which anticipate and deal with future or presumed issues.

Reactive marketing is a marketing strategy which can be seen as a response to, or a defence against, activities carried out by the competition. As such, reactive marketing can be seen as the direct opposite of proactive marketing, which involves a more systematic planning, implementation and control of marketing strategies and activities.

Realized strategy

A realized strategy is the sum of the planned or intended strategies and the unplanned or **emergent strategies** which have been effectively put into action.

Reasoning by analogy

Reasoning by analogy is often considered a compromise means of problem solving and decision making, as it falls between two conflicting goals. The technique involves trying to associate the current situation closely enough to a previous situation to help guide the manager in thinking through the actual situation.

The main problem with this is that in many cases the previous situation was simpler than the actual situation, and it is therefore difficult to draw useful conclusions.

Long, Derek and Garigliano, Roberto, *Reasoning by Analogy and Causality: A Model and Application*. Crystal City, VA: Ellis Horwood, 1993.

Recruitment and selection

The exact nature of a recruitment and selection procedure will tend to be based on exactly what the preferred methodology may be and whether the recruitment is occurring internally, externally or via an external recruiter. Recruitment procedures will inevitably begin with the recognition that a specific post, either existing or newly created, exists as a vacancy. Exactly how the organization chooses to fill this vacancy may depend on previous experience, taking into account any successes or failures that may have been encountered in the past.

Having drawn up a job description, job specification and person specification from a job design, the organization then proceeds to create documents upon which decisions related to the recruitment will be based. Whether internal recruitment or external recruitment is used, the organization now needs to advertise the post and attempt to attract suitable candidates. In the case of internal recruitment, this may simply mean a suitable advertisement in the organization's newsletter or a document posted on a notice-board.

In the case of external recruitment, the organization may choose to place an advertisement in a local or national newspaper, in a trade magazine, or on the internet (e-recruiting). Alternatively, at this stage it may decide to enlist the services of either a government agency or an employment agency to attract and perhaps shortlist candidates on its behalf. If the organization wishes to carry out the recruitment themselves, through their own human resource department, there will now be a requirement to respond to enquiries, based on the criteria which have been outlined in the job advertisement. This may, of course, involve dealing with CVs or résumés, letters of application and application forms. A process then needs to be established in order to assess the various applications that may have arrived by the date determined in the advertisement. At this stage the organization has the choice of whether to pursue employment references or whether to postpone this aspect until the candidates have been shortlisted.

The shortlisting process aims to identify the most suitable candidates to fill the post, on the basis of the information primarily provided by the candidates themselves. A series of checks may be made prior to the confirmation of the shortlist, perhaps using external agencies to carry out background checks on a limited number of individuals.

The interview process may require the shortlisted candidates to answer a number of questions related to their past working experience, reasons for applying for the post, aspirations, and other more personal issues. If nothing else, the interview process allows those on the interview panel to make a direct comparison between what they have read

R

and what they now see. As part of this process, candidates may also be required to undergo a medical evaluation, or consent to taking a personality test. At the end of the interviewing process a decision needs to be made as to the most suitable candidate.

Prudent organizations will offer the most suitable candidates the opportunity to confirm whether they wish to take up the job offer before informing those that were not successful that, on this occasion, they have not been selected. This means that should the most suitable candidate change his mind, then the next most suitable candidate can now be offered the post. Unsuccessful candidates are often grateful for objective comments about their performance and a short statement as to why they were not suitable for the advertised post, although there is no legal obligation to provide these.

Once the suitable candidate has accepted the job offer, the next stage in the recruitment process is to draw up a contract of employment and agree a start date. The new employees will normally begin their working relationship with the organization by undertaking an induction programme, which can be seen as an integral part of the recruitment process as it serves to orientate the individual into the organization itself.

Wood, Robert and Payne, Tim, *Competency-based Recruitment and Selection: A Practical Guide*. New York: John Wiley, 1998.

Re-engineering

Re-engineering is alternatively known as recycling, de-manufacturing, reclamation and remarketing, and involves the various means by which products or components can be re-used, either by the original manufacturer, or by an organization specifically set up to deal with this material. Re-engineering is an integral part of an increasing trend towards sustainable product design and sustainable manufacturing, as it not only accommodates demands that the lowest possible percentage of a product is discarded once it has reached the end of its useful life, but also recognizes that many parts or components of products can, in fact, have secondary value.

Regular formal measures

Regular formal measures are most closely associated with a management information system, in as much as they are organizational performance measurements which are automatically collected and tracked. These regular formal measures indicate standard performance measurements, such as inputs, outputs, the number of defects and other criteria.

See also **regular informal measures.**

Regular informal measures

Regular informal measures are organizational performance measurements which are not automatically gathered or tracked. These measurements are gathered on a periodic basis and may be tracked project-by-project on the direction of the manager, for internal use within that business unit. Generally speaking, these informal measurements do not find their way into the management information system and are not widely available as information throughout the organization.

See also **regular formal measures.**

Related diversification

Related **diversification** involves a business diversifying and achieving a strategic fit, thus complementing its existing **value chain**. Related diversification allows a business to build shareholder value by capturing cross-business fits, which include:

- the transference of skills and capabilities from one business to another;
- the sharing of resources or facilities in order to reduce costs
- the achievement of leverage through the use of common brand names;
- the combination and deployment of resources to create new competitive strengths and related capabilities.

Relative market share

Relative market share is one of the many different ways in which an organization can compare its success or failure in a given marketplace. Normally, relative market share refers to the ratio of the organization's market share to the **market share** which is controlled by the largest competitor in that industry.

R

Research and development

New product development and the bright ideas associated with such an endeavour must be tempered with the practicalities of production. Whilst many good ideas appear to be workable on paper, the realities of the situation may mean that the product cannot be produced in a cost-effective and efficient manner.

An organization has to assess whether it is looking for a new product which its current production process is capable of producing. It would serve no purpose for an organization to develop an idea for a new product only to discover that the actual production process has to be carried out elsewhere, possibly by subcontractors or business partners. After all, one of the key considerations in developing new products, regardless of their design, is that the organization should make full use of its production facilities.

The design of new products is often changed gradually as the organization becomes aware that the current design presents problems. This process, although not enjoyable for the designer, needs to be considered in terms of efficiency and overall benefit to the organization. Whether the design process is undertaken by the organization itself or by external organizations, the business must ensure that it carries out feasibility studies. These are undertaken at the earliest possible stage to ensure that resources are not wasted in the development of a new product design when there is no likelihood of it being produced in a cost-effective way. This screening process needs to be rigorously enforced to make sure that the business does not invest funds in product designs that are impractical and will never come to fruition. The development of new products can be not only time-consuming but expensive. The desire to develop new products should be tempered by an awareness that many small businesses fail as a result of over-investing in new product development. However, the success of new products is central to the long-term success and growth of the organization. It should be noted that only a small percentage of new products are ever successful. It is imperative for an organization to plan its new product development using the following steps:

- Allow an initial screening period in which an investigation is carried out to assess how the product fits in with current products and services.
- Investigate whether the new product could be produced using current production methods.
- Test the production process.
- Fully cost the production process.
- Carry out the necessary market research.
- Produce a test batch of new products and test market them.

Resource dependency

The concept of resource dependency takes the view that organizations are rather like living creatures, and that they are dependent upon their external environment. In other words, they require certain resources to prosper and survive. The relationship between the organization and its resources is illustrated in Figure 50.

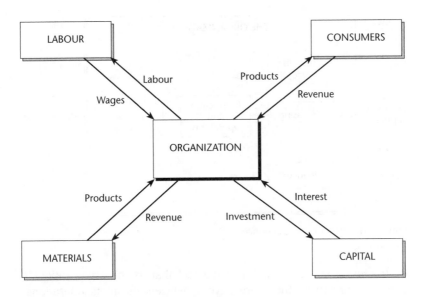

Figure 50 Relationship between organization and resources

Resource dependence has a direct impact on the organization's strategies and structures; as such, it often determines the structures and the opportunities to implement strategies.

Typically, organizations will seek to create linkages with their key resources and possibly to gain control over them. It is often the case that businesses include what are known as boundary spanning units in order to control their most important resources. These will achieve the following:

- They will provide insights into the external environment, and perceive and monitor impacts on resources.
- They will understand how external factors can affect the business's policies and procedures.

Resource dependence can be managed in the manner shown in Figure 51.

This model illustrates how the functional departments of a business can, in effect, buffer products and operations from resource dependency.

Restructuring

Simply a mention of the word 'restructuring' brings enormous dread and negative connotations to both an organization and its employees.

R

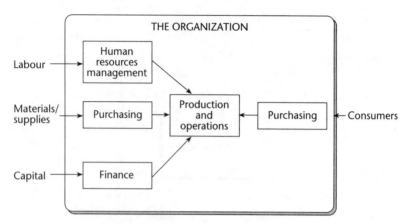

Figure 51 Resource dependence

Restructuring is a recognition of the fact that as the organization is currently structured there are severe deficiencies in its operations. Inevitably, for employees and human resources departments, any restructuring exercise will involve a huge degree of upheaval. Restructuring tends to occur either when a business is teetering on the brink of disaster, or as a pre-requisite demanded by a financial institution as a priority issue before funds will be released to the organization.

For human resources, restructuring can mean dealing with a potentially large percentage of the employees as casualties of the process. Those that remain may have their jobs entirely redesigned or realigned to match the new structure, which aims to be more efficient and productive.

Retrenchment strategies

The retrenchment strategy is exemplified by moves which businesses may seek to make in difficult times, or when the markets or the external environment are unpredictable. They may opt for a scaling down of operations, perhaps identifying the current areas of business activity which are most under threat. They will partially or completely remove themselves from weaker parts of the market, or divest themselves of some business operations in order to refocus on stronger areas of the business. Retrenchment often involves a considerable regrouping through both cost and asset reduction as a result of a reverse or a trend of declining sales and profits.

Retrenchment is often referred to as a turnaround or a reorganization strategy. In essence it seeks to strengthen the business and force it to return to its distinctive **core competences**. Retrenchment can involve the sale of land or buildings, the reduction of production lines, the closing of marginally profitable businesses, the closure of an obsolete manufacturing unit or automated processes, a reduction in the number of employees, or the institution of stringent expense-control systems.

Davis, Fred, *Strategic Management Concepts*. New York: Prentice-Hall, 2001.

Return on investment (ROI)

This is the US equivalent of return on capital employed (ROCE). Whilst management may use this formula – assessing profit, before tax and interest, as a percentage of total assets – shareholders are more interested in the figure for profit after interest, and comparing this with the assets less the liabilities.

Return on investment is a ratio which seeks to identify the net profit (after tax) as a percentage of the total assets of the business. The ratio is:

$$Return\ on\ investment = \frac{net\ profit\ (after\ tax)}{total\ assets} \times 100$$

This ratio is extremely important as it measures the profits available after all charges have been deducted, compared with the assets owned by the business. Typically, the total assets figures are the year-end figures, but they can be an average of the opening and closing figures.

A business with a net profit of $250,000 (after tax) and total assets to the value of $3,200,000 would calculate as follows:

$$\frac{250,000}{3,200,000} \times 100 = 7.81\%$$

This figure would then be compared with the industry standard. A complication may be the age and depreciation of the fixed assets of the business. If depreciation is a factor then the business will reveal a higher ROI. Conversely, if the business has relatively new fixed assets, valued at or near the purchase price, then the ROI will be significantly lower.

Troy, Leo, *Almanac of Business and Industrial Financial Ratios*. New York: Aspen Publishers, 2003.

Walsh, Ciaran, *Key Management Ratios: Master the Management Metrics that Drive and Control your Business*. London: Financial Times, Prentice-Hall, 2003.

Return on stockholder/shareholder's equity

Shareholder's equity, or net asset value, means the total assets of a business less its liabilities, which include any debentures, loan stock or preference shares (preferred shares).

Shareholder's equity is often referred to as the actual net worth of the business. A related issue is the net asset value per share, which has the following calculation:

$$\frac{Net\ asset\ value}{Total\ number\ of\ ordinary\ (common\ stock)\ shares}$$

Return on total assets

'Return on total assets (ROTA)', as the term implies, is a measurement of whether or not a business is effectively using the assets which it owns. Typically, the equation takes the following form:

$$\frac{Income\ before\ interest\ and\ tax}{Fixed\ assets\ +\ current\ assets}$$

Troy, Leo, *Almanac of Business and Industrial Financial Ratios.* New York: Aspen Publishers, 2003.

Walsh, Ciaran, *Key Management Ratios: Master the Management Metrics that Drive and Control your Business.* London: Financial Times, Prentice-Hall, 2003.

Risk management

Risk management is an integral part of managerial responsibility. Risk management does not just apply to managers in senior positions, as it takes place on a daily basis at various levels of risk. There are no tried and trusted methods of risk management, but there have been several attempts to create a standard model, as can be seen in Figure 52.

Figure 52 Standard risk management model

This is, however, a rather simplistic means of assessing risks and dealing with the risk management procedure, since it suggests that risks can be addressed one-by-one, and in fact risk management often involves dealing with several risks simultaneously. Therefore a more complex risk management model, such as in Figure 53, may be employed.

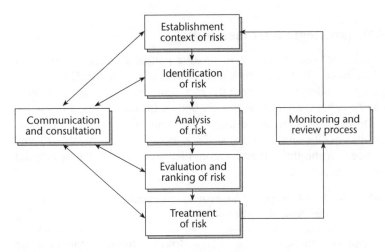

Figure 53 Complex risk management model

Other businesses prefer to take a more proactive approach with regard to risk management and may well evaluate the probability of risks and their impacts prior to the risk even threatening to take place. An example of this form of proactive risk management is given in Figure 54.

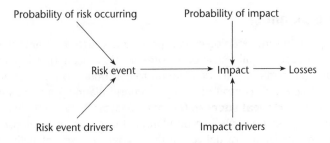

Figure 54 Proactive risk management model

Smith, Preston G. and Merritt, Guy M., *Proactive Risk Management: Controlling Uncertainty in Product Development.* Shelton, CT: Connecticut: Productivity Press, 2002.

SBU (strategic business unit)

A strategic business unit is a separate part of a business organization which has distinct missions and objectives of its own. An SBU can therefore plan independently from the rest of the business. Typically, an SBU can be either a division, a product line or, in some cases, a brand.

Organizations recognize that the establishment of SBUs can lead to significant efficiency and cost savings, as can be seen in Table 25, which focuses on the finance and accounting aspects, comparing traditional structures with SBUs.

Table 25   Transformation of financial and accounting functions from a traditional structure to an SBU

Traditional structure		Strategic business unit structure	
Decision support	10%	Decision support	50%
Control	30%	Control	10%
Reporting	20%	Reporting	20%
Transaction processing	40%	Transaction processing	20%

Scenario planning

Scenario planning methodologies can provide a structured framework which can be used at all levels of an organization. Scenario planning allows different parts of the organization to contribute to the strategic planning process and central planning. Scenario planning involves an evaluation of the **critical success factors** which are required to deliver particular goals. Key actions can be identified in order to develop the organization's capability of delivering these goals, consistent with the most likely scenario. Scenario planning involves the definition of corporate visions and values, which will ultimately underpin exactly how the organization will go about achieving its objectives.

Although there is no clear model for scenario planning, a typical scenario planning model is outlined in Figure 55.

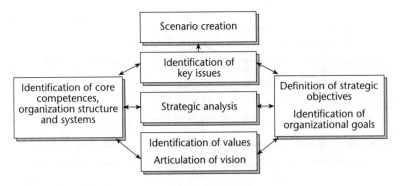

Figure 55   A typical scenario planning model

Lindgren, Mats and Bandhold, Hans, *Scenario Planning: The Link Between Future and Strategy*. Basingstoke: Palgrave Macmillan, 2002.

Self-regulation

Self-regulation is either a private agreement or a set of standards which have been agreed by members of an industrial sector. These self-regulating standards may be either substantive or procedural. Although it is not always the case, self-regulation may mean the absence of government regulation. However, many governments enter into an agreement with the industry and may provide a safety net.

Theoretically, self-regulation reduces, but perhaps does not eliminate, the need for government regulation or involvement. Self-regulation can be more flexible than government regulation as it can be changed to reflect the impact of new technologies. Self-regulation is also valuable in establishing a dialogue between customers and the industry, and establishing trust between them.

Self-regulation, however, is less transparent and potentially subject to manipulation or collusion by the industry. Equally it may be the case that customers and the government will lack the means to enforce industry compliance.

Self-regulation is appropriate in some circumstances, but not in cases where there is a monopoly provider.

S

Seven S framework

The Seven S framework is a tool used to describe the inter-relationships between seven key factors which determine the way in which a business operates. It is illustrated in Figure 56 and Table 26.

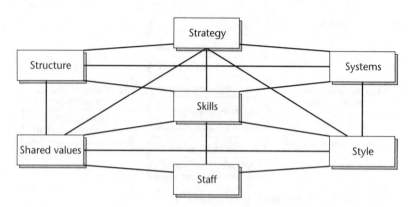

Figure 56 The Seven S framework

Table 26 Elements of the Seven S framework

S Factor	Description
Strategy	The environment, competition, customers.
Structure	Organizational chart, inter-relationships, authority, power and control.
Shared values	Central beliefs and attitudes towards quality, objectives and other factors.
Staff	Employees, in terms of functionality, education and background.
Style	Behavioural patterns and common traits (of both managers and employees).
Systems	Procedures and processes.
Skills	The core competences of the organization.

Pascale, Richard Tanner, Gioja, Linda and Milleman, Mark, *Surfing the Edge of Chaos: The Laws of Nature and the New Laws of Business*. New York: Three Rivers Press, 2001.

Shake-out stage

The term 'shake-out stage' relates to a stage in the **industry life cycle model** where demand has approached saturation level.

Share building strategy/share increasing strategy

These two associated corporate-level investment strategies aim to either build or increase **market share**. The key differences between the two strategies are:

- Share building involves building the actual market share itself by developing a unique, but stable, **competitive advantage** and primarily addressing consumers who have not bought from the business in the past.
- Share increasing focuses on attracting the customers of weaker businesses that are in the process of leaving the market.

Simple structure

Simple organizational structures are primarily geared to optimize administrative procedures and streamline coordination and communication. In such structures, there is a clear distinction between managerial roles and managerial levels. In essence, they seek to optimize all aspects of operations and control by simplifying the steps needed to maintain or attain organizational objectives. Simple structures tend to be 'flat' organizations with few levels of management or hierarchy.

Single-dimensional measure

Unlike means of **performance measurement** such as **multi-dimensional measures**, single-dimensional measures deal with one basic unit of performance. Typically these would include the number of errors, number of employees, cycle time or number of hours.

Situational analysis

Situational analysis primarily focuses upon two different considerations. These are:

- The business's external or **macro-environment**, which incorporates the industry conditions and competition.
- The business's internal or **micro-environment**, which addresses its **core competences**, resource strengths and weaknesses, and capabilities.

Typically, an assessment of the industry or competitive conditions would include the following:

- the economic traits of the industry;

- the strengths and weaknesses and the nature of the competition;
- the causes of changes in the industry;
- the competitive position of other businesses;
- the strategic plans of competitors;
- key success factors;
- industry attractiveness.

With regard to the internal business situation, the following would be considered:

- present strategy;
- SWOT analysis;
- cost comparisons with competitors;
- current strength of the business's competitive position.

Having carried out this strategic analysis, the business is able to identify its strategic options and then choose the best strategy for the future.

Soft metrics

Soft metrics can be differentiated from **indices** or **hard metrics** in the sense that they seek to measure perceptions. In other words, soft metrics are more concerned with the qualitative aspects or human dimension rather than with quantitative metrics or mathematical and financial figures.

Span of control

The span of control is the number of subordinates for whom a manager has direct responsibility. The ideal number frequently quoted is between five and nine individuals under the control of one manager. Beyond this it becomes increasingly difficult to react or respond to their specific needs. Therefore, additional levels of hierarchy need to be inserted, both above and below each manager, in order to reduce the span of control to a manageable level.

Stability strategies

In uncertain markets most businesses would settle for a degree of stability. Indeed one of the safest growth stances is stability, even if it can only be achieved for a short time. Stability does not necessarily mean that the business is stagnating, but it may suggest that the business is pausing or is cautious for a period of time while it grows. Three stability strategies are normally used by businesses. These are:

- *Pause and then proceed* – this is a stability strategy in which the business essentially takes time out for a period. It may need to rest, or consolidate, after a period of rapid growth, before continuing a more aggressive growth strategy. Equally, 'pause and then proceed' is appropriate if an organization is moving into what it perceives to be an uncertain or hostile environment, where it cannot predict what may or may not occur in the short to medium term. The organization will remain in this holding pattern until either the situation changes, or it is more clear about the nature of the environment.
- *No change* – in some respects 'no change' could be considered a rather timid approach to change, but for the most part businesses that adopt this policy may be operating in mature, stable environments, where there are few competitors and therefore there is no immediate need to move out of stability and into uncertainty.
- *Taking profits when you can* – essentially this is only a short-term strategy, founded upon the ability of the organization to make profits while the situation remains stable, but ignoring the fact that the general market conditions are unstable and probably deteriorating.

Stakeholder

A stakeholder is an individual or a group who are either affected by, or have a vested interest in, a particular business. Stakeholders can include customers, managers, employees, suppliers and the community, as well as the organization itself. Each business attaches a degree of importance to each stakeholder and will attempt to understand what its stakeholders require of it, and will take these views into account when making decisions.

Rahman, Sandra Sutherland, Andriof, Jorg, Waddock, Sandra and Husted, Bryan (eds), *Unfolding Stakeholder Thinking: Theory, Responsibility and Engagement*. Sheffield: Greenleaf Publishing, 2003.

Stakeholder analysis

'Stakeholder analysis' refers to a range of tools and activities which aim to identify and describe the **stakeholders** of a business according to the following criteria:

- their attributes;
- their inter-relationships;
- their interests in relation to given issues;

- their interest in and influence over given resources.

Stakeholder analysis takes place for a variety of reasons, including:

- to empirically discover the existing patterns of interaction and inter-relationships;
- to improve interventions;
- to provide a management approach to policy making;
- to provide a prediction tool.

In essence, stakeholder analysis attempts to identify the key 'actors' in the system and assess their respective interests in it. In another sense, stakeholder analysis helps a business understand what can often be a complex and potentially turbulent business environment. There is also a notion that the management of the organization has a desire to manage a stakeholder relationship in some way. Typically, stakeholders are described as either internal or external, as can be seen in Table 27.

Table 27 Internal and external stakeholders

Internal stakeholders	External stakeholders
Management (both direct and functional)	Government (regulators, legislators, legal systems, courts, political parties)
Employees (groups, teams and unions)	Competitors
Sponsors	Community (special interest groups, local population)
Owners (stock or shareholders, board of directors, venture capitalists, finance providers)	Media (radio, television, internet data services and newspapers)
Functional departments (accounts, HRM, engineering, marketing, etc.)	

There are also groups which straddle the divide between the internal and the external. These could include the following:

- customers;
- vendors;
- suppliers.

Stakeholder analysis seeks to identify the following features of stakeholder groups:

- the relative power and interest of each stakeholder;
- the importance and influence of each stakeholder;

- the multiple interests which they have, or indeed multiple roles;
- the networks and coalitions to which they belong.

A flexible set of steps to accomplish stakeholder analysis would therefore include:

- an identification of the main purpose of any analysis;
- a development of the organization's understanding of the stakeholder system and of decision-makers in that system;
- an identification of the key stakeholders related to the organization;
- an identification of stakeholder interests, their characteristics and their sets of circumstances;
- an identification of any related patterns of interaction between stakeholders;
- a definition of any options for the organization.

In order to assess the relative power and participation of any potential stakeholders, a model of stakeholder involvement can be constructed, as can be seen in Figure 57.

This model reveals that the larger groups (consumers etc.), although significant in numbers, are not overly involved in an organization, whilst those stakeholders who are fewer in number (such as the board of directors) are closely involved. The diagram in Figure 58 suggests that there

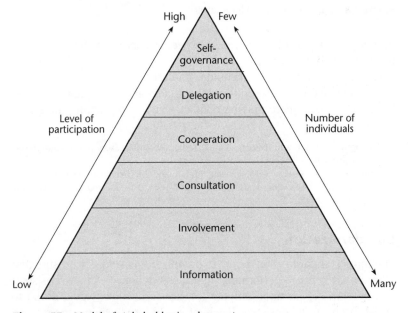

Figure 57   Model of stakeholder involvement

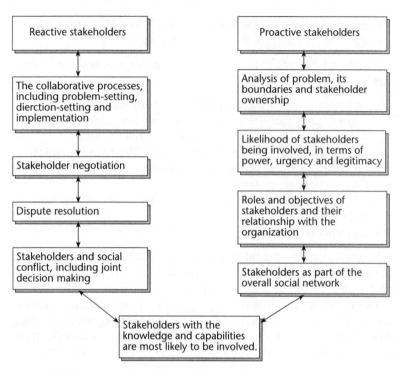

Figure 58   Bases for stakeholder analysis

may be as many as nine different perspectives upon which to begin any form of stakeholder analysis.

On the proactive side, stakeholder analysis is relevant when there is no immediate crisis between the stakeholders and the organization. On the reactive side, there may be conflict which is prompting the stakeholder analysis.

Scharioth, Joachim and Huber, Margit (eds), *Achieving Excellence in Stakeholder Management.* Berlin and Heidelberg: Springer Verlag, 2003.

Hemmati, Minu, Dodds, Felix, Enayati, Jasmin and McHarry, Jan, *Multi-Stakeholder Processes for Governance and Sustainability: Beyond Deadlock and Conflict.* London: Earthscan, 2002.

Standardization

The term 'standardization' refers to organizations' efforts to ensure that all their workers are performing their tasks or activities in a consistent manner. An organization striving for standardization would do so to assist in ensuring consistent levels of safety, productivity, and quality.

The term 'standardization' may also refer to an organization's desire to standardize the parts and components it uses.

In international business, standardization very much relies upon the specific arrangements required by overseas nations in moving towards standardized procedures and classifications.

See also **globalization of markets.**

Star

'Star' is one of the categories of product or service which can be found on the **Boston growth matrix**. Stars are successful products which enjoy a significant level of market demand. Invariably, stars were formerly question marks. Like **cash cows** they enjoy leading market positions. Stars are typified by products or services which are continuing to grow rapidly (this enables them to maintain their position in the market). Stars provide a business with a significant amount of income, but significant investment in marketing and advertising is required in order to support their continued success.

Stars have the potential to penetrate into other existing markets. They are usually the targets for improved distribution, product extensions and other marketing techniques in order to sustain their continued appeal. Ultimately, when the market in which a star is placed slows down, the product or service becomes a 'cash cow'.

Strategic alliance

Strategic alliances are either short-term or long-term alliances between two businesses with the purpose of sharing resources. Strategic alliances may include **joint ventures**, but in general they are a business relationship in which the two businesses pool their strengths, share risks and try to integrate their business functions for mutual benefits. Unlike any other form of close cooperation, both business entities remain independent throughout the arrangement. Strategic alliances are an important way of being able to break into new markets, acquire new technical skills and improve the business's competitive position. Businesses may create a strategic alliance in one of the following three ways:

- through internal growth;
- through merger and acquisition;
- through spin-offs.

The alliance strategy is particularly attractive to international businesses that wish to operate in foreign markets that are relatively politically stable, or in developing countries which have free market systems (and are not suffering from high inflation or a high level of private-sector debt). Strategic alliances can be used to offset many of the risks associated with pioneering costs as the risks are spread.

There are, in effect, six different ways in which a strategic alliance could assist international businesses in entering a foreign market. These include:

- Exporting – which has all the advantages of avoiding the set-up costs of manufacturing in an overseas market, but may have the disadvantage of higher transport costs and potential trade barriers. A strategic alliance could be used to form an association with a marketing subsidiary in the host country.
- Turnkey projects – this allows an international business to become involved in an overseas market where there may be prohibitions related to foreign direct investment. In essence, the international business exports only its process abilities and understanding, but this may inadvertently create a competitor in the longer run.
- Licensing – this involves framing a strategic alliance on the basis that a host country's industry undertakes to manufacture products in accordance with the trademarks and patents of the international business. The international business may risk losing control over its licences and will be passing on technological know-how to a potential long-term competitor.
- **Franchising** – this involves a strategic alliance with a host country business which will bear the risks and the costs of opening up a new market. With distant franchisees, there are often problems of dealing with quality control issues.
- **Joint ventures** – this involves establishing a strategic alliance based on the sharing of costs and risks and the gaining of local knowledge and perhaps political influence. Again the international business may lose a degree of control over, and protection of, its technologies.
- **Wholly owned subsidiary** – whilst the international business will have to bear all of the costs and risks in opening up the overseas market, a wholly owned subsidiary offers tighter control of technology and other aspects of the business operation.

In order to make strategic alliances work, both businesses need to have sophisticated formal and informal communication networks and take steps to build trust between each other. Both parties need to take proactive steps in order to learn as much as they can from the operations of their partner.

Doz, Yves and Hamel, Gary, *Alliance Advantage: The Art of Creating Value through Partnering*. Boston, MA: Harvard Business School Press, 1998.

Strategic business unit

See **SBU (strategic business unit)**.

Strategic change

'Strategic change' is a general term which is used to describe the actions undertaken by an organization in its pursuit of a **competitive advantage**. Strategic change is exemplified by moves by an organization away from its current posture and operations to an altered state which facilitates the achievement of a competitive advantage.

Strategic choice

On the one hand, a basic definition of strategic choice revolves around decisions made by an organization which are determined by its operational contingencies, but this misses many of the additional aspects.

'Strategic choice' can also refer to the personal preferences exercised by leaders of organizations, which can influence the organizational direction. This form of strategic choice is, essentially, a political process. Strategic choice, in this sense, therefore involves considerable influences on:

- the organizational environment;
- the interactions between different parties within the organization;
- the relationship between the organization and its external environment.

More broadly, there are four different approaches to strategic choice:

- A focus on decisions to be made during a planning process, with reference to issues such as timescale and overall impact.
- A subtle form of judgement which can handle uncertainties, whether they involve technical, political or procedural issues.
- A choice based on incremental changes, rather than addressing the longer-term, more all-embracing policies. These choices would focus on what has to be decided, how, and what can be deferred to a later date.
- An interactive form of choice, largely based on the collaboration between individuals with complementary skills, which should produce a practical approach to making choices.

Imparato, Nicholas and Harari, Oren, *Jumping the Curve: Innovation and Strategic Choice in an Age of Transition*. New York: Jossey-Bass Wiley, 1996.
Lake, David A. and Powell, Robert (eds), *Strategic Choice and International Relations*. Princeton, NJ: Princeton University Press, 1999.

S

Strategic commitment

Strategic commitment can be seen as an organization's determination to achieve a particular goal. It forms an integral part of a broader set of policies which could include the following issues:

- the reshaping of the **organizational culture**;
- the building of strategic commitment;
- the enhancement of capabilities;
- the desire to serve the organization and its **stakeholders**;
- the building of teams and groups within the organization to achieve this aim;
- the satisfaction of customers;
- the realignment of the organization in order to achieve this aim.

Ghemawat, Pankaj, *Commitment: The Dynamics of Strategy*. New York: Free Press, 1991.

Strategic competence

Typically, businesses will compete on the basis of their available resources (either acquired or internally generated). The resources, broadly speaking, can be identified as falling into one of two categories:

- Intangible or tangible resources which can be bought and sold on the market, provided the funds are available.
- Skills, know-how or inherent competences (resources) which are within the organization itself.

The second category of resources is, in essence, the organization's **core competences**; they are organization-wide and specific to that business. These strategic competences are at the heart of what the business does and what it can offer its customers. They essentially represent the nature of that business's **competitive advantage**. Not all businesses have strategic or core competences and many that do, find it difficult to identify the exact nature of the competences, and have severe difficulties in trying to put procedures in place to nurture and develop them.

At corporate or strategic levels of management, the core competences are difficult to manage and may well be at variance with forms of organization which are primarily (and probably only) concerned with the generation of profit. If the organization is sufficiently successful at profit generation, then there is a tendency for its strategic competences to be taken for granted and not developed or supported.

Strategic competences can pass and become obsolete, as competences can become outdated and no longer of any great value to the organization. Consequently, an organization may choose to divest itself of its core competences and seek to develop new ones.

Strategic competences can be seen as a useful foil against senior management's tendency to focus on the dynamics of the market and the impact of these on the organization's products and services. Strategic competences, assuming they are carefully managed, remain the backbone of the business and ensure that it remains competitive and is heading in a clear direction.

Sanchez, Ron and Heene, Aimé, *The New Strategic Management: Organization Competition and Competence*. New York: John Wiley, 2003.
Tidd, Joe (ed.), *From Knowledge Management to Strategic Competence: Measuring Technological, Market and Organisation Innovation*. London: Imperial College Press, 2000.

Strategic control

'Strategic control' describes management's attempts not only to monitor activities associated with the organization, but also to take action when required in order to realign or affect the performance of the business.

Strategic control is a complex issue. Normally control is asserted in the following situations:

- when there is a degree of ambiguity in relation to objectives;
- when performance needs to be measured, either qualitatively or quantitatively, for purposes of judgement;
- when possible outcomes are unknown;
- when the organization undertakes activities which are not repetitive – often these are one-off situations.

Strategic control is not an exact science and its nature very much depends upon the situation and context in which a decision must be made. In 1981, Geert Hofstede suggested that there may be as many as six different forms of strategic control, each of which are deployed in specific circumstances according to the nature of the situation facing the management. An interpretation of his suggestions is shown in Figure 59.

In order to explain the six different forms of control it is necessary to investigate these a little further. They are described in Table 28.

Goold, Michael and Quinn, John J., *Strategic Control: Strategic Milestones for Long-term Performance*. London: Financial Times, Prentice-Hall, 1993.
Hofstede, Geert, 'Management Control of Public and Not-for-Profit Activities', *Accounting, Organisations and Society*, 6 (3) (1981), pp. 193–211.

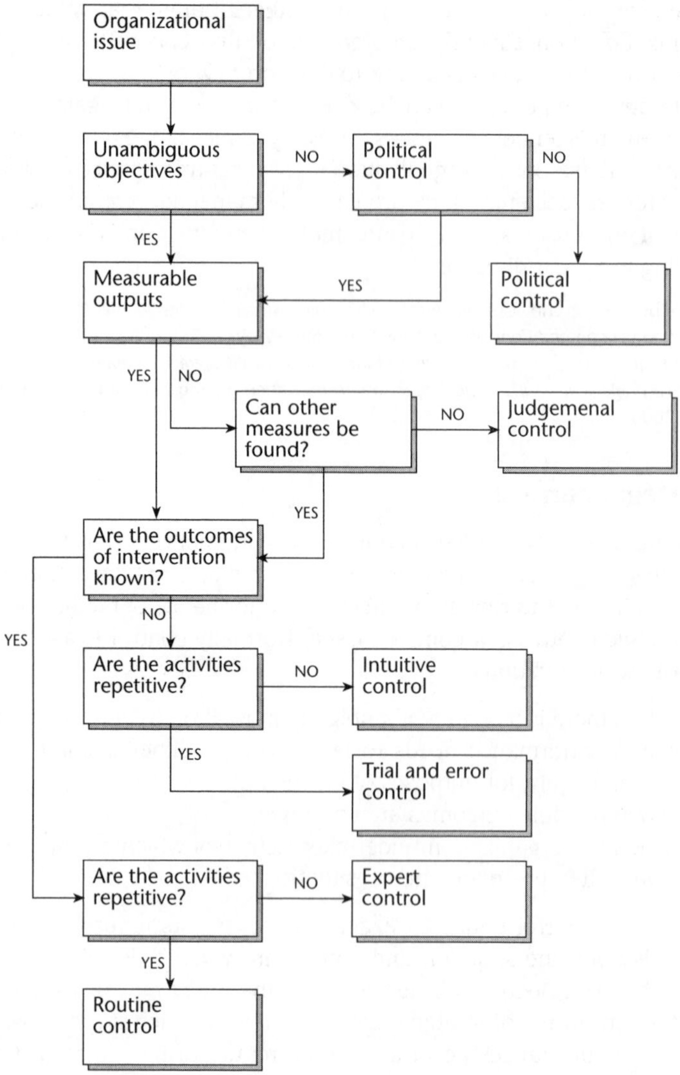

Figure 59 Forms of strategic control

Strategic control systems

Strategic control systems are associated with formal systems which aim to set targets, carry out measurements and provide feedback regarding organizational operations and activities.

Table 28 The six forms of strategic control

Form of control	Description
Political	This form of control relies upon the management's ability to use skills in negotiation and persuasion. They may have to manipulate the situation in their favour.
Judgemental	This is essentially a subjective decision made by the management.
Intuitive	This is essentially an art rather than a science. Each situation will require a different approach, often based on spurious assumptions.
Trial and error	The management employs control which may or may not be applicable in the current situation.
Expert	Usually part of the planning and monitoring process. Actual outcomes are compared with projections, control is concerned with dealing with the variances.
Routine	This is control associated with situations where there is little ambiguity between objectives and where performance is measurable. Variations are dealt with by negative feedback and decisions regarding the removal of the deviations.

Essentially, strategic control systems aim to provide the senior management with a means by which to assess the progress of the business in relation to its objectives. Typically, the following would be measured:

- efficiency;
- quality;
- innovation of development;
- responsiveness to customer needs and enquiries;
- implementation of policies.

See also **strategic control**.

Strategic groups

The term 'strategic groups' usually refers to situations where groups of two or more businesses seek to follow similar lines of policy. The strategic groups tend to either agree on particular ways of doing business, or follow the lead of the most successful business in the group.

The strategic groups are differentiated from other organizations in the same market or industry by virtue of the fact that they have strategies that are distinct from those of other businesses.

Strategic intent

'Strategic intent' refers to the intention of a business to coordinate and drive the whole of the organization towards predetermined sets of **goals** or **objectives**. Typically, the business would set goals or objectives which may, on the face of it, appear to be somewhat ambitious. The strategy formulation process recognizes that the goals may be difficult, but the intent and purpose of the management is to configure operations, resources and capabilities to achieve them. Essentially, this is a strategic approach driven by senior management.

Strategic leadership

Strategic leadership is the concept of the organization being driven by the senior management's ability to construct, express and impose a practical series of applications or actions which aim to address the organization's strategic vision.

The key to strategic leadership is not only the successful conversion of this vision into actual activities or steps, but also the motivation and drive needed by other managers and employees to see the vision and why certain activities must be undertaken. In essence, strategic leadership requires senior management to successfully sell the idea of the vision.

Strategic management

At its simplest, strategic management provides an organization with the ability to:

- determine its long-term direction;
- assess its long-term performance;
- ensure that plans are correctly and expertly formulated;
- monitor and implement plans effectively;
- carry out a continuous evaluation of the business and its performance.

The strategic management seeks to ensure:

- that the missions of the organization are translated into **objectives** (clear and obvious);

- that these become strategies which can be employed;
- that goals are then set arising out of the strategies;
- that these goals (and hence the mission, objectives and strategies) are superimposed upon any project or programme of activities.

Strategic management seeks to integrate the organizational functions and processes into a broad, cohesive strategy. It also seeks to coordinate the various functional elements of the organization, ensuring that they interact and use their interdependencies in a positive and constructive manner.

Strategic management is, in effect, the processes by which the organization, in a dynamic and, above all, interactive manner, seeks to ensure that it responds to its **general environment**.

See also **strategic management process**.

Hannagan, Tim, *Mastering Strategic Management*. Basingstoke: Palgrave Macmillan, 2002.

Jenkins, Mark and Ambrosini, Véronique, *Strategic Management: A Multi-perspective Approach*. Basingstoke: Palgrave Macmillan, 2002.

Strategic management process

The strategic management process can be seen as an ongoing management function involving a complex series of decisions and actions. These decisions and actions aim to:

- formulate strategy;
- implement strategy;
- monitor and respond to performance measures.

The process itself tends to be forward looking in the sense that it is concerned with the achievement of **objectives** in relation to and interacting with the organization's environment. Most models of the strategic management process include four stages, as shown in Figure 60.

Alternatives could include a distinctly different set of processes, such as:

- environmental scanning;
- formulation;
- implementation;
- evaluation and control.

Any strategic management process, regardless of its configuration, should address the following:

- Where is the organization at the moment?

S

- Where does the organization wish, or need, to be?
- How will the organization get there?

Figure 60 Stages of the strategic management process

De Wit, Bob and Meyer, Ron, *Strategy: Process, Content, Contest: An International Perspective*. London: Thomson Learning, 1998.

Strategic marketing

Strategic marketing seeks to identify and exploit marketing opportunities or check whether marketing threats have a strategic link or relevance to the organization. Strategic marketing also seeks to develop and maintain marketing activities to support the functions and competences of the organization. It is the role of strategic marketing to determine the long-term marketing plans which will support the long-term **strategic planning**.

See also **strategic marketing planning**.

Strategic marketing planning

The strategic marketing planning process seeks to identify and answer a number of questions and make decisions regarding the following issues:

- What is the present position of the organization and what steps were taken to achieve this position?
- What does the future hold for the organization?
- Where does the organization intend to be in the future?
- What steps are required to get the organization to this position in the future?

- What are the costs associated with these steps?
- What are the reasonable performance measures involved in the progress to this position?

See also **strategic marketing.**

Aaker, D. A., *Strategic Marketing Management*. New York: John Wiley, 2002.

Strategic planning

A strategic plan is an overarching series of activities which aim to implement and develop a new concept, deal with a problem, or establish the foundation of the business's objectives in the coming period. As Figure 61 shows, there is a close relationship between the implementation and the strategic development process.

Strategic planning should, as the diagram illustrates, be a continual process, with the monitoring and control procedures providing the information for the development of this and future strategic plans.

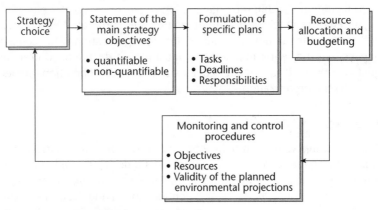

Figure 61   Implementing strategic planning

Strategic planning gap

The strategic planning gap represents the difference between an organization's current position and where it hopes to be at some point in the future.

The strategic planning gap can also be seen as the difference between the organization's vision (of where it wishes to be) and the forecast (based on historical figures) of where the organization is heading.

The organization may recognize that over a period of time a gulf is opening up between the forecast, in terms of the ideal performance, and the actual performance of the organization. This strategic planning gap may be filled by:

- a market penetration strategy;
- a market development strategy;
- a product development strategy.

Alternatively, the organization could consider:

- backward integration;
- forward integration;
- vertical integration;
- horizontal integration;
- diversification.

Strategic responsibility

Strategic responsibility is the notion that senior management is concerned with, and ultimately responsible for, long-term planning and overall guidance within the organization.

Strategic responsibility is the domain of the corporate headquarters and its staff in a multinational or larger organization. The concept implies that the senior management must have a degree of control and guidance over all functional activities and business operations undertaken by the organization.

Strategic thinking

Strategic thinking is essentially a process in which senior management confronts significant issues and undertakes a decision-making process in order to deal with them. Strategic thinking may involve either organizational or personal decisions, the identification of and decision-making surrounding, important issues, or simply understanding a situation. Strategic thinking implies the generation of alternatives and the evaluation of these alternatives in an objective manner. It therefore incorporates creative ideas, idea generation, divergent thinking and, above all, logical and rational thought. Typically, strategic thinking would include some, or all, of the following characteristics:

- the identification and then the focusing on important issues;
- the selection of key information;
- the identification of any linkages, patterns or interactions;
- the distinguishing of cause and effect;
- the clarification of assumptions;
- the looking at issues or situations in a broad context;

- long-term view;
- an understanding of implications and consequences;
- the generation of alternatives and the objective evaluation of them;
- flexibility;
- using logical, rational thinking alongside creative idea generation.

Strategic turnaround

A strategic turnaround is essentially concerned with issues arising out of the recovery process of a business. Clearly, any decreasing revenue, depletion of cash reserves, negative earnings, or periods of sustained loss can adversely affect the fortunes of the business. Strategic turnaround involves dealing with these issues and taking measures in order to address what could swiftly become a crisis. Businesses aim to strengthen their **cash flow** or income problems by adopting strategies which seek to either maintain or increase sales. In effect, strategic turnaround involves an immediate intervention at operational level to reduce expenses or increase efficiency.

Alternatively, the strategy could revolve around reducing debt or increasing revenue through pricing or advertising changes. Other businesses might seek to redeploy their assets or strategically reposition the business.

Strategy formulation

Strategy formulation needs to ensure that any planned course of action is consistent with the general strategy of the business and with the business's ability to achieve these objectives. Normally, strategic formulation takes place at three different levels of an organization:

- Corporate level – where strategy formulation is based on objectives and strategies for achieving these objectives.
- Business level – which is often known as competitive strategy formulation, and deals with strategy formulation in relation to every area in which the organization is involved.
- Functional level – which is strategy formulation related directly to ensuring that either corporate level or business level strategy can be achieved through the manipulation of current functional activities.

Sun Tzu

Sun Tzu's *Art of War* is one of the oldest military treaties yet discovered and pre-dates **Carl von Clausewitz** by over 2000 years. The book addresses the inter-relationships and interpersonal relationships primarily concerned with diplomacy. However, much can be learned from the book in relation to business strategy. Sun Tzu's writing has been used as an important source for strategic management.

Tzu, Sun, *Art of War*. New York: HarperCollins, 1994.

Sustained competitive advantage

A sustainable competitive advantage can be typified as being a **competitive advantage** of either an international business or a specific country, which cannot easily be imitated and will be difficult to erode over a period of time. In order to have a sustainable competitive advantage a business or a nation needs to have a unique **core competence** which is difficult to copy, unique in itself, sustainable, superior to the competition and, above all, applicable in a number of different situations. Typical forms of sustainable competitive advantage include:

- A vastly superior product in terms of quality.
- Well-established and extensive distribution channels.
- A positive reputation and a strong brand equity.
- Low-cost production techniques and processes.
- The ownership of patents or copyrights.
- A monopoly in the form of government protection.
- A superior management team and/or superior employees.

Switching costs

Switching costs are either the physical or the perceived costs of changing from one brand to another, or from one supplier to another. Indeed, switching costs may be associated with any form of transference from a prior supplier to a new supplier.

Synergy

Synergies are the benefits which can result from combining different aspects of an organization, rather than allowing them to act separately. In other words, organizations will seek to group complementary activities in situations where there is a strong possibility of collaboration. This means that a mutual benefit can be enjoyed, particularly when common work or activity form the basis of the alliance.

Synergies can also be enjoyed between organizations where complementary skills or production processes, or indeed knowledge of a specific market, can be brought together in order to achieve far more than the two organizations could possibly have hoped for individually. Synergies can either bring about short-term project-based alliances between businesses, or may well prove to be the foundation of a longer-term relationship.

'Business synergy' is a term often applied to **franchising** operations, in as much as when individuals purchase a franchise they become part of a larger 'family'. All the members of the family work together and the most effective ideas are shared.

S

Tactical planning

See action planning.

Take-over constraint

The term 'take-over constraint' has implications as far as strategic management is concerned in as much as it limits the actions of senior management. In an ideal world, senior management want to pursue their own strategies, and take actions in relation to the organization which might not necessarily directly, or immediately, benefit the stock-holders or shareholders of the business. Should they pursue their own intended policies and strategies, then the stockholders or shareholders might be adversely affected, which could lead them to assume that the business was no longer a reasonable investment proposition. This could, in turn, reduce the market value of the stocks or shares, leaving the business open to potential take-over, on either a hostile or a friendly basis, from a third party.

Tangible resource/asset

Tangible resources, or tangible assets, are items which have a physical substance and may well be used as part of the production or supply of products and services. In accounting terms, tangible assets also include leases or company shares. They are, in effect, the fixed assets of the organization and can be differentiated from intangible assets, such as goodwill, trademarks or patents, which do not have a physical substance but are still valuable concepts and assets.

Damodaran, Aswath, *Investment Valuation: Tools and Techniques for Determining the Value of Any Asset*. New York: John Wiley, 2002.

Gardner, Mona, Mills, Dixie and Cooperman, Elizabeth, *Managing Financial Institutions: An Asset/Liability Approach*. London: Thomson Learning, 1999.

Taper integration

Taper integration can describe two different forms of integration: one in relation to suppliers and the other in relation to distributors. Taper integration as far as suppliers is concerned relates to the purchasing of raw materials, components or products, from both independent suppliers and suppliers which have come under the ownership of the purchasing business. In effect, this reflects the reality of partial vertical integration. In respect of distributors a similar set of circumstances arises, in as much as the business sells its products or services through outlets which are part of the overall organization, acquired through vertical integration. They will also sell their products and services through independent outlets.

Target

See **goals** and **performance goal**.

Taylor, Frederick Winslow

During his research, Taylor (1856–1915) began with the assumption that employees only work for money. He developed a series of work study techniques which he considered would enable employees to reduce the amount of time it would take to carry out different tasks, leaving the planning and organization of tasks for the managers and supervisors. He believed that encouragement to work harder and the promise of additional benefits, such as money, as a reward for this would make employees sufficiently motivated to work harder.

Taylor, however, was proved wrong. He discovered that employees would only work harder when they were being supervised, but would return to their normal pace of work once the supervision was removed.

Since Taylor's writing on 'scientific management', much emphasis has been placed on job design. Henry Ford developed Taylor's principles into what has become known as 'Fordism'.

Bratton, John and Gold, Jeffrey, *Human Resource Management: Theory and Practice.* Basingstoke: Palgrave Macmillan, 2003.

Kanigel, Robert, *The One Best Way: Frederick Winslow Taylor and the Enigma of Efficiency.* London: Little Brown, 1997.

Taylor, Frederick Winslow, *Principles of Scientific Management.* London: W. W. Norton, 1967.

Summary of Taylor's work at www.accel-team.com/scientific/scientific_02.html

Technical strategy

'Technical strategy' refers to a model adopted by businesses that seek to protect their technical advantages. Figure 62 illustrates these strategies.

High protection ability/low technical advantage	High protection ability/high technical advantage
Defender	*Innovator*
Needs:	Needs:
• Value-added features • Cost/performance advantages • Product extension • Market entry barriers	• To be less dependent on compulsory assets • Resources are a problem • Could be market leader
Low protection ability/low technical advantage	**Low protection ability/high technical advantage**
Exposed	*First mover*
Needs:	Needs:
• Better price, service and features • Problem is lack of uniqueness • Good geographical location	• Secrecy and protection • Complementary assets • Market leader reputation • Quicker time to market

Figure 62 Technical strategies

Technological myopia

Technological myopia is often described as a business's inability to understand, appreciate or utilize the potential benefits of technology. Technological myopia has been exemplified in recent years by the failure of many businesses' intranets. Whilst these businesses had secured the technical expertise to install and set up the infrastructure for the intranet, they had failed to train managers and employees sufficiently and had also failed to fully utilize the benefits of the new system.

Wyman, J., 'Technological Myopia: The Need to Think Strategically about Technology', *Sloan Management Review*, 26(4) (1985), pp. 59–65.

Technology management

The management of technology involves the linking of engineering, science and management in order to:

- plan technological capabilities;
- develop technological capabilities;
- implement technological capabilities.

This management system seeks to shape and accomplish the technological goals, both strategic and operational, of the business. This is achieved in a three-part process:

- accomplish the goals of the organization by creating value through technological development;
- focus on the development of technological capabilities which can be used to improve or create production/service processes;
- establish linkages to all other parts of the organization.

Technology management has developed considerably since the 1950s, as can be seen Table 29.

Table 29 Development of technology management

Factor	1950	1970	1980	1990
Management paradigm	Research and development	Innovation strategy	Technology strategy	Value management
Resources	Plentiful	Reduced	Accountability	Accountability
Innovation	Internal development	New venture divisions	Business links	Technology focus
Resource allocation	Funding of research and development	Funding of new technologies	Funding of market opportunities	Funding of business development

Times covered ratio

The times covered ratio examines the extent to which a business's gross profit covers its annual interest payments. The usual formula is:

$$Times\ covered\ ratio = \frac{Profit\ before\ interest\ and\ tax}{Total\ interest\ charges}$$

The normal interpretation of the ratio suggests that if the times covered ratio declines to less than 1, the business will be unable to meet its interest costs. The net result of this is that the business is technically insolvent.

Timing of entry

'Timing of entry' refers to a decision made by a business as to when it will become involved in a particular market. It is a basic entry decision which all businesses must take, identifying the most opportune moment for them to enter what to them appears to be an attractive market.

Top–down change

Top–down change is exemplified by leaders and managers who seek to dominate the organization in which they operate by controlling situations and attempting to predict the actions of everyone in the organization. Top–down change is actually driven by managers who are essentially responsible for transforming the visions or values of the organization into reality. Typically, top–down change is driven by mechanisms including:

- business planning;
- quality and performance management;
- employee involvement;
- team briefings;
- consultation initiatives.

Top–down planning

Top–down planning is a feature of many businesses with a formal hierarchical structure. The philosophy of these organizations is to ensure that decision making, and consequent instructions or orders, emanate from the higher levels of the hierarchy and are filtered down, through the layers of the organization, being translated into a series of tasks by the levels of management. Top–down planning does not necessarily take into account the realities of the organization, and assumes that plans framed by the senior management can be fully implemented further down the structure.

Top–down planning does not seek to incorporate the ideas or positions of the subordinate managers or those carrying out the tasks. It also means that these organizations do not tend to involve their staff in the decision-making process, unlike **bottom-up planning**, which is a more consultative leadership style, promoting employee participation.

Total asset turnover ratio

This ratio is a variation on the fixed asset turnover ratio and also measures the business's effectiveness in using its assets to generate sales. In this case, the formula is:

$$Total\ asset\ turnover\ ratio = \frac{Sales}{Total\ assets}$$

Suppose that a business which has sales of some £3,200,000 and a total asset figure of £2,850,000. Again, the figure for the total assets may be calculated as an average of the opening or closing values (used for expanding businesses primarily) or simply the closing value of the assets at the end of the year. The relevant calculation would therefore be:

$$\frac{3,200,000}{2,850,000} = 1.12 \text{ times}$$

The total asset turnover ratio therefore reveals that the business is generating £1.12 in sales for every £1 invested in assets.

A low ratio suggests that the business is having productivity problems. A high ratio may suggest that the business is over-trading on its assets. In other words, the business does not have sufficient assets to support the sales which are being generated. This is often a problem that faces new businesses which are expanding. As sales increase, they do not have sufficient cash to invest in additional fixed assets and may also have working capital difficulties. Ultimately, the business may suffer from liquidity problems, which means that they may not be able to supply customers as they do not have sufficient funds to replace their stock.

Temple, Peter, *Magic Numbers: The 33 Key Ratios that Every Investor Should Know*. New York: John Wiley, 2001.

Total quality management (TQM)

The concept of total quality management (TQM) has been stimulated by the need for organizations to conform with regard to quality levels. This need has been brought about in essence by an increased demand from customers and suppliers for higher-quality products, parts and components. The fundamental principle behind total quality management is that the management of quality is addressed at all levels of an organization, from the top to the bottom. Improvements are made on a continuous basis by applying the theories and approaches of management theorists in an attempt to improve quality and decrease organizational costs. The emphasis, primarily on quality, is also very much on people and their involvement, particularly with regard to suppliers and customers. The fundamental principles of TQM are summarized in Table 30.

Bank, J., *The Essence of Total Quality Management*. London: Prentice-Hall, 1999.
Oakland, John S., *Total Quality Management: The Management of Change through Process Improvement*. Oxford: Butterworth-Heinemann, 1993.

Total shareholder return

Total return is usually taken to mean the full return on any particular investment. The total return would include any income which has been

Table 30 Principles of total quality management

TQM principle	Description
Committed and effective leaders	A commitment to, and a belief in, the principles of TQM by those key decision-makers at the top of the organizational structure is essential. They have to portray this commitment to the lower levels of management in an effective style of leadership by providing resources to make changes happen.
Planning	It is imperative that all changes are planned effectively, particularly as the TQM approach may be fundamentally different from the approach currently adopted by an organization. All planned changes must be integrated through the whole organization with cooperation throughout all levels and functions. With quality, or improved quality, as the key dimension, a longer-term strategy will be adopted throughout the organization's functions, from new product design through to getting the product to the end-user.
Monitoring	A continuous monitoring system will be put into place so that the process of continuous improvement can be supported and developed. Problem identification and the implementation of solutions will be sought.
Training	Without education and training, employees and management will lack expertise and awareness of quality issues. It will be difficult to implement changes in organizational behaviour unless there is a comprehensive and effective educational scheme which not only seeks to provide the initial information and understanding of techniques, but constantly updates those techniques in order to reinforce understanding. Without this investment, short-term TQM benefits will be difficult to achieve, as will the long-term impact of TQM through conventional measurements such as increased efficiency and general growth.
Teamwork	The development of empowered cooperative teams is an essential prerequisite of TQM. Under this system teams are encouraged to take the initiative and often given responsibilities which would have formerly been management roles. Without this involvement and empowerment TQM is almost impossible to implement as it requires both the participation and the commitment of individuals throughout the organization.

$\Rightarrow$

T

Table 30 Principles of total quality management (*continued*)

TQM principle	Description
Evaluation and feedback	It is imperative that individuals within the organization see the fruits of their labour. TQM means that there should be an integral system which not only provides positive feedback but also rewards for achievement. The evaluation and feedback of TQM will invariably involve the measurement of achievement in both internal and external targets, notably through **benchmarking**.
Long-term change	As TQM becomes embedded and very much a fact of life in the ways in which employees think and processes are carried out, there is a permanent change to the way in which attitudes, working practices and overall behaviour are approached.

derived either from a dividend or from interest and will incorporate any appreciation or depreciation in the value of the investment over a given period. Total return figures can be calculated on a yearly basis or at the end of a specific project, or in some cases at the end of an asset's useful life.

Total return can also be referred to as 'yield'.

Madden, Bartley J., *CFROI: Cash Flow Return on Investment Valuation: A Total System Approach to Valuing the Firm*. Oxford: Butterworth-Heinemann, 1999.

Transfer pricing

Transfer pricing is a form of internal pricing policy which requires a particular part of a business, or group of businesses, to ensure that they still meet their profit targets, even when supplying products and services to another business, or division, under common ownership.

Feinschreiber, Robert, *Transfer Pricing Handbook: Transfer Pricing International: A Country-by-Country Guide*. New York: John Wiley, 2002.

Transformational change

Transformational change is a root-and-branch change process which seeks to fundamentally improve the way in which a business may operate. It requires considerable planning, coupled with an overarching strategy and commitment across the entire organization. There are seven steps associated with transformational change:

T

- Defining the change strategy – which assesses the need and readiness for change, the best change configuration and how the process of change will be controlled.
- Management commitment – this entails developing a sense of ownership amongst the management, and working towards a strategic vision for the change, as well as identifying how that vision relates to each manager.
- Creation of the change strategy – creating a change strategy that will be meaningful to all employees, and defining the way in which the vision can be communicated to all **stakeholders**.
- Building employee commitment – the creation of the means by which the change can be 'sold' to the employees and the identification and management of resistance to that change.
- Development of a new culture – incorporating the development of new values for employees and new behaviours which are aligned to the vision, including the regular review of support required.
- Reconfiguration of the organization – redesigning roles, competences, structure and the identification of appropriate individuals who will assume those roles.
- Managing performance – the creation of a new working environment with relevant **performance measurement** and the alignment of business performance to individual objectives.

Anderson, D. and Anderson, L. S. A. (eds), *Beyond Change Management: Advanced Strategies for Today's Transformational Leaders.* New York: Jossey-Bass Wiley, 2001.

Transitional change

Transitional change seeks to achieve a known desired state that is different from the existing one. Its foundation is based on the work of Kurt Lewin, who believed that the change process consisted of three stages. First the organization needs to accept the need to change, and make positive steps towards that change. The organization then moves to the new position and refreezes itself in a new equilibrium position.

Amado, Gilles and Ambrose, Anthony, *The Transitional Approach to Change.* London: Karnac Books, 2001.
Lewin, Kurt, *Field Theory in Social Science.* New York: Harper Row, 1951.

Transnational strategy

See **global learning** *and* **global strategy**.

Turnaround strategy

See **strategic turnaround.**

Two-boss employees

Two-boss employees occur naturally within a **matrix and matrix structure** and within a **global matrix structure**. These individuals, who are involved as participants in project teams, have two forms of management control. These are:

- The direct managers within the project team, who are responsible for the internal communication and coordination.
- The managers of functional departments, who are tasked with the communication and coordination of their activities with the project team.

T

Unrelated (conglomerate) diversification

This form of **diversification** involves moving out of the traditional areas of the organization's activities. Normally, this would be undertaken as a result of the business attempting to find opportunities for growth elsewhere. It may have funds available for investment, but feel that reinvesting the funds in current operations would be less advantageous than finding new opportunities elsewhere.

Existing opportunities may be less attractive and new opportunities may be more attractive in the longer term, particularly if the line of business the organization is involved in is showing signs of decline. Equally, the business could choose unrelated diversification in order to make better use of its **core competences**.

Value chain

The term 'value chain' was coined by Michael Porter in 1985 and is used to describe how the activities of an organization are linked to the maintenance of a competitive position within the market. The value chain can be used to describe activities both within and external to the organization, relating them to its competitive strength. The analysis itself values each activity which adds to the organization's products or services. In other words, it considers the organization's employees, available funds, as well as machinery and equipment. The supposition is that the ways in which these resources are deployed determine whether the organization is able to produce products and services at a price which customers are prepared to pay. By successfully organizing the resources, the business may be able to achieve a degree of **competitive advantage**.

As can be seen in Figure 63, Porter identified five main areas, or primary areas, related to the delivery of a product or a service. These were inbound logistics, operations, outbound logistics, marketing and sales, and service. These activities are supported by procurement, tech-

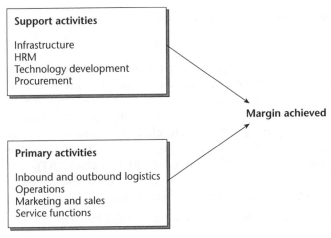

Figure 63 Activities contributing to the value chain

nology development, human resource management and the overall infrastructure of the organization. On this diagram Porter also incorporates a margin, which refers to the profit margin between the costs of the primary and support activities and the price which the customer is willing to pay.

In the majority of industrial sectors, however, the organization's value chain is simply part of a larger structure, which incorporates the supplier's value chain, the distribution channel's value chain and the customers' value chains. The position of the organization can be seen in Figure 64.

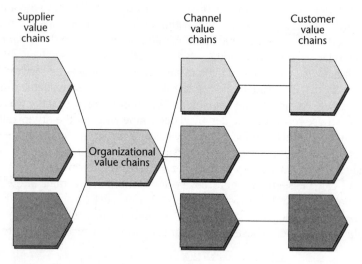

Figure 64 The structure of value chains

This more holistic impression of the overall system suggests that the progress of raw materials, components and products across the entire value chain requires consideration of the other elements' requirements for a profit margin. In other words, depending upon the relative strength of these elements within the value chain, margins can be squeezed or enlarged. Internally, at least, an organization can seek to improve its margins by adopting tactics such as **just-in-time (JIT)**, whilst not passing on any of the associated cost savings up the value chain, but retaining these as an additional profit margin.

Porter, Michael E., *Competitive Advantage*, London: Free Press, 1985.

Value chain analysis

Value chain analysis involves the analysis of activities which directly relate to an organization's ability to create a **competitive advantage**. The **value chain** can be expressed as in Table 31.

Table 31   The value chain

Chain activity	Description
Inbound logistics	Receiving goods, warehousing and inventory control.
Operations	Transforming the inputs into a finished product.
Outbound logistics	Warehousing, order fulfilment.
Marketing and sales	Advertising, pricing, etc.
Services	Maintaining and enhancing the product or service (repair and support).

In addition to this set of value chain activities, the business supports the primary functions with the following:

- Procurement – obtaining for inbound logistics and operations.
- Technology – for research and development, but also for all steps in the value chain.
- Human resources management – for all steps in the value chain.
- Infrastructure – to support all areas of the value chain (legal, financial, quality management).

Value chain analysis assists businesses in being able to obtain a competitive advantage by mapping the process flows and isolating the value creating or value adding activities.

The value chain clearly identifies linkages, as costs and decisions affect other parts of the value chain. In order to optimize the value chain, this analysis is essential.

Walters, D. W., *Operations Strategy: A Value Chain Approach*. Basingstoke: Palgrave Macmillan, 2002.

Values

Values are beliefs, perhaps enshrined in a mission statement or a philosophy which has meaning to a business. It is widely believed that the development, adoption and implementation of values is one of the key success factors in high-growth, high-profit businesses. Typical values include the following:

- continuous improvement;
- customer delight;
- people development;
- innovation;
- society commitment;
- maximum utilization.

Vertical hierarchical structure

Vertical hierarchical structures are essentially the traditional and easily recognized pyramid structure configuration adopted by many organizations. Within these traditional vertical hierarchical structures, power and authority are clearly recognized by the imposition of successive layers of management throughout the levels of the structure itself. Organizations such as these will tend to take a traditional view regarding the division of labour and the standardization of parts and products. They will see control as the primary and most important aspect of management.

Vertical integration

Vertical integration is a business acquisition process which aims to secure adjacent levels of the supply chain. Typically, a manufacturer will seek to acquire either a supplier or a distribution business or retailer in order to gain stronger control over the supply network.

Virtual corporation

In literal terms, a virtual organization does not exist. However, the term is used to describe a flexible organization which does not have a physical presence or central organizational structure but relies on a network of remote employees engaged in a variety of telecommuting and telework activities. It can also refer to an organization which employs outworkers, paid on a piece-rate system. The virtual organization acts as a provider of work and a fulfilment service or intermediary between the outworkers and the customer.

Vision statement

Vision statements relate to the seemingly unchanging ideals of a business, which are normally expressed in their **mission statement**.

Whilst mission statements tend to communicate the organization's core ideologies and **goals** (in a visionary sense), they have three components, one of which directly or indirectly states the organization's vision statement. These components will answer the following questions:

- What are the core values of the organization?
- What is the central purpose of the organization?
- What are the visionary goals of the organization?

Theoretically, at least, the core values and the purpose of the organization should remain fairly constant. The mission statement itself simply expresses how the business currently sees itself and what it aspires to achieve. This is where the vision statement differs, as it is the sum of the:

- core values;
- core purpose;
- key visionary goals.

The core values themselves are closely held values which are independent of all else which may come and go (the current state of the environment or the management direction). In distinguishing a core value from any other value, it has to be held as being crucial, even if the organization (all but temporarily) considers the value to be something of a liability in the given climate. Typical core values, therefore, remain, despite changes or trends. They may be stated simply as 'integrity', 'creativity' or 'excellence in customer service'. More often than not they are ill-defined notions open to interpretation.

Core purposes are those which aim to set the organization apart from its competitors. Some are idealistic in nature; they would not be clearly defined purposes, such as 'to make a profit' or 'to return value to investors'. Core purposes, therefore, tend to relate to how the business actually is, rather than to a goal or an aspiration.

The visionary goals of the organization are the key aspirational objectives; they can be long-sighted with regard to accomplishments. Visionary goals tend to follow one or more of the following:

- A target – simply a quantitative or qualitative goal.
- Competitor orientation – to replace the current market leader over a period of time.
- Role model – to set up another business as the ideal or the role model, and aspire to its values and presence in the market.
- Transformation – internal configuring in order to become the leading (or next to leading) player in all markets in which the organization operates.

Von Clausewitz, Carl

Von Clausewitz (1780–1831) was a Prussian military strategist and acknowledged to be one of the most important writers on military history. He remains one of the most frequently cited writers as his theories can be applied to almost any form of human strategy.

His book *On War* provides a social and economic blueprint which has been much quoted and much applied to business. His writing reveals the logic behind strategic thinking and practice and suggests that friction, being the difference between planned activities and what actually happens, is an intrinsic part of strategy itself.

Von Clausewitz, Carl, Howard, Michael and Paret, Peter, *On War*. Princeton, NJ: Princeton University Press, 1989.

Von Clausewitz, Carl, von Ghyczy, Tiha, von Oetinger, Bolko and Bassford, Christopher, *Clausewitz on Strategy: Inspiration and Insight from a Master Strategist*. New York: John Wiley, 2001.

V

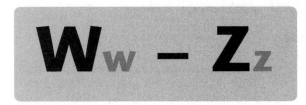

Weber, Max

Max Weber (1864–1920) based his conclusions about bureaucracy on his studies of such disparate organizations as the Catholic Church, the Prussian army and the empire of the Egyptians. He concluded that employees frequently suffer from inequity in most areas of work from selection to promotion. His key points are summarized in Table 32.

Table 32 Max Weber's views of bureaucracy

Principle of bureaucracy	Description
Division of labour	The workforce is split into specialized areas according to expertise.
Chain of command	There is a pyramid-shaped organizational structure which defines the hierarchy and the authority of the organization.
Rules and regulations	There are formalized rules governing the running of the organization, which assist the organization in dealing with the potential disruption caused by changes in management.
Impersonality	Management is detached from the workforce to ensure that sentimentality or familiarity does not impede decision making.
Selection and promotion	Selection of employees and their subsequent opportunities for advancement in the organization are strictly governed by their utility as far as the organization is concerned. Friendship plays no part, and the advancement is usually based on seniority and on express achievements.
Documentation	There is a meticulous system of document creation, completion and storage to chart all activities for the purposes of monitoring and evaluating those activities.

$\Rightarrow$

Table 32 Max Weber's views of bureaucracy (*continued*)

Principle of bureaucracy	Description
Centralization	All decision making is made from the upper strata of the organization, where individuals reside who have seniority and clearly recognizable achievements over a period of time.

White spaces

'White spaces' refers to a more effective deployment of an organization's **core competences**. The notion of white spaces suggests that the business could create new products and services by more creatively, or effectively, redeploying, recombining or re-coordinating the core competences which the organization enjoys.

Wholly owned subsidiary

A wholly owned subsidiary is a business which is entirely owned, usually by a holding company, or alternatively by another business that owns the majority or all of its stock or share capital. Wholly owned subsidiaries are common in business, particularly when the purchasing organization wishes to expand its overall influence and control in a given market, yet wishes to retain the acquired business as a separate legal identity. This may also be for practical and commercial reasons, such as retaining brand names and trademarks under their existing names. Wholly owned subsidiaries are also commonplace in respect of multinational businesses, who seek to acquire foreign businesses and bring them into common ownership, under a holding company, in order to facilitate the parent company's entry and operations in an overseas market.

W

Numbers

5 Forces model

See **Five Forces model.**

7s framework

See **Seven S framework.**

Index